IMAGES
of America

SWIFT COUNTY
MINNESOTA

IMAGES
of America

SWIFT COUNTY MINNESOTA

Swift County Historical Society

ARCADIA
PUBLISHING

ISBN 978-0-7385-0796-5

Published by Arcadia Publishing
Charleston, South Carolina

Printed in the United States of America

Library of Congress Catalog Card Number: 00-107496

For all general information contact Arcadia Publishing at:
Telephone 843-853-2070
Fax 843-853-0044
E-mail sales@arcadiapublishing.com
For customer service and orders:
Toll-Free 1-888-313-2665

Visit us on the Internet at www.arcadiapublishing.com

Contents

ACKNOWLEDGMENTS

The photographs and information for this book were taken from the archives of the Swift County Historical Society. The Swift County Historical Society is a non-profit organization, founded in 1929 to preserve local history. The society operates a museum and research library at Benson, Minnesota.

The society appreciates everyone who has donated pictures to the Swift County Historical Society's archives during the past 71 years. Thank you to Frank Eckhardt, collector and dealer in postcards, for loaning postcards of Swift County to the society so that copies could be made for our archives.

A special thank you to the society's director, **Marlys Klang-Gallagher**, for the hours put into compiling this volume.

INTRODUCTION

Swift County is located in the west central part of Minnesota, surrounded by Kandiyohi County on the east, Chippewa and Lac qui Parle on the south, Big Stone on the west, and Stevens and Pope on the north. The county is rectangular in shape, 42 miles long by 18 miles wide. It has three tiers of townships with seven townships in each tier. Except for Appleton Township, which has its southwestern corner cut off by the Minnesota River, each township is 6 miles square. The total area is 757 square miles or 484, 945 acres.

Swift County is divided into two major drainage basins: the Pomme de Terre and the Chippewa Rivers. The Pomme de Terre River flows through the western part of the county and enters the Minnesota River about 3 miles southwest of the town of Appleton. The Chippewa River flows through the center of the county and drains into the Minnesota River in Chippewa County.

The greater part of Swift County varies from nearly flat to undulating in topography. However, topography is steep and choppy in the northeast corner and in small areas throughout the county.

The climate in Swift County is marked by wide variations in temperature. The average growing season is 134 days, with the last killing frost around May 15th and the first around September 26th.

After the Civil War had ceased and the fear of further Indian outbreaks had died out, the westward march of the pioneers was renewed in earnest. In its first years, Swift County represented only a patchwork of settlements. Scandinavians and Germans were in decided majority among these early settlers. A number of them came with the honor and privileges of Civil War veterans. Others came directly from their mother land.

These early settlers had to live simple, primitive, and strenuous lives. Because of the scarcity of trees in Swift County, there were few log cabins. Many of the houses out on the level prairie were built out of sod, laid piece on piece after the manner of laying bricks. These proved durable and were in use by some for several decades. What little furniture there was was usually homemade. Stoves were a luxury. When wood was scarce, twisted hay served as fuel.

By 1869, the St. Paul and Pacific Railroad had reached Willmar, and the following year went as far west as Benson. In 1879, the Hastings and Dakota Railroad was completed through Appleton as far as Ortonville. By the spring of 1887, the Great Northern Railroad had connected Benson and Appleton with Watertown, South Dakota.

The first roads in Swift County were simply wagon tracks—short cuts across the prairies from the homestead to the nearest neighbor and trading center. Extensive construction of improved roads was thought little of until the arrival of the automobile.

While the pioneer settlers were busy with the cultivation of their crops and laying the foundations for prosperous trading centers, some thought had to be devoted also to the organization of the county government, the establishment of townships and school districts, the building of roads, the construction of buildings for county offices, and the raising of taxes in order to carry out these projects.

Agriculture has been and still is the main industry in Swift County. The first homesteaders would usually break 5 to 15 acres that was mainly planted to wheat. Wheat grew well on the virgin soil, and with each succeeding year more wheat was planted. After 1900, other principal crops exceeded wheat in acreage. The average size of the farms in Swift County in 1880 was 170 acres, and in 1910 it reached 265 acres. In 1930, the size was down to 242 acres, but since 1950, the acreage continues to increase.

This book deals with the settlement of Swift County and its development up to the 1930s. The photographs provide a glimpse of Swift County in the formation years, including the growth of trading centers, how the spiritual and educational needs were met, how the county was governed, and the social life of its founders.

The Swift County Historical Society receives numerous genealogy requests. People are tracing family roots and want to know what life was like for their ancestors. It is the hope of the Swift County Historical Society that this book will help to answer their questions.

One

Trading Centers

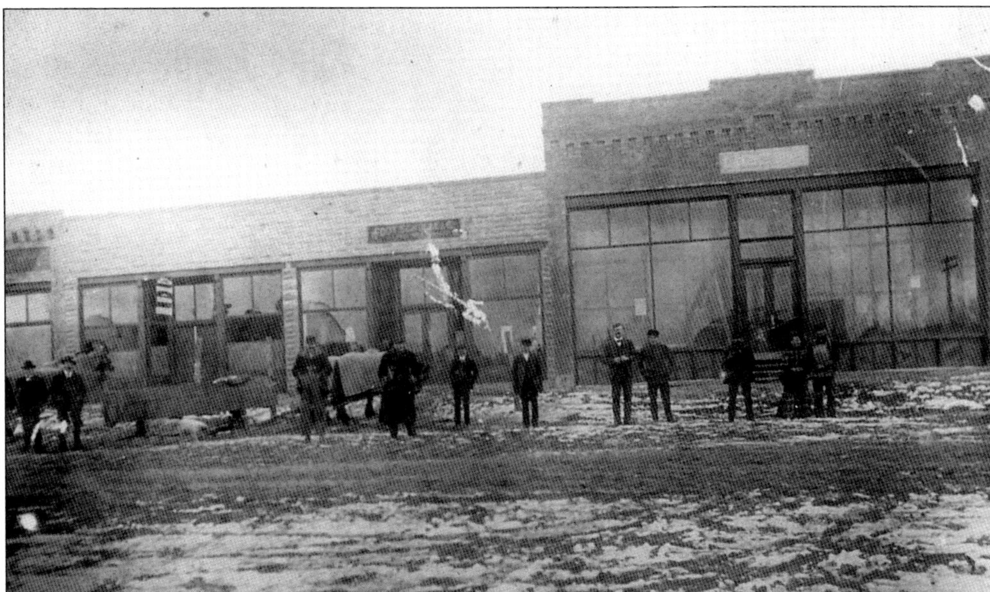

Among the trading centers in Swift County, there were eight incorporated as villages. Swift Falls is the only one appearing on Minnesota maps that was never incorporated. Holloway, originally named Norton and located in Moyer Township, was plotted in 1887, and incorporated as a village in 1903. The population was 2 in 1900 and 215 in 1910.

In January of 1907, a fire in Holloway wiped out an entire business block, destroying a bank, three stores, the post office, and a saloon. The losses reached $57,000. Every trading center in the county experienced losses due to fires.

This postcard view of main street Holloway was taken in 1910. The building on the right was Latzke Brothers store.

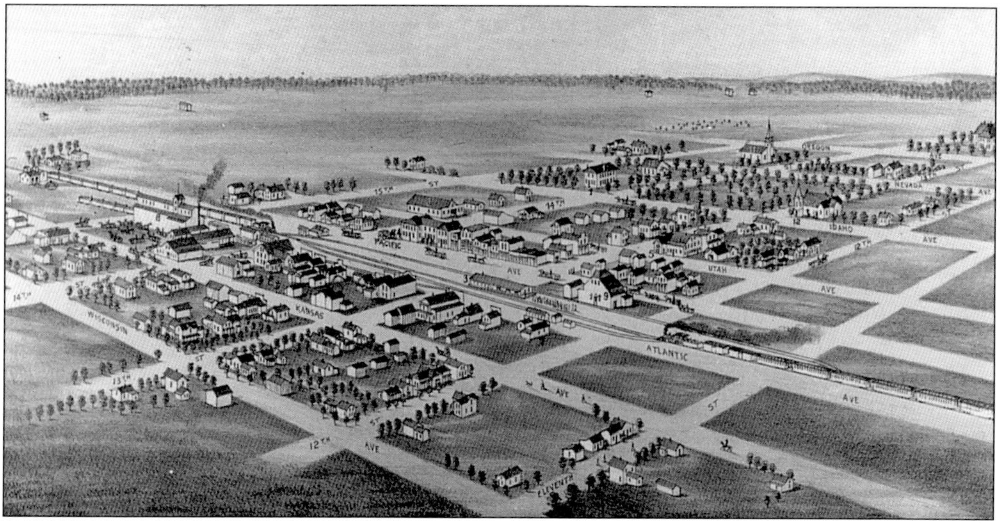

In the spring of 1870, a group of ambitious young men who were aware of the coming of the railroad had set up business on the Chippewa River. That summer, they had to move their places of business. The railroad had chosen a site east of the river as the end of the line and the site of a new trading center, Benson. This 1880 lithograph shows the location of Benson and the Chippewa River (tree border in background).

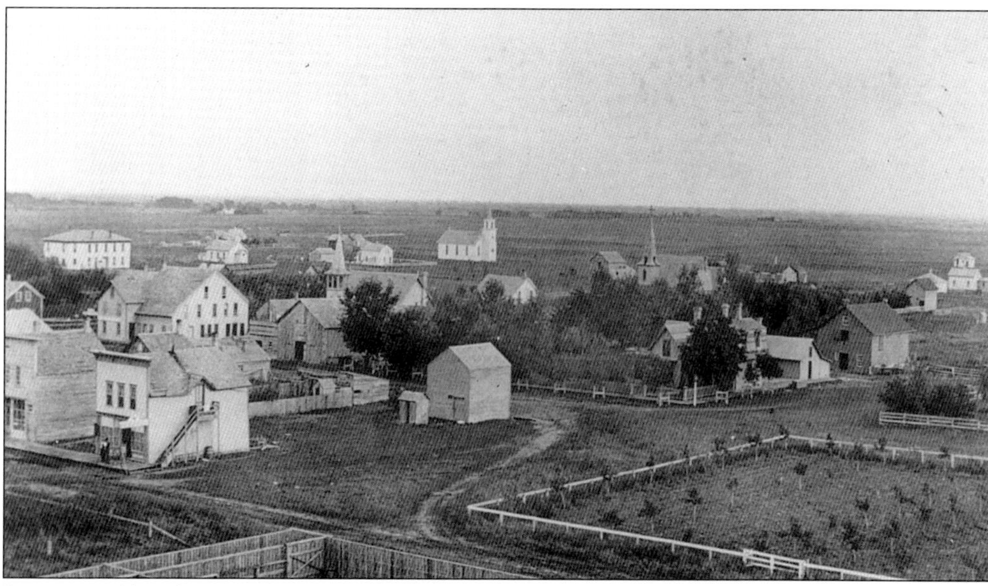

By an act of legislature, Benson was chosen as the county seat. The buildings in the background from the left are the first county courthouse and Benson's first school building.

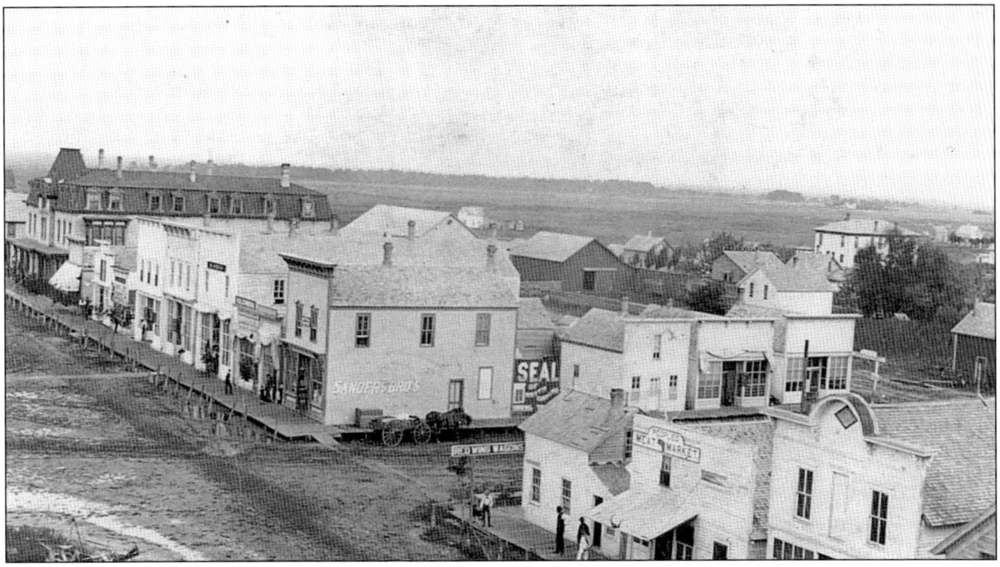

The business district of Benson developed on both sides of the railroad tracks. To the north was Atlantic Avenue. Some of the first businesses were hotels (Aldrich Hotel on left) and general stores (Sanders Brothers, end of block in center of photo). Benson was platted on wet ground, as can be seen in this *c.* 1880s photo.

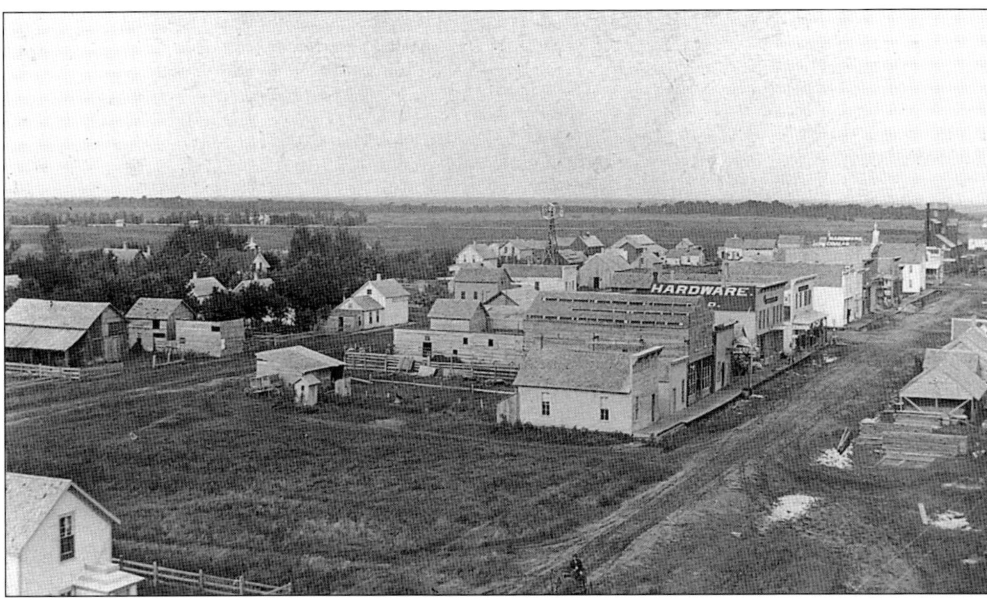

This *c.* 1880s photo is of Pacific Avenue, located south of the tracks in Benson. Ten short years from the arrival of the railroad in 1870, Benson had expanded to 30 business interests and a population of 456. The fact that Benson served as a railroad terminus for the first year and as the trading center for 100 miles to the west, north, and south resulted in the development of a lively trading center.

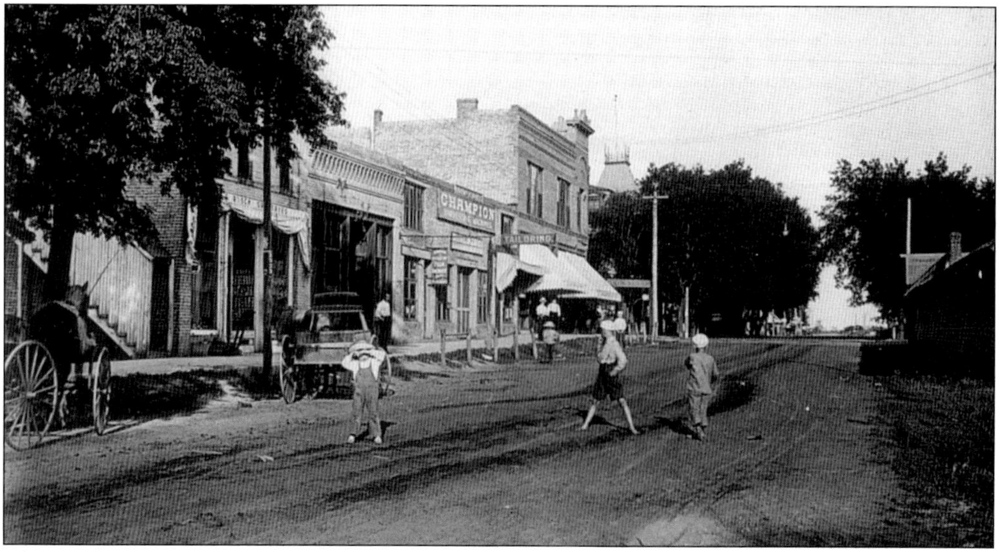

This is the west end of Atlantic Avenue as it appeared in 1908. The population of Benson had reached 1,670 by 1910. Stores extended to three city blocks east and west along Atlantic Avenue. Buildings constructed of brick were replacing wood structures. Trees were now providing ample shade.

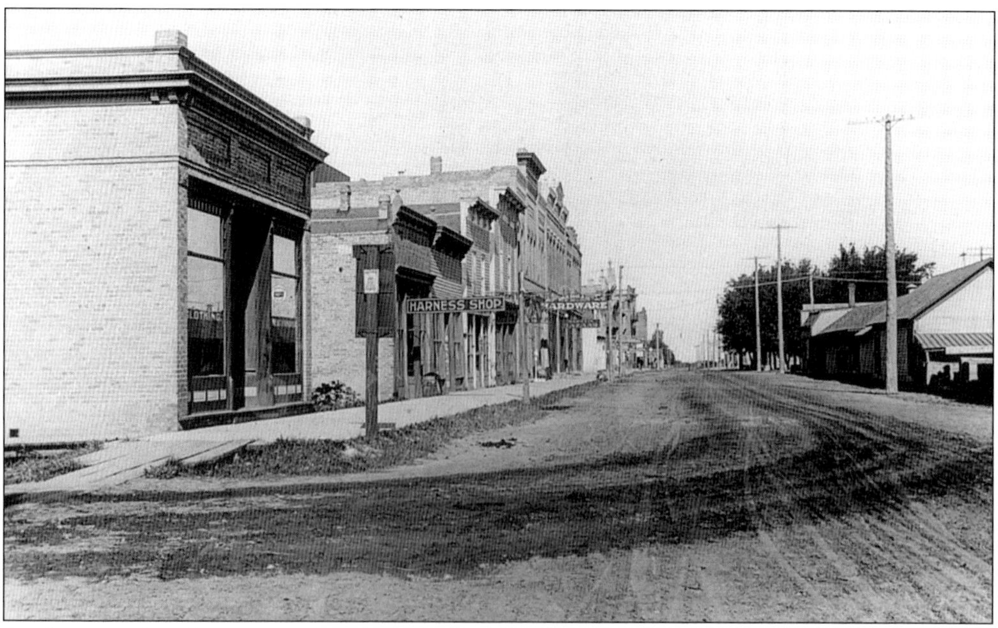

At the time this photo was taken in 1908, brick buildings were prominent on Pacific Avenue. Poles for telephone and electric wires and cement sidewalks adorned Benson streets. Benson's first telephone line was installed in 1893, the first electric plant in 1897, and construction of cement sidewalks began in 1901.

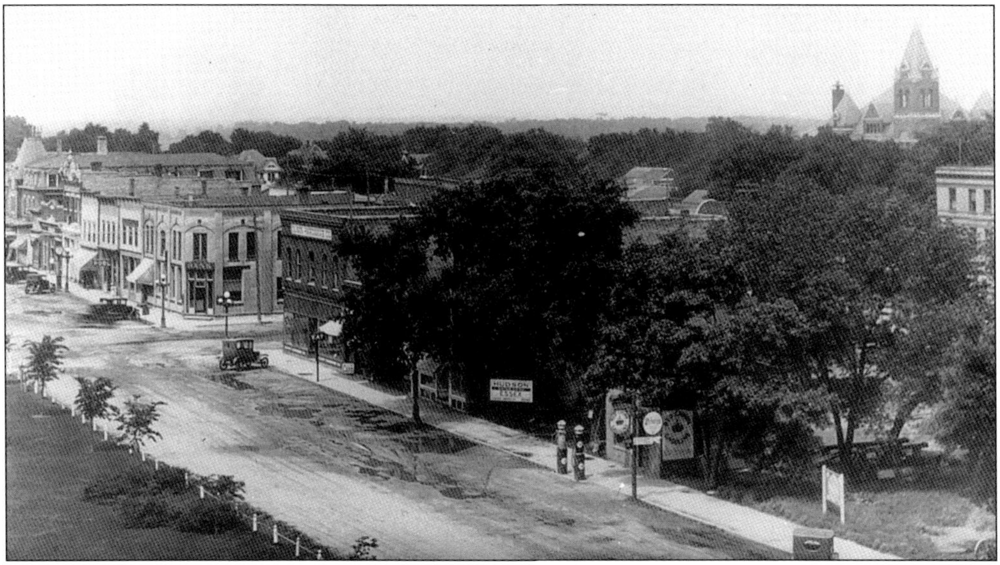

From 1908 to the 1920s, there were not as many changes in the buildings on Atlantic Avenue as there were in the pioneering years. The biggest difference was the appearance of automobiles on the streets of Benson and a new type of business, gas stations.

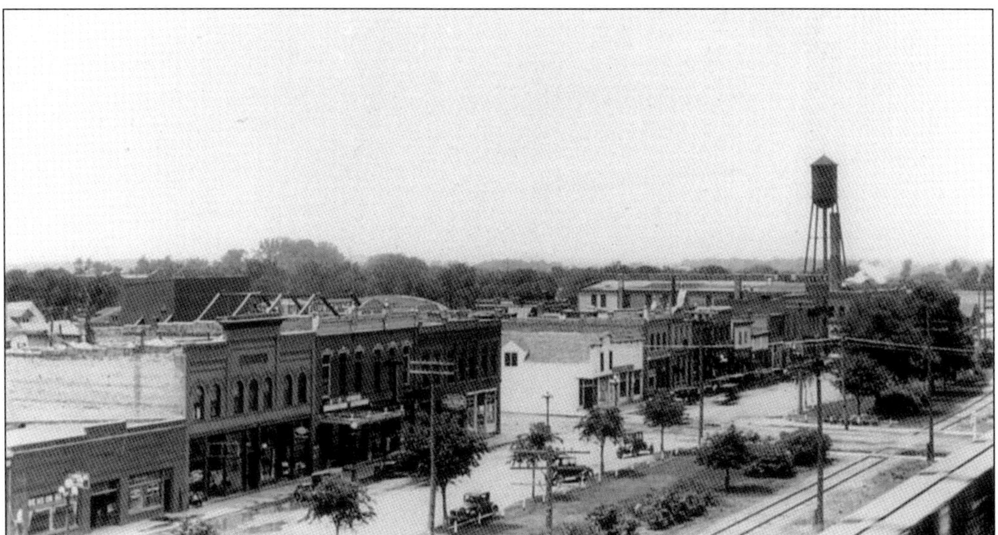

On the left of this *c.* 1925 photo of Pacific Avenue is a garage and auto sales business, which had been the location of a harness shop. In 1926, Benson began paving the streets in the business district to accommodate the increasing number of automobiles.

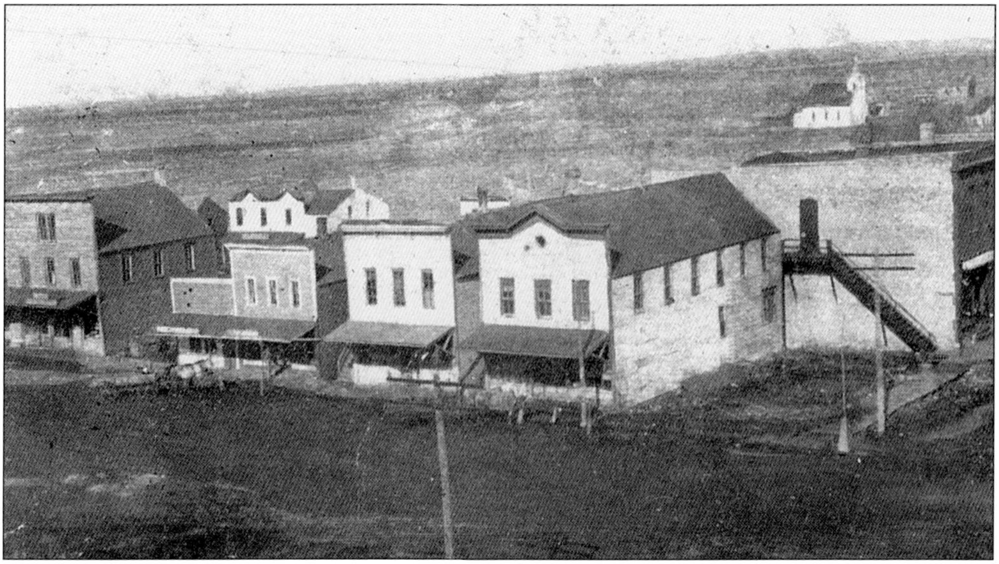

This *c.* 1890s photo is of Kerkhoven, which is located on the eastern end of Swift County. Kerkhoven was one of the trading centers determined by the railroad in 1870. It was incorporated as a village in 1881, and given the name Pillsbury due to its central location in Pillsbury Township. However, two years later the citizens decided to return to the name Kerkhoven.

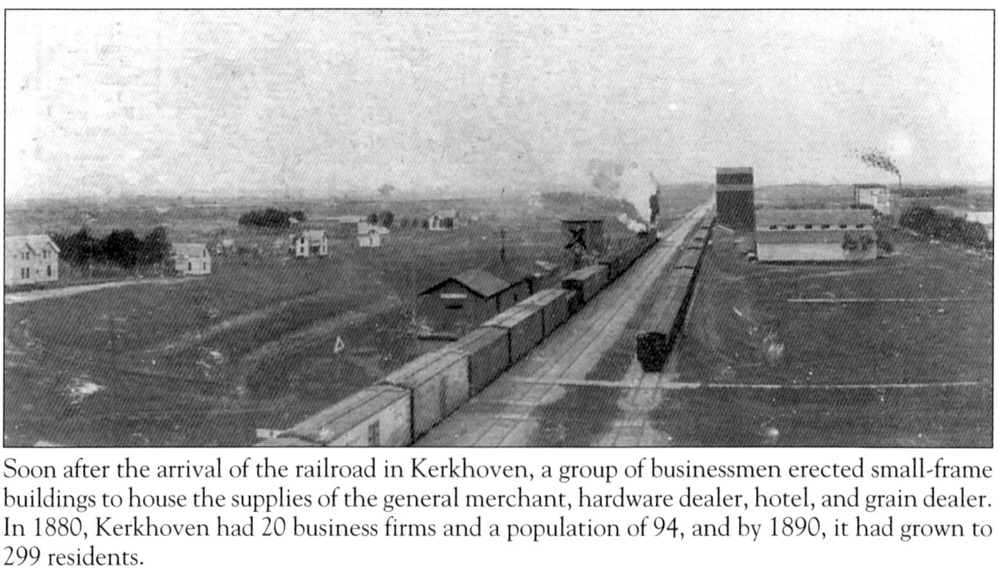

Soon after the arrival of the railroad in Kerkhoven, a group of businessmen erected small-frame buildings to house the supplies of the general merchant, hardware dealer, hotel, and grain dealer. In 1880, Kerkhoven had 20 business firms and a population of 94, and by 1890, it had grown to 299 residents.

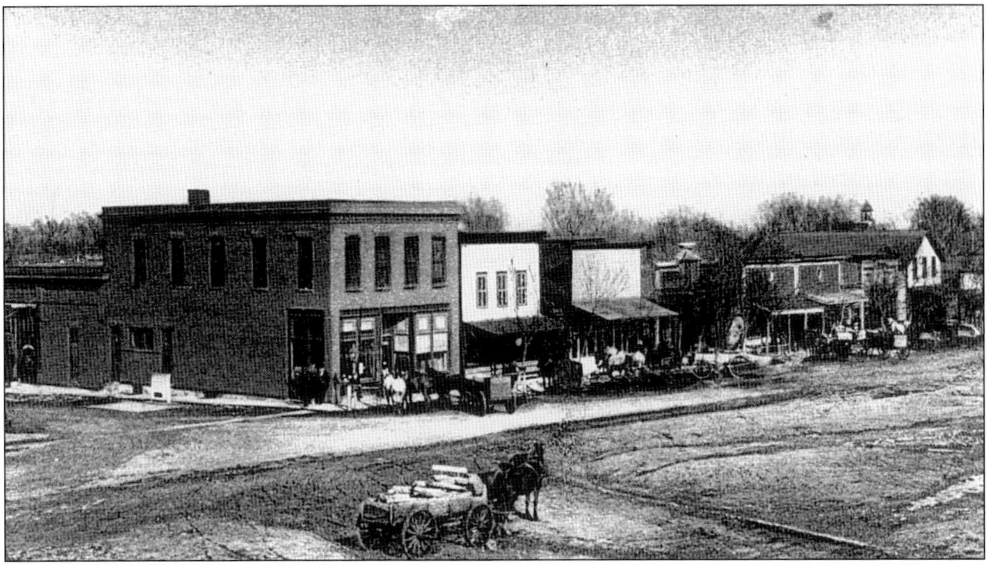

This photo of Atlantic Avenue in Kerkhoven was taken after 1902. Atlantic Avenue was the name given to one of the main streets in each of the first town sites plotted by the railroad—Kerkhoven, DeGraff, and Benson.

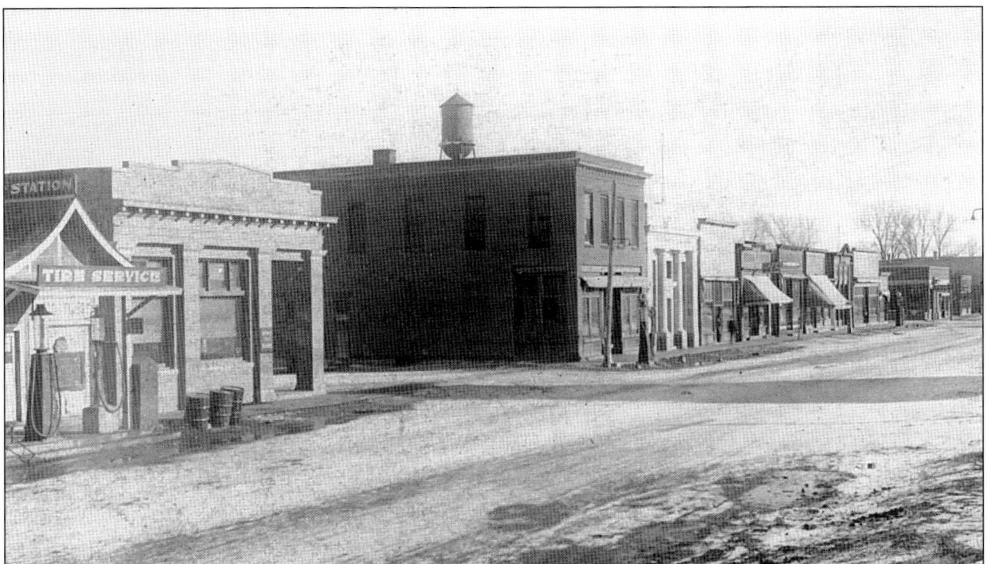

The building on the left is one of the gas stations which were established in Kerkhoven after the arrival of the automobile. This gas station was located on Atlantic Avenue. C.A. Rosengren had a filling station on Pacific Avenue, south of the tracks, with a visible gas pump in 1919.

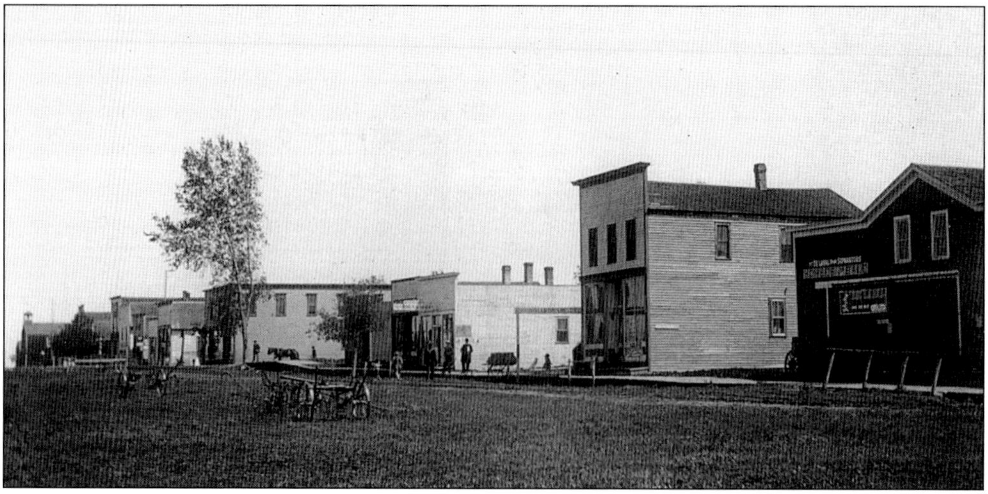

In 1875, DeGraff was founded in Kildare Township. DeGraff became one of the colonies for the Catholic Bureau of Colonization in 1876, when the bureau was formed to encourage Catholics in the eastern states to move to Minnesota. Groups of families immediately settled in the area. July of 1876 brought two years of grasshoppers that wiped out the crops, slowing the rate of immigration, and leaving mortgaged and deserted farms. The bright future for DeGraff had faded.

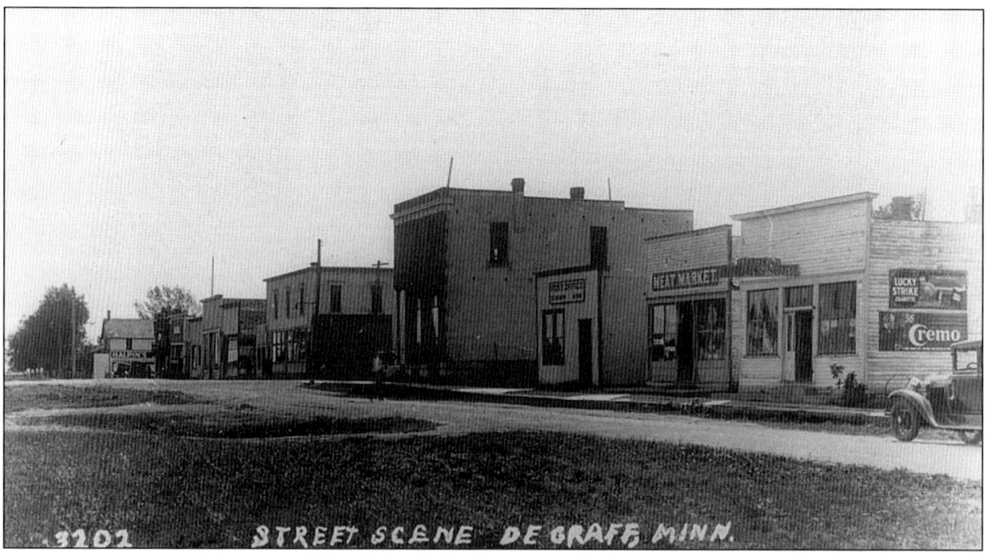

DeGraff was much like other trading centers in the formation years. Businesses included general stores, hotels, hardware stores, banks, post office, meat markets, and harness shops. This photo was taken in 1932, before the Depression of the 1930s resulted in the closure of businesses in DeGraff and many other small towns.

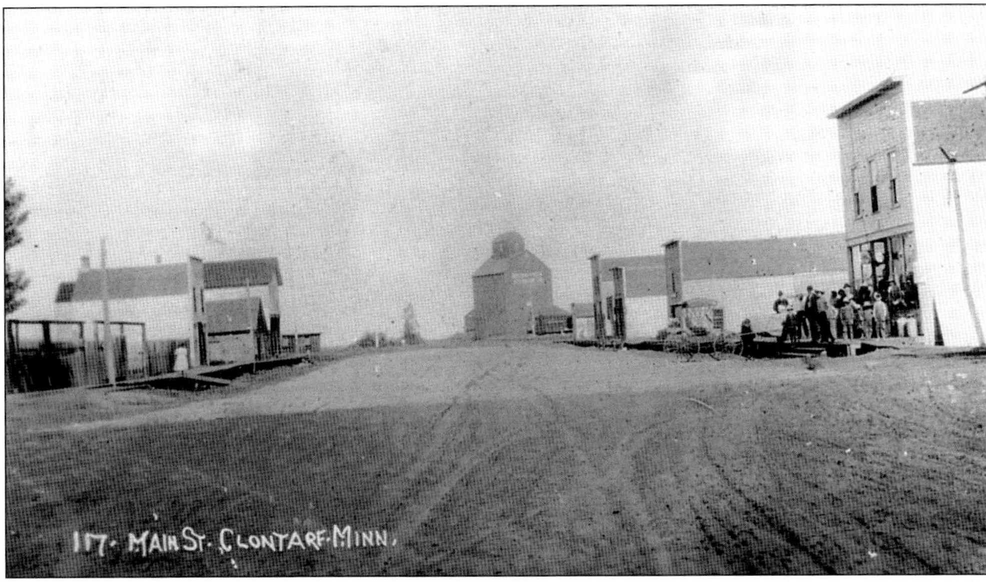

In 1871, the railroad was completed from Benson to Breckenridge. A railroad siding, 7 miles northwest of Benson and intended as a town site, was named Randall Station. In 1876, Randall Station was selected as the site of the second colony for the Bureau of Catholic Colonization. The colony lumberyard was established about 1 mile south of Randall. In 1877, the name Randall was changed to Clontarf. In addition to the lumberyard, post office, and elevator (1878), other early enterprises included Fallihee & Nolan General Store, John Green's Yard Goods Store, D.M. McDonald—carpenter, and Frank Roll—sewing machines. Clontarf is located in Clontarf Township.

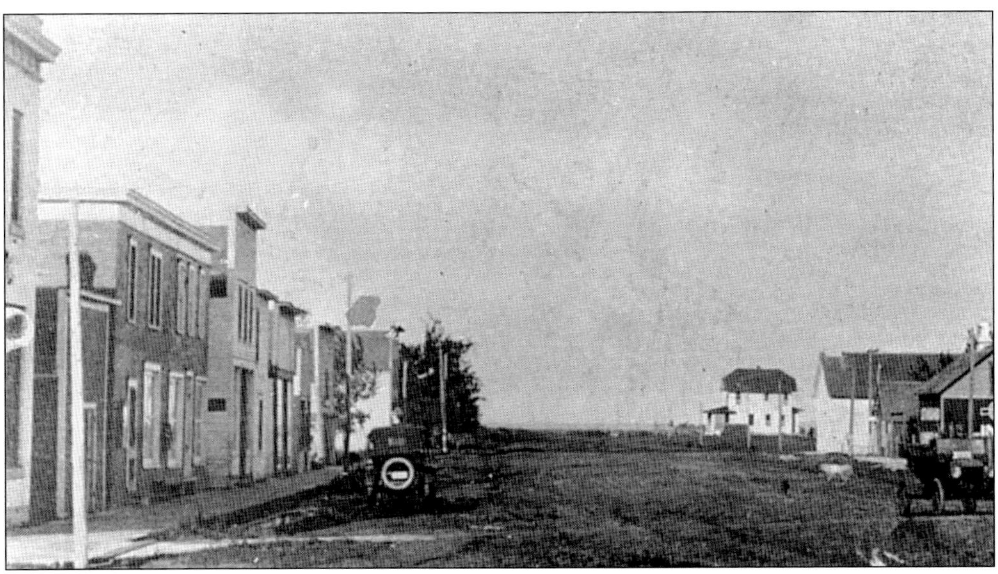

The building on the extreme left was the Farmers State Bank of Clontarf. In 1920, a Christmas Eve fire destroyed all the buildings between the bank and Mikkelson-McDonald store.

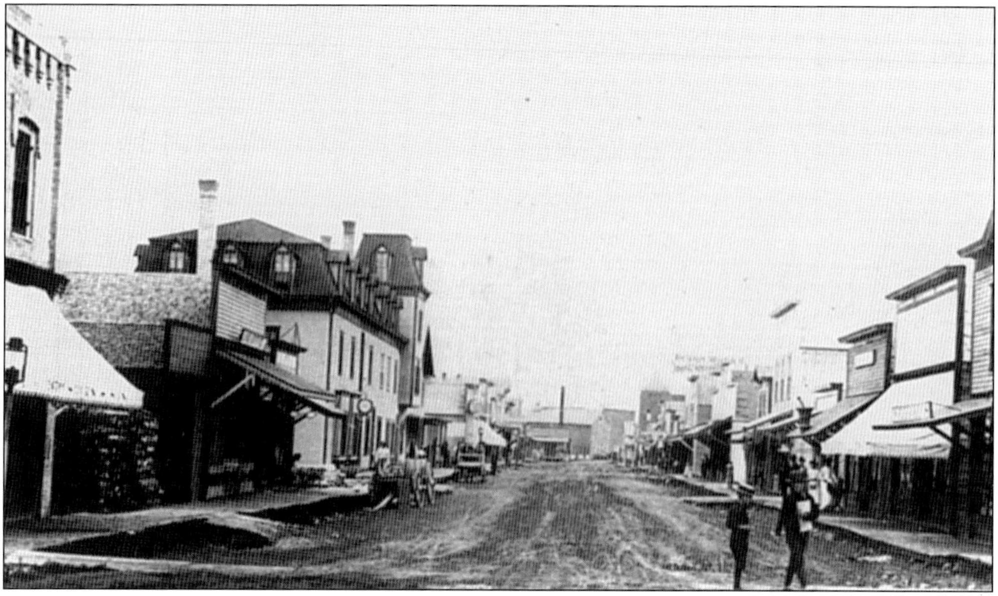

In 1874, the Village of Appleton contained one store, one hotel, one blacksmith shop, one mill, and about a half-dozen dwellings. There were more than 60 business establishments in 1892. This photo of Main Street, Appleton, shows the rapid growth in the second largest trading center in Swift County. Appleton is located in Appleton Township.

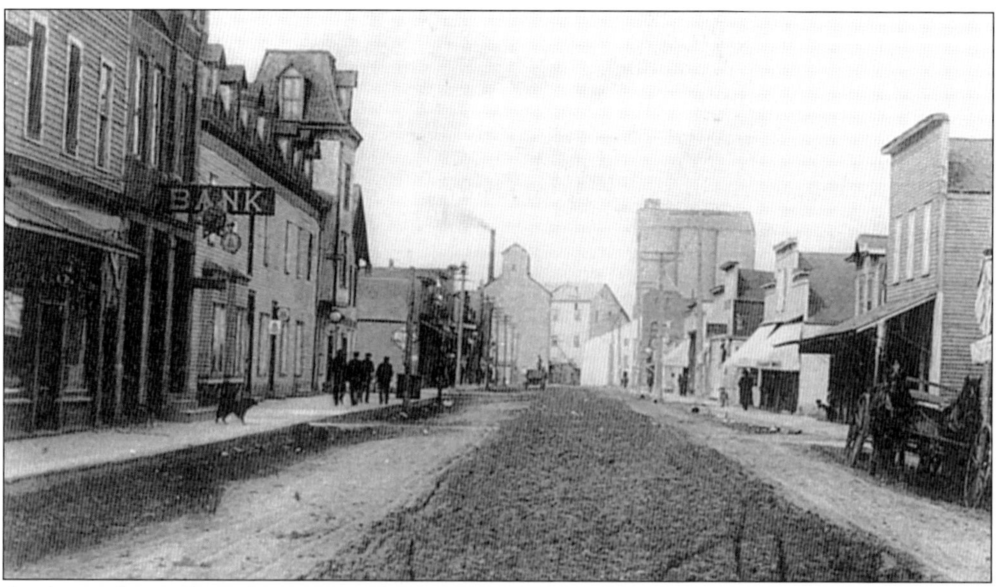

Appleton, located on the Pomme de Terre River on the west end of Swift, was one of two waterpower sites in the county. A flourmill was completed in 1872, with a second one in 1878. Prior to the Appleton mill, farmers had to depend on the New London mill (approximately 50 miles northeast of Appleton) or the market at Benson or Kerkhoven. The flourmill can be seen at the north end of Main Street in this *c.* 1908 postcard view.

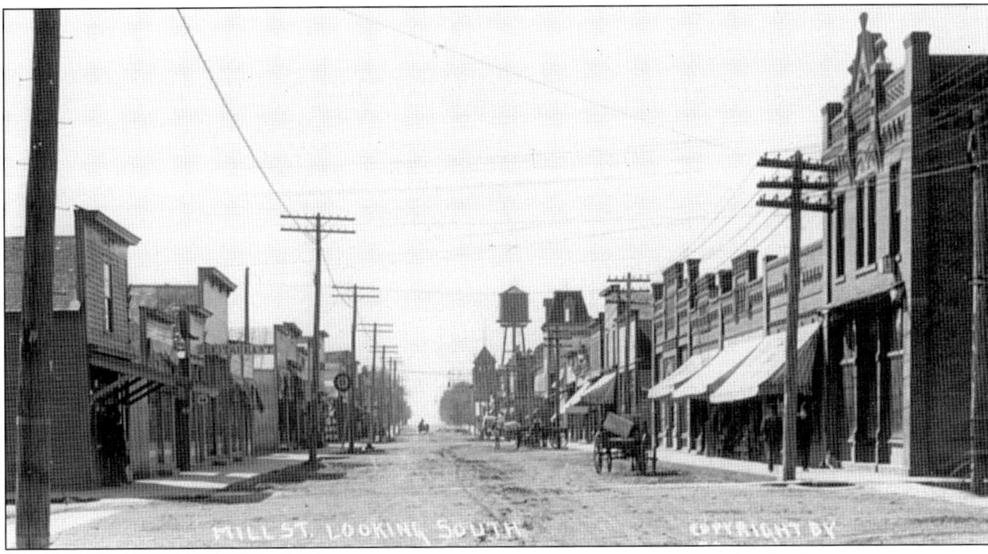

In 1897, an electric light and power company was organized and a local telephone exchange put into operation at Appleton. A resolution was passed to replace the boardwalks with cement in 1901. This photo was taken in 1911, looking south down Mill Street in Appleton.

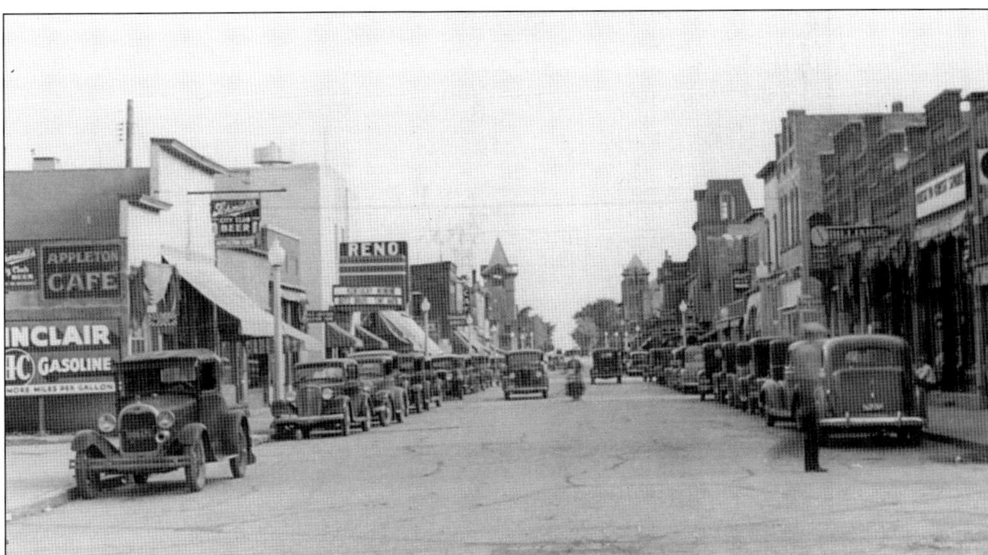

By the 1930s, Mill Street in Appleton had seen many changes. Automobiles now filled the street. The Reno Theater, on the left, was in its third building, the first two having been destroyed by fire. The Scenic Theater, as it was called in 1910, was opened by Reno Risch, who previously operated a grocery store in Benson.

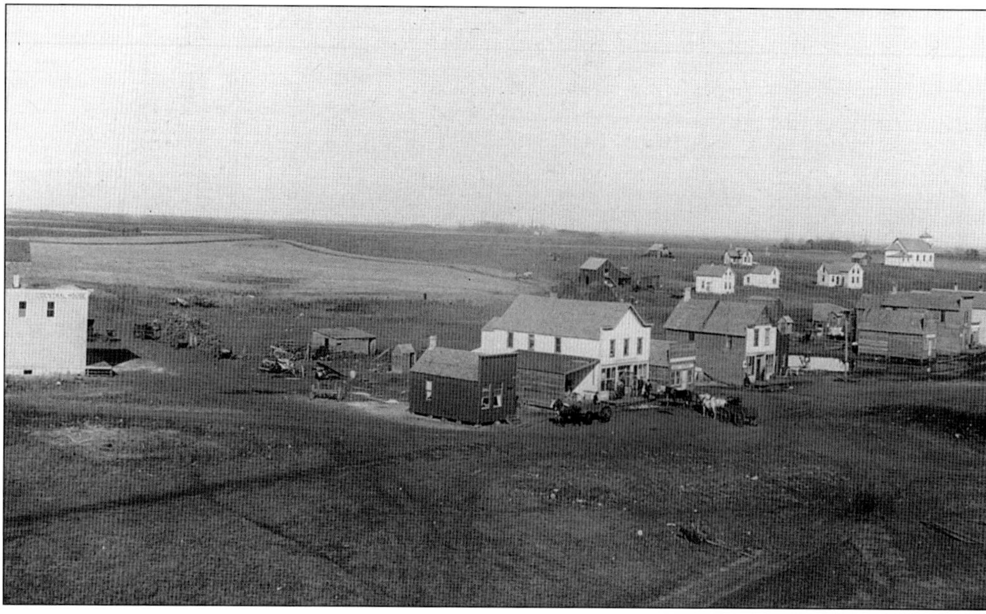

Another railroad town, Danvers was platted in 1887. The first business activity was in a 12 by 16-foot store operated by Andrew H. Mattheisen. This photo of Danvers was taken in the late 1890s. In the background on the right is the first Catholic church built in 1892. Danvers is located in Marysland Township.

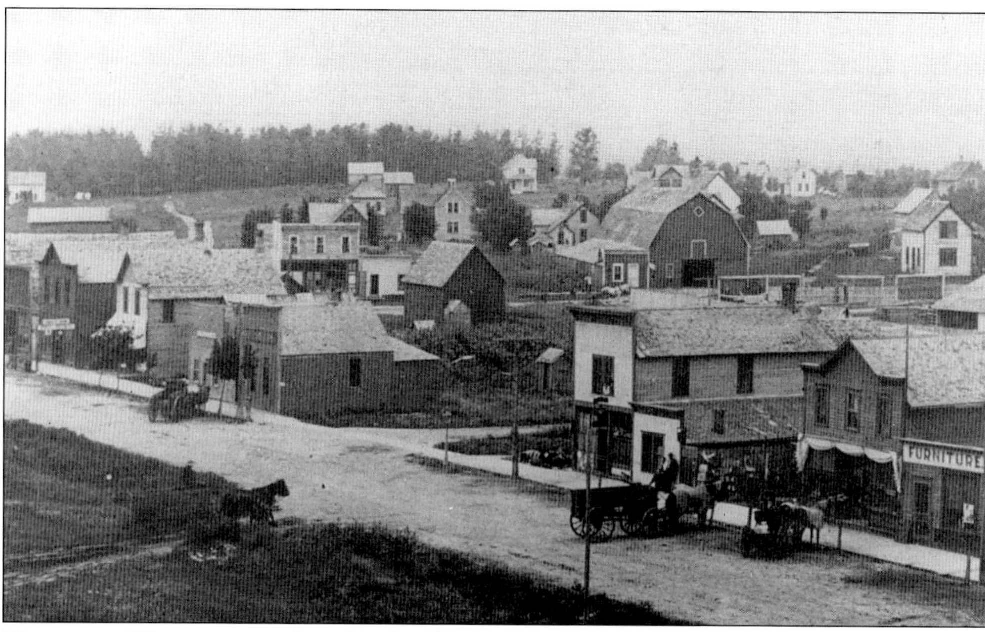

This view of Danvers was taken shortly after 1900. By 1900, Danvers had 20 business interests and a population of 112. There were three hotels, saloons, feed mill, blacksmith shop, hardware and harness shop, livery stables, and Edmund Juvet's general and furniture store (on the right). The barn-shaped building towards the center of the photo was one of the stables.

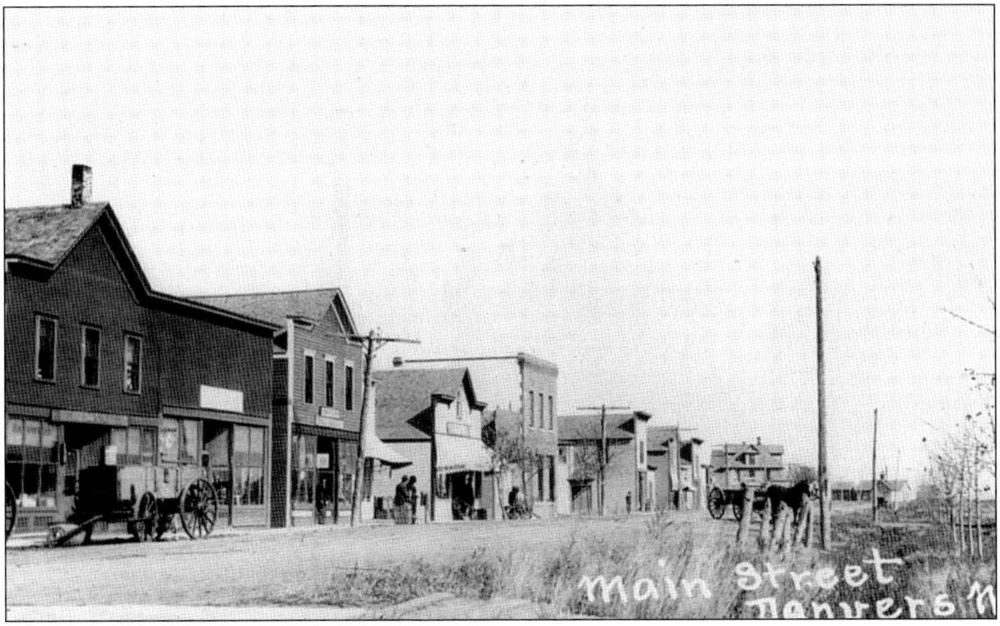

Kerosene and gas streetlights served Danvers from 1906 until 1922, when a municipally-owned lighting system served the village. In 1925, electric power was contracted with Otter Tail Power Company. The brick building in the center of the photo was the State Bank of Danvers, which was built in 1912. Danvers Rural Telephone Company occupied its second floor.

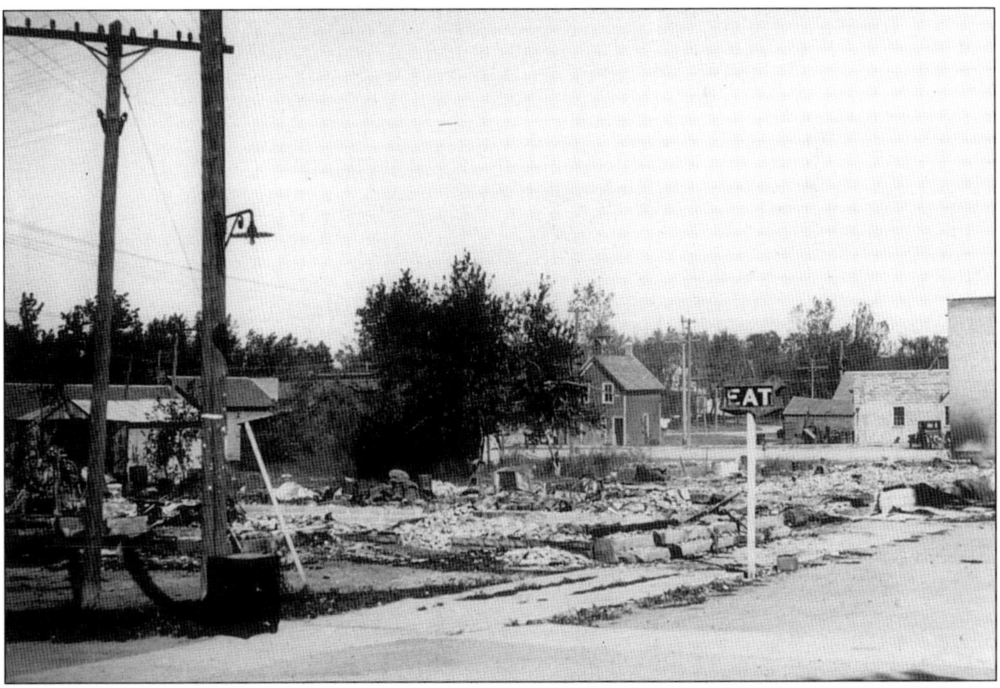

In October of 1931, an entire city block in Danvers was destroyed by fire. The wood-frame buildings were reduced to ashes. The only building remaining was the State Bank of Danvers, which was constructed of brick. Largely due to the Depression of the 1930s, merchants who had lost their businesses were unable to recover.

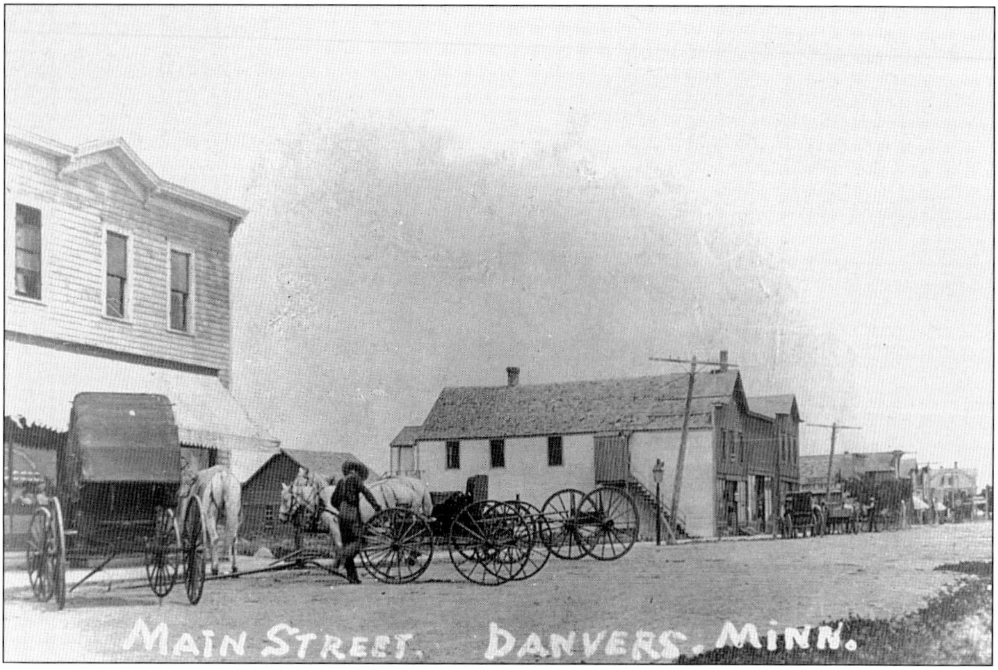

On the left is the Rykken and Tiegen general store, which was established in Danvers in 1901. Mr. Tiegen also sold machinery and livestock. The next building to the right was owned by Charles Dolan. It housed a butcher shop, lunch room, and hotel. This picture was taken before the 1931 fire.

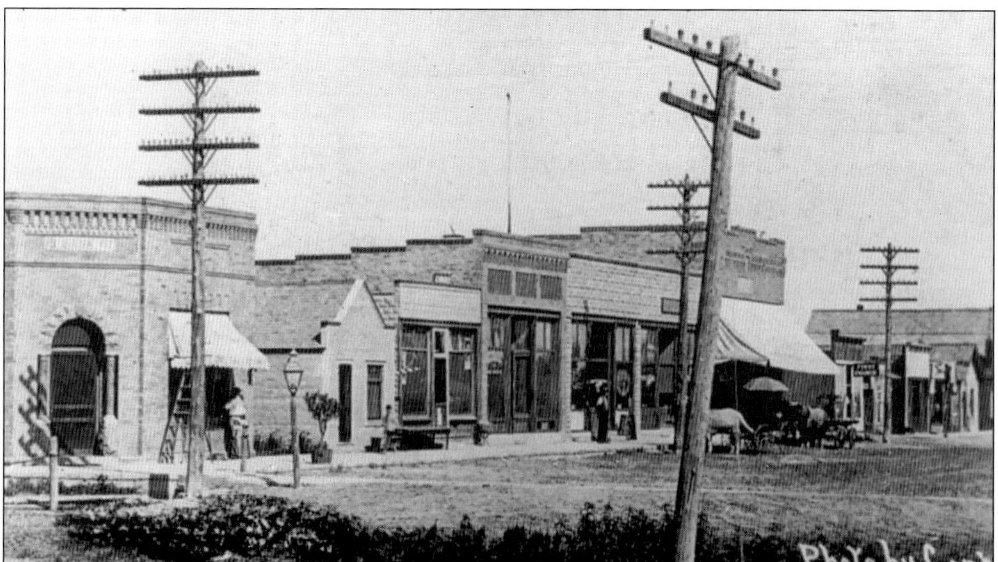

This is a view of Main Street, Holloway, looking north. The building on the left is the Bank of Holloway, built in 1907. Holloway's first bank building had been destroyed by fire. The community had three banks that consolidated in 1923.

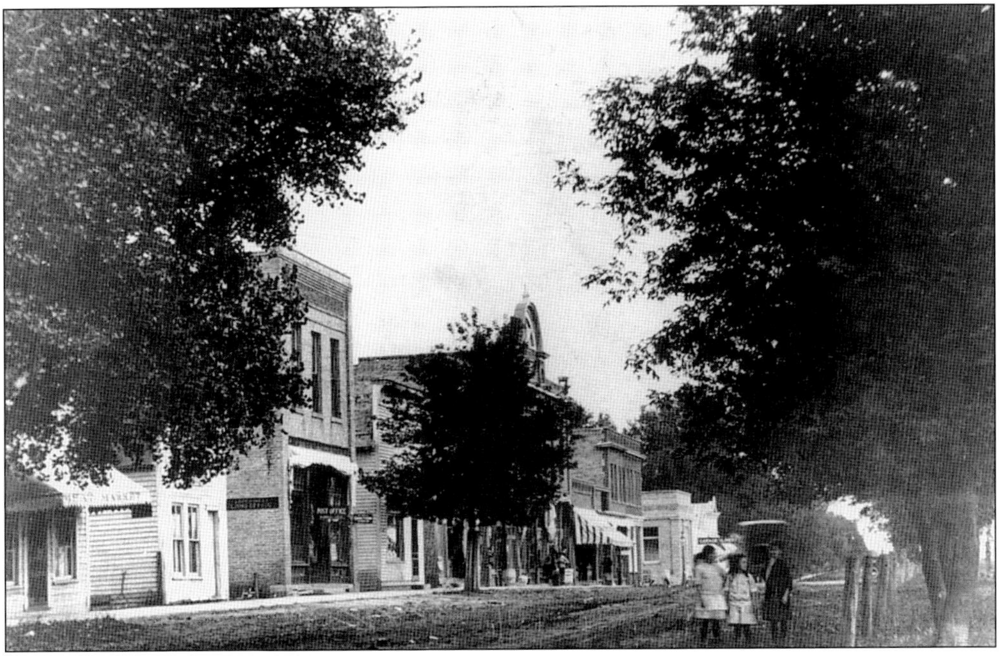

In 1876, Samuel Murdock, along with Joseph Schaaf, began to lay out the plans for a town site between Kerkhoven and DeGraff. It was given the name Murdock after its founder. By 1879, Murdock had three hotels, a drug store, a blacksmith and machine repairer, and a lumberyard. Murdock is located in Dublin Township.

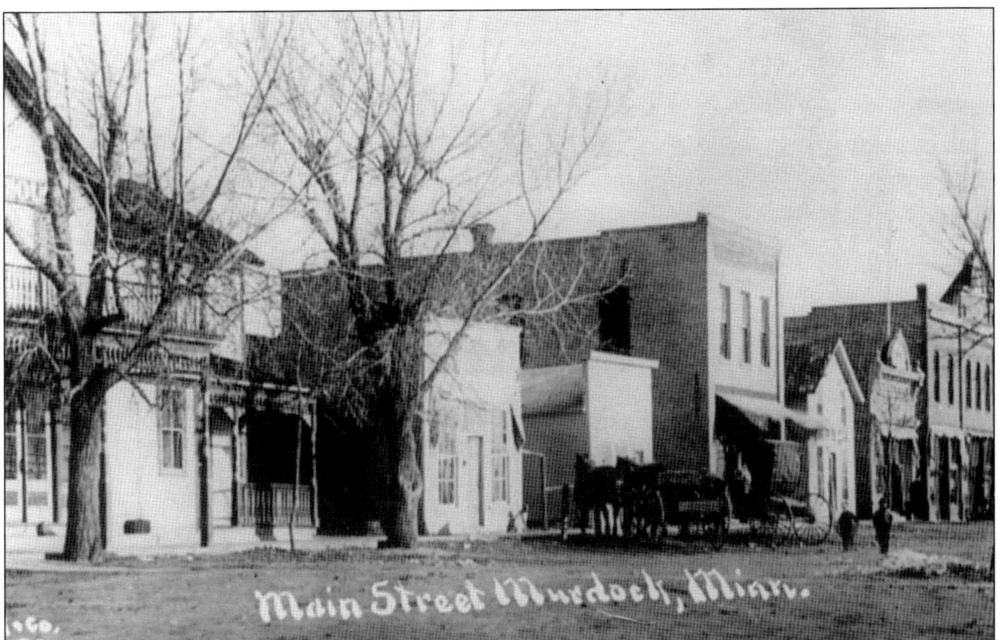

The Schlagel Hotel is the building on the left in this Murdock street scene. In 1892, Matthew Schlagel purchased the hotel from John Weber, who had operated the hotel under the name of the Murdock House. The original Murdock House was established in 1879. It burned in 1881, and this building was constructed.

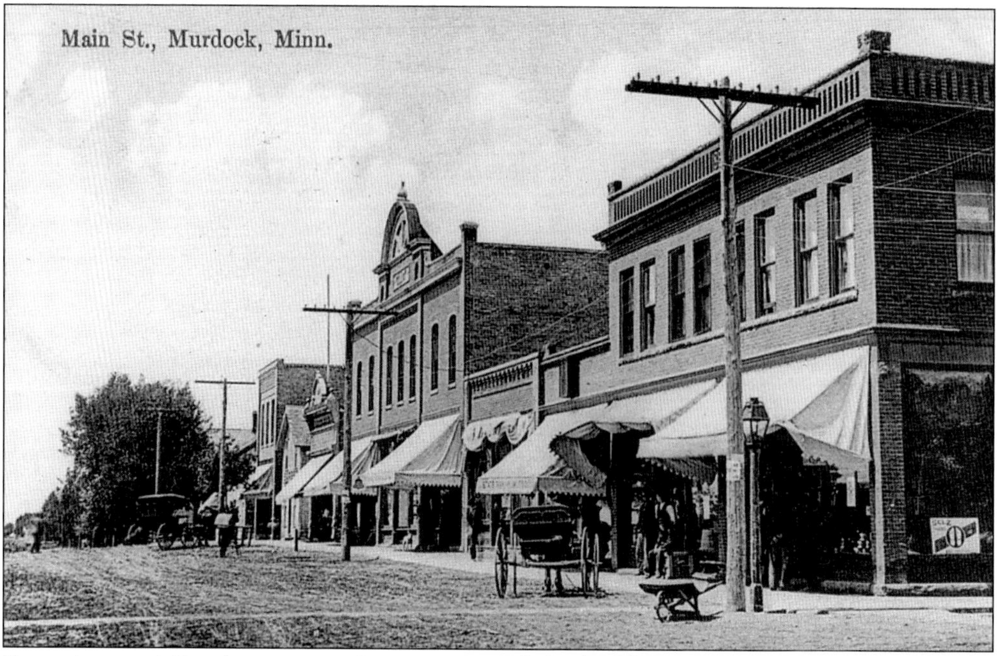

Samuelson and Rundquist general store occupied the building on the right in this Murdock street scene. They began their business in 1896, with a capital of $1,500. The small building next to it was the Bank of Murdock, founded in 1892. In 1916, the bank moved into a new building and was called the First State Bank of Murdock.

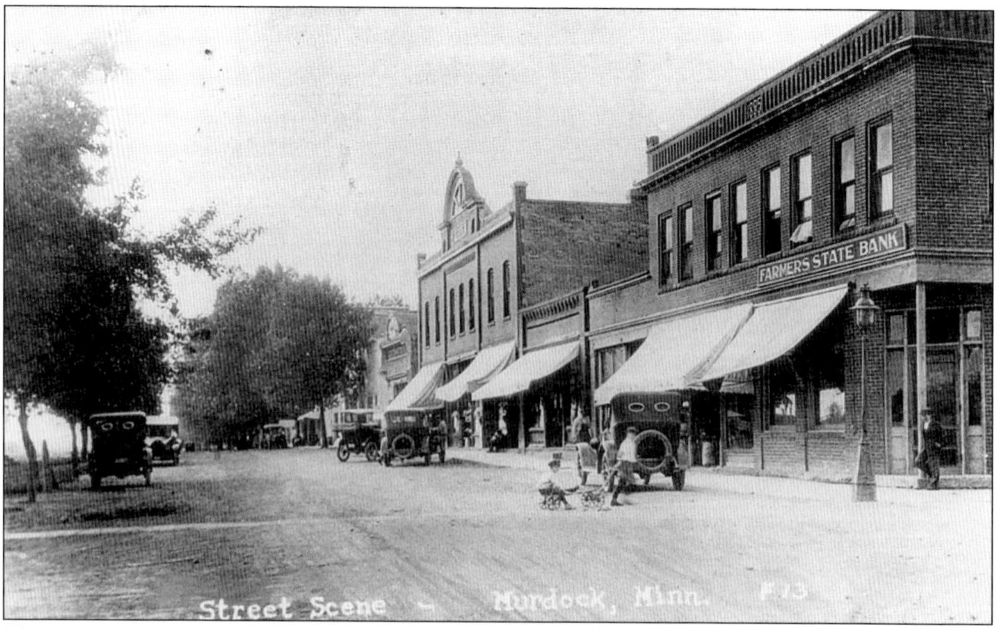

The Farmers State Bank also occupied the building that housed Samuelson and Rundquist general store. It was the second bank in Murdock. In 1915, a group composed mostly of farmers started the bank with a capital of $25,000 and surplus of $5,000. The bank was hit by the Depression of 1929 and was forced to close.

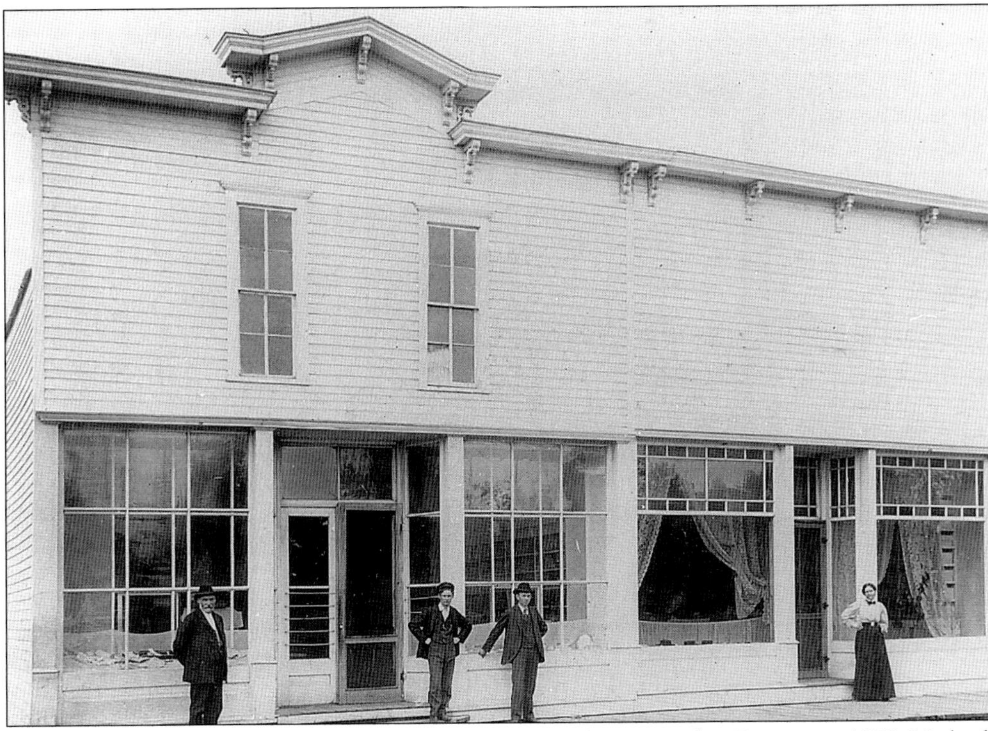

Theodore Hansen purchased a ticket on the first train that arrived in Benson in 1870. He built a small wood frame building for his general store. In 1878, he had the building in this photo constructed just north of his old store on the corner of Pacific Avenue and 13th Street. From left to right are Theodore Hansen, his son Harold Hansen, Harold Olson, and Mrs. Joe Hendrickson who rented part of the building for her millinery shop.

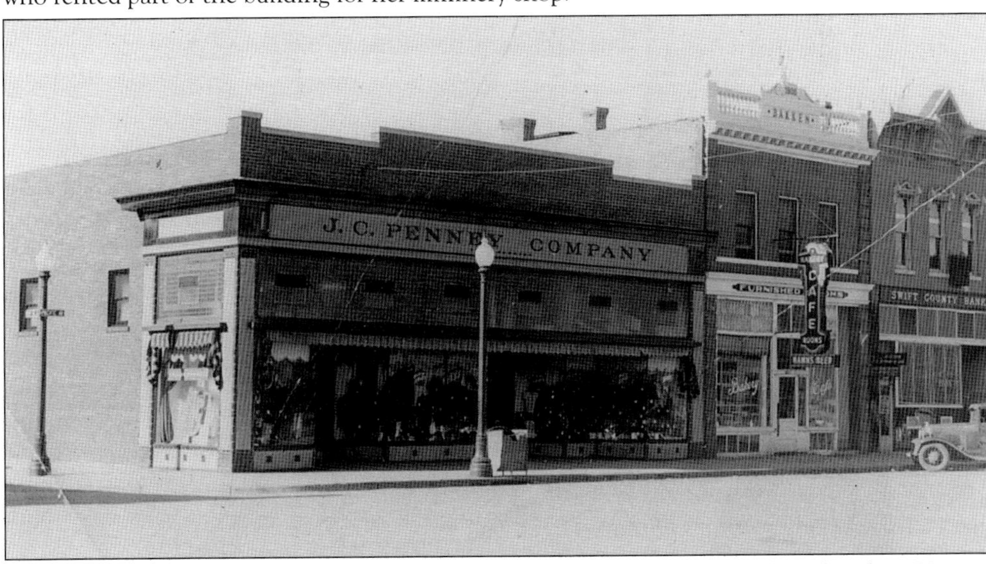

In May of 1929, J.C. Penney Co. secured a 15-year lease in Benson. The Theodore Hansen building was razed and a new building erected on its site. The J.C. Penney store opened for business on December 12, 1929. The building to the right was built in 1900 by S.H. Bakken for a restaurant and hotel. The second floor contained about 20 bedrooms for rent.

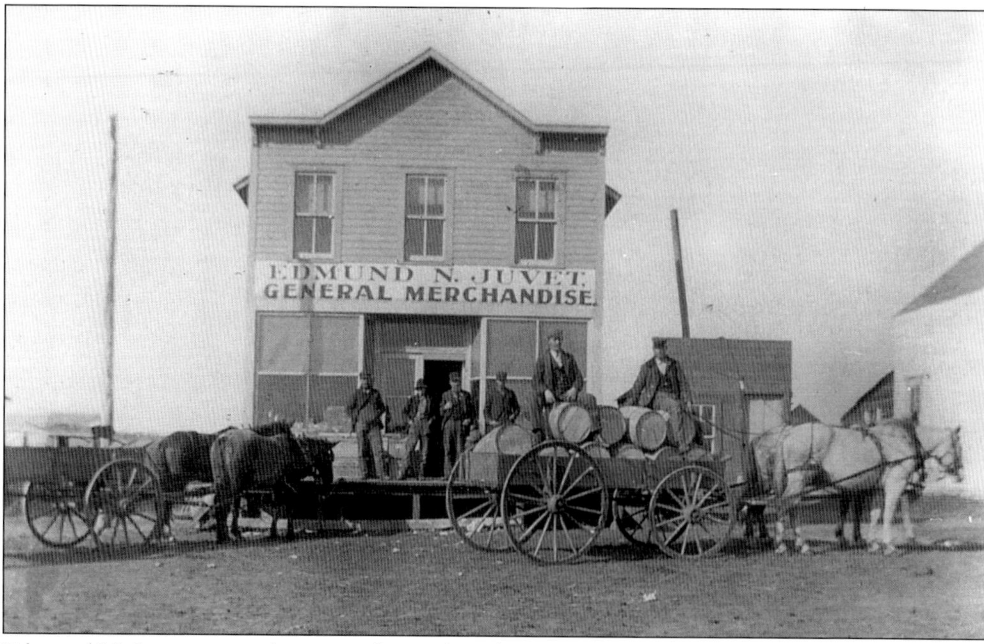

Edmund N. Juvet opened a general merchandise store in Danvers in 1898, and also served as postmaster for the village. In 1905, he sold his store to Robert B. Coy, who ran the store until his death in 1909. Mr. Coy's three sons took over the business and changed the name to Coy Brothers.

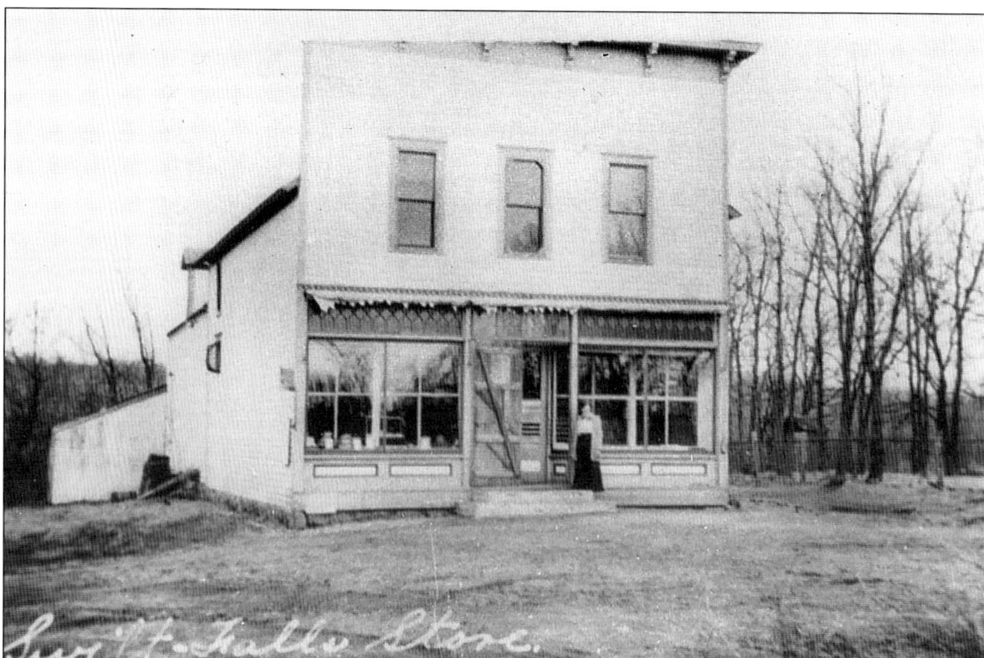

J.M. Danelz erected this general merchandise store at Swift Falls in 1871. Additions were added at various times, including a cafe in 1918. Alfred Flaten purchased the store in 1927, and changed the name to Swift Mercantile Company. During the Depression years, the store became a focal point for social affairs, including the rabbit hunt headquarters.

The Swift County Bank was started in 1876 by Z.B. Clarke and H.W. Stone with a capital of $5,000. The institution operated as a private bank until it was incorporated in 1907. Clarke and Stone had this building erected for their bank in 1881. It is located on Pacific Avenue in Benson.

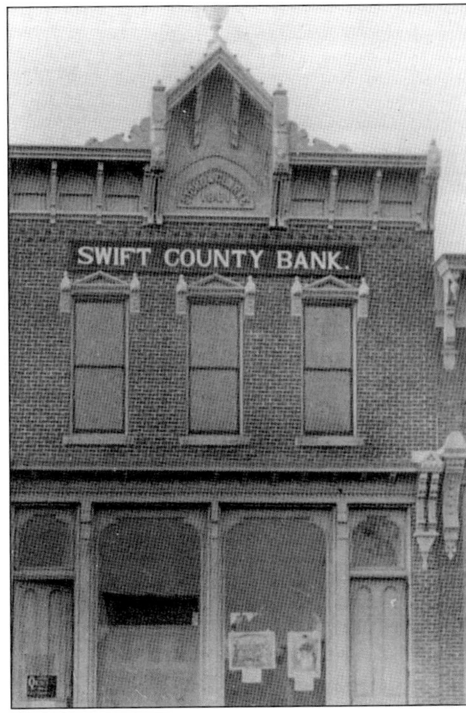

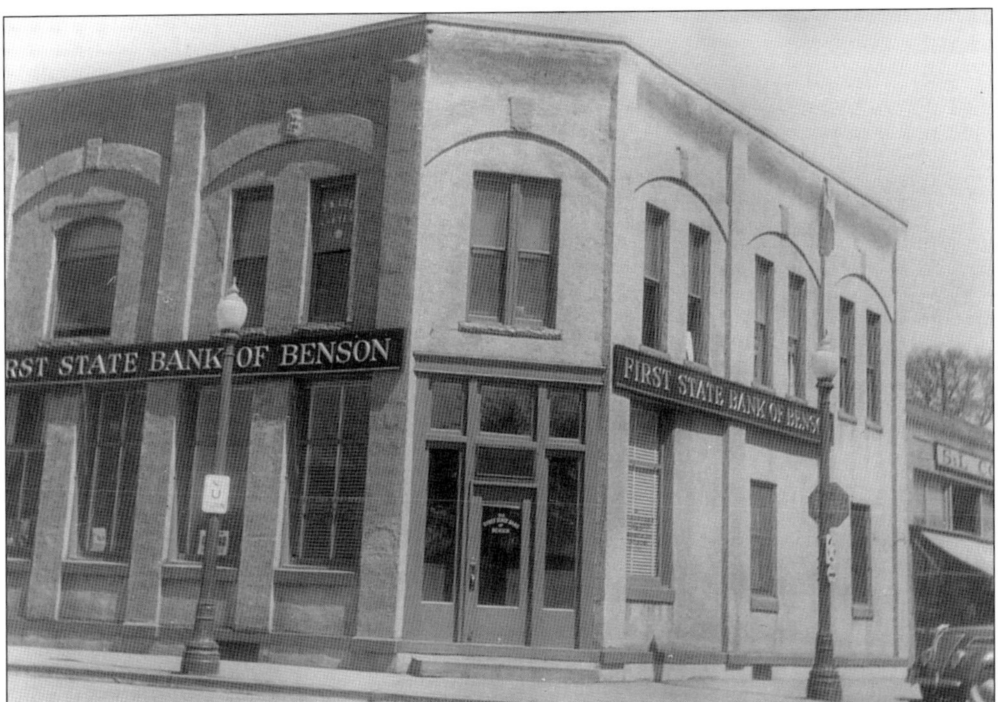

Large brick buildings like the one in this photo were often referred to as a block. In 1891, R.R. Johnson had the building constructed on the corner of Atlantic Avenue and 13th Street South. It was known as the Abstract Block and the leading office building in Benson.

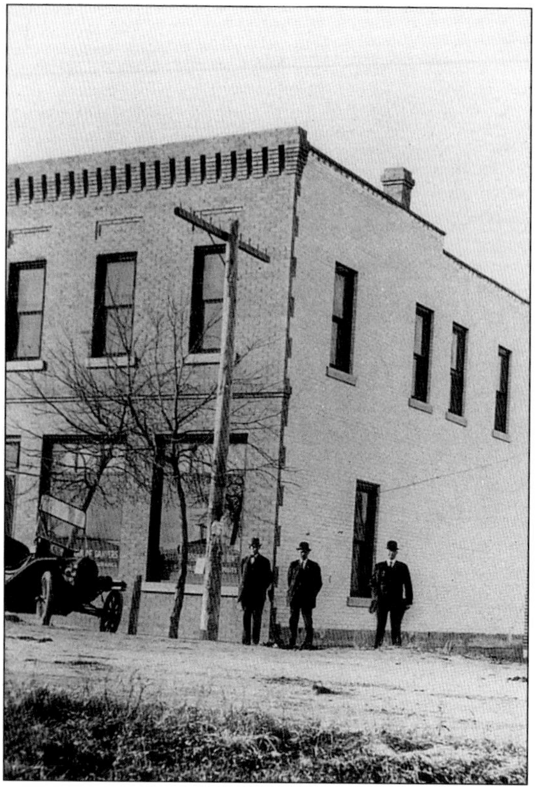

The Bank of Danvers was opened in 1902. Later, Thomas H. Connelly and Leslie Matthews purchased the bank, with Connelly assuming management. It was renamed the State Bank of Danvers in 1907. This brick building was constructed in 1912 on the same location as the first bank. Connelly was an automobile enthusiast and was one of the first auto owners in the county.

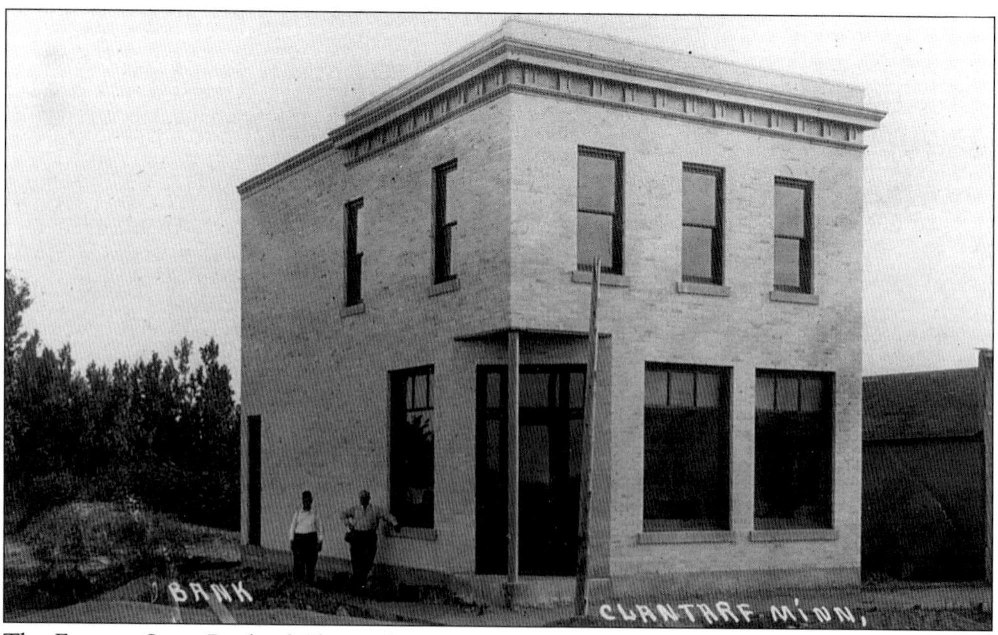

The Farmers State Bank of Clontarf was organized in 1912. Bruno Perrizo was the president and William J. Perrizo the cashier. In 1931, the bank was purchased by the First Bank Stock Corporation of Minnesota and merged with the First State Bank of Benson. The bank building was then converted into a cafe. Photo was taken about 1915.

The T. Knudson building in this photo was located on Atlantic Avenue. It was built in 1878 for a cost of $2,800 and believed to be the first brick business structure in Benson. Two years later, a fire broke out in a saloon and wiped out every business on the city block including T. Knudson's general store.

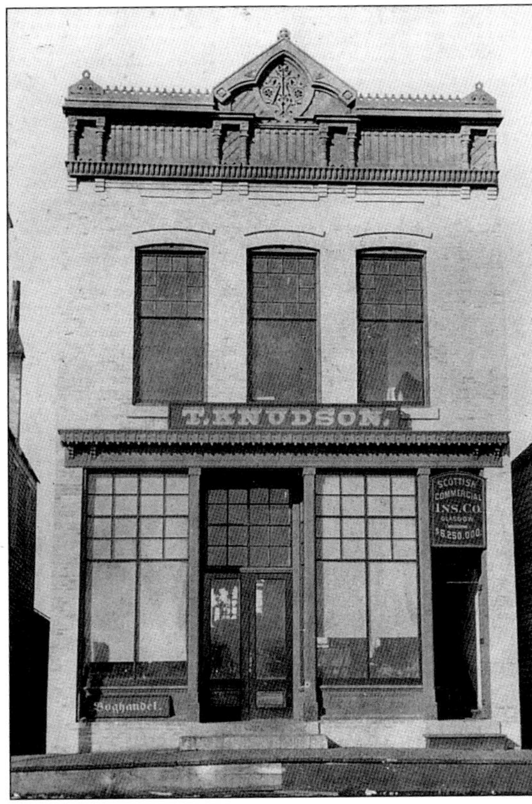

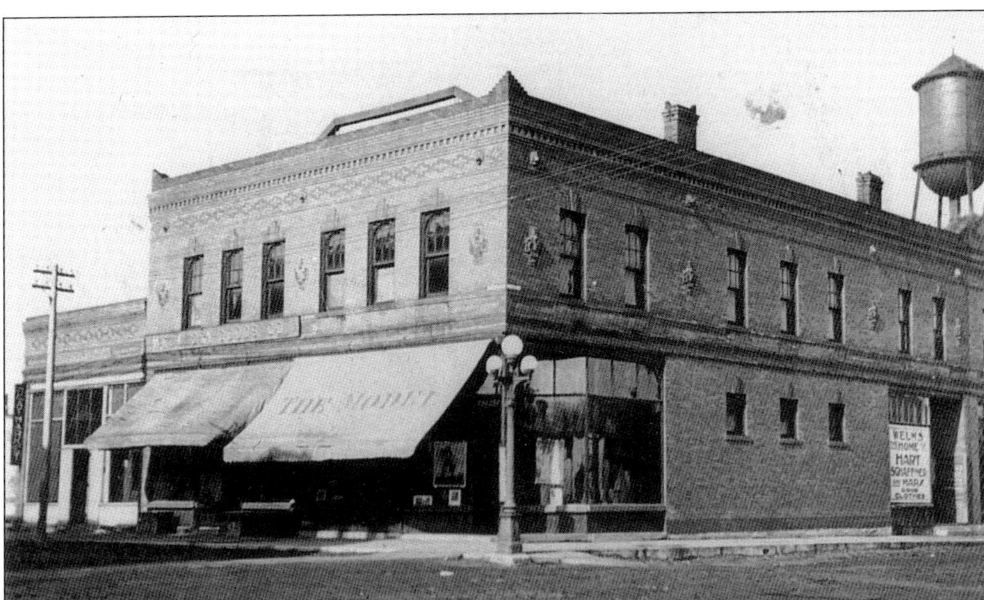

The Benson Times newspaper of July 31, 1900, reported "work will commence at once on S.H. Hudson and John Lee's new block to be located on the corner of Pacific Avenue and 14th Street South. The first floor will accommodate two stores, and the second floor will be fitted up for lodge purposes with a large main hall and anterooms."

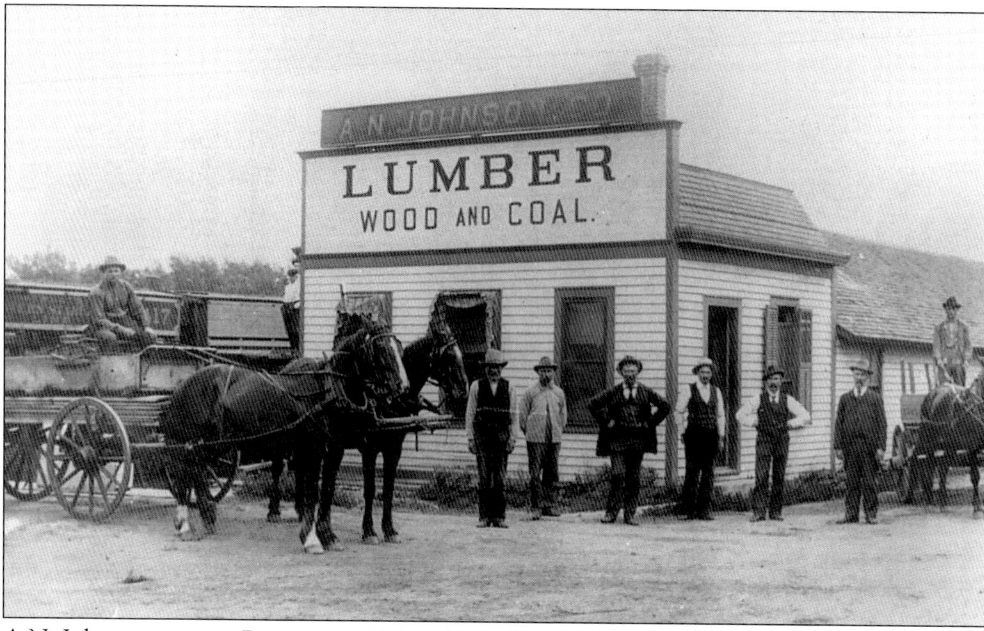

A.N. Johnson came to Benson in 1875 and purchased an interest in a general mercantile store. His sales ran up to $60,000 in the last eight months of 1875. In 1884, he had a new store built on Pacific Avenue. Later he was engaged in the lumber business. The business in this photo was located next to the railroad tracks between Atlantic and Pacific Avenues.

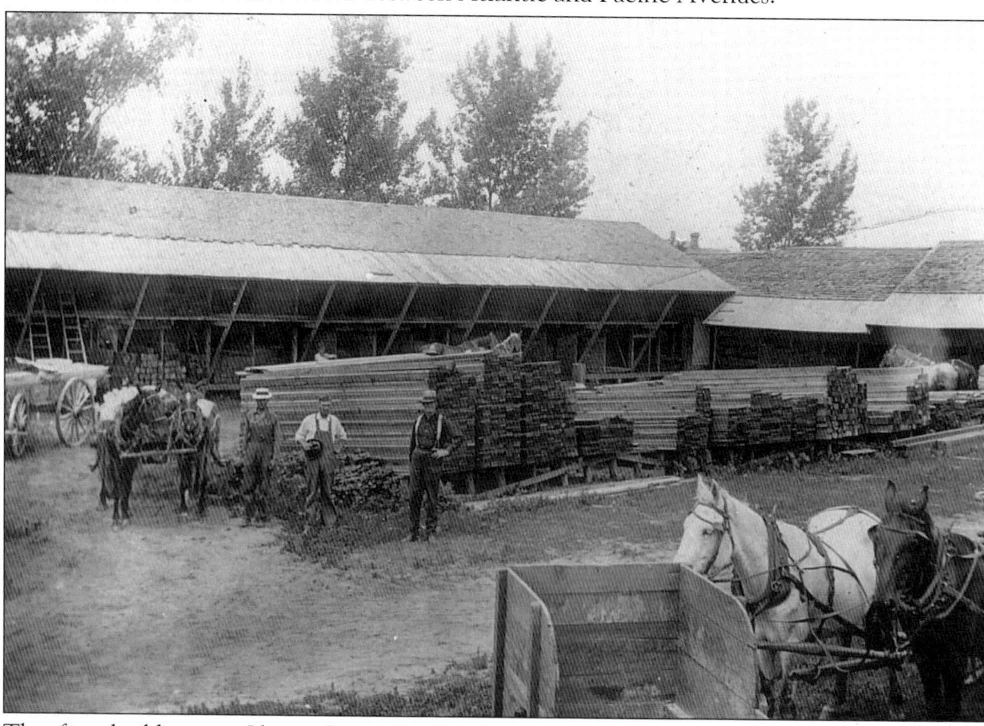

The first building in Clontarf was the lumberyard established by the Catholic Bureau of Colonization in July of 1876. Dominic McDermot was asked by Bishop John Ireland to be in charge of managing the yard.

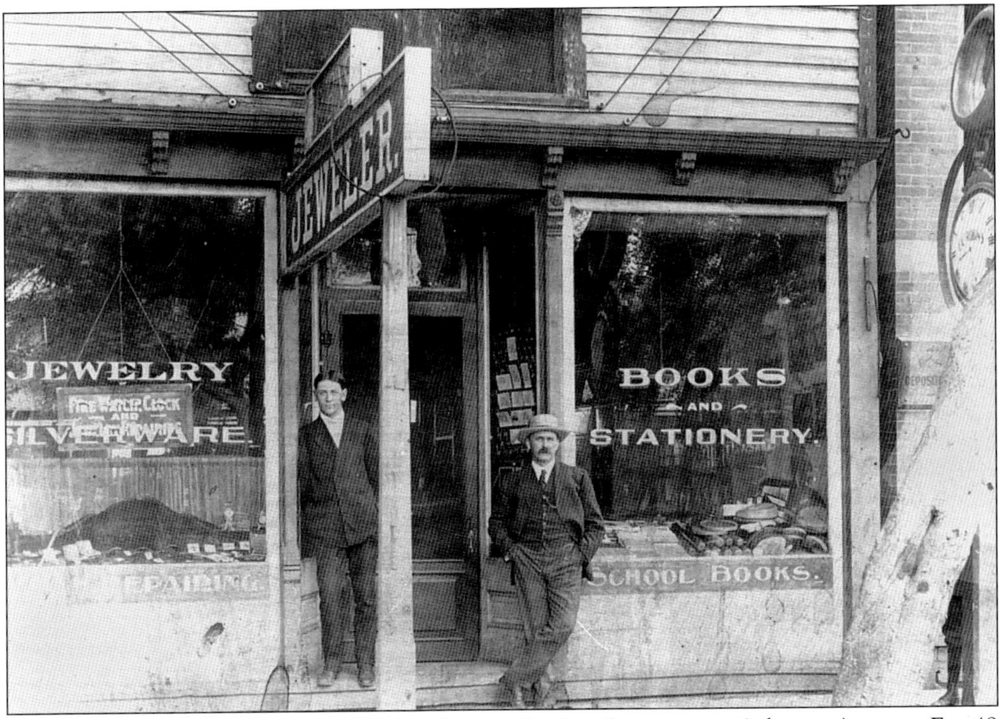

F.C. Robins came to Benson in 1884 and opened a jewelry store on Atlantic Avenue. For 49 years, "The Sign of the Big Clock" was recognized as Robins Jewelry. Standing in front of Robins Jewelry is Oscar Arne (an apprentice) and F.C. Robins on the right.

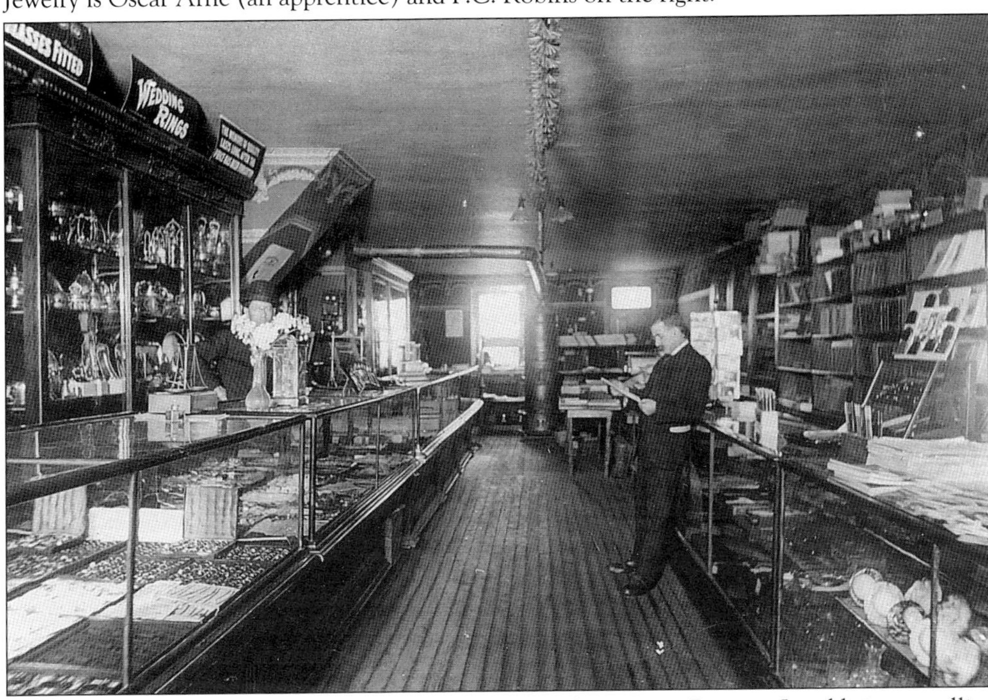

Leaning against the counter is F.C. Robins in his jewelry store in Benson. In addition to selling jewelry, Mr. Robins sold books, stationery, novelties, and maintained a florist service.

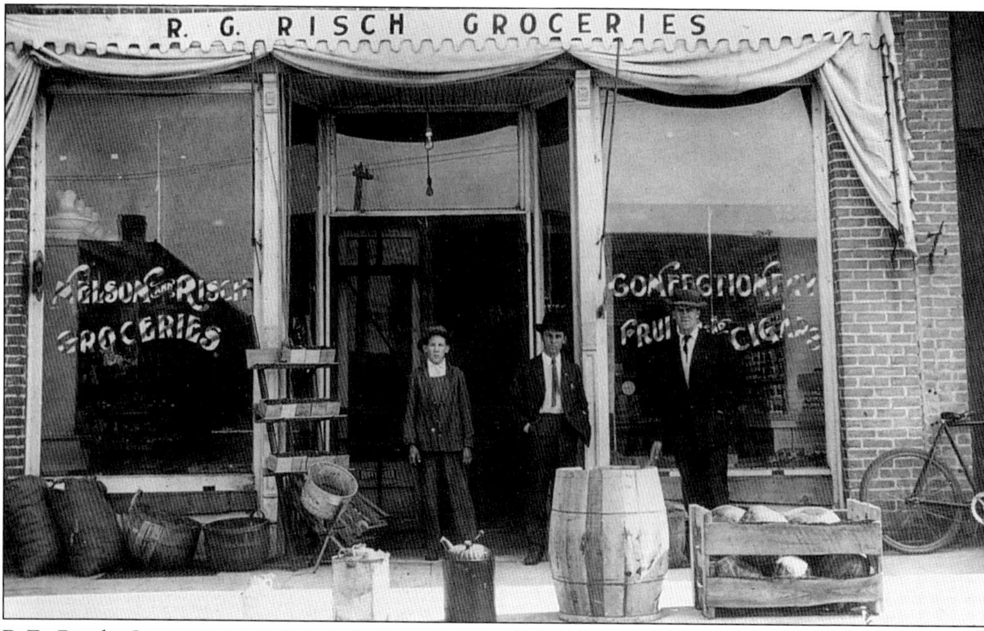

R.E. Risch Groceries was located on Atlantic Avenue in Benson. Reno Risch was born in Benson Township where he attended country school. After two years of high school, he went to the Humes Academy in Benson. He taught two terms of school before entering the grocery business, and in 1910, he moved to Appleton and opened a movie theater.

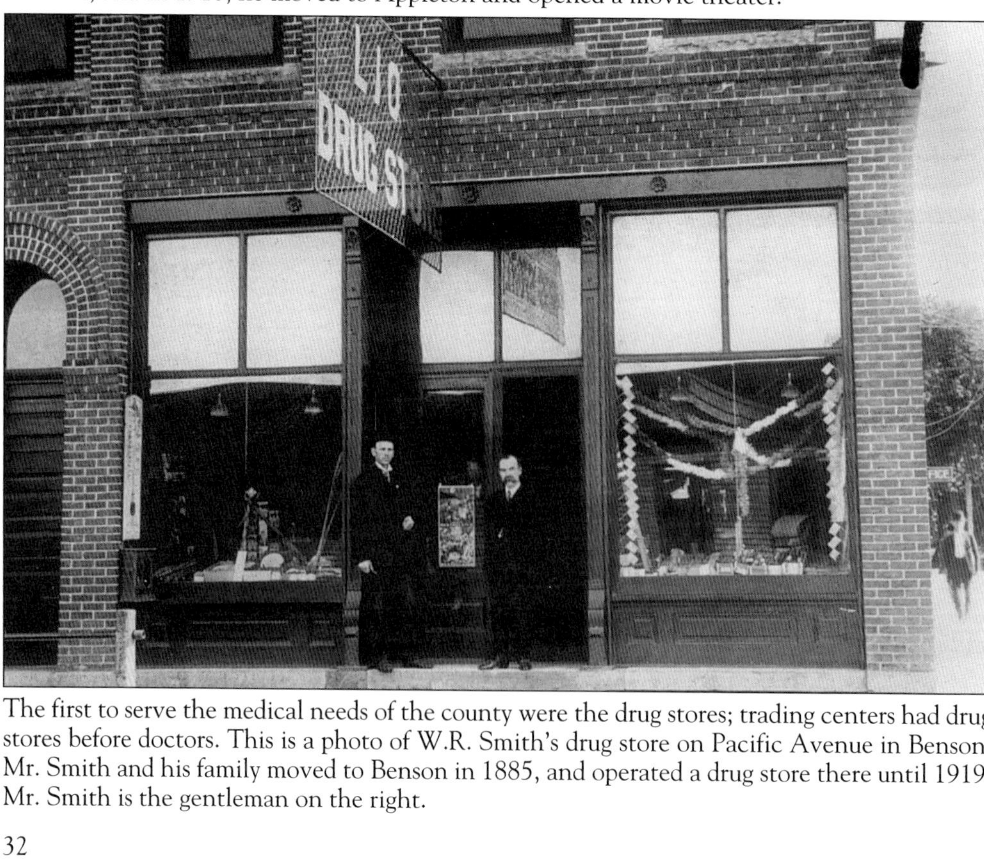

The first to serve the medical needs of the county were the drug stores; trading centers had drug stores before doctors. This is a photo of W.R. Smith's drug store on Pacific Avenue in Benson. Mr. Smith and his family moved to Benson in 1885, and operated a drug store there until 1919. Mr. Smith is the gentleman on the right.

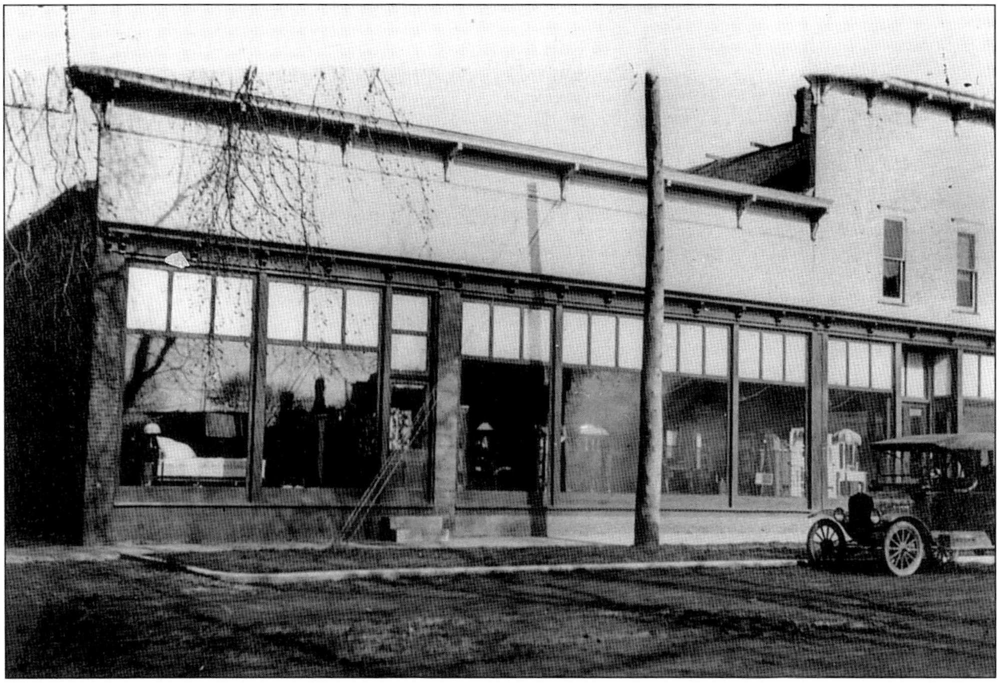

A.J. Hoiland arrived in Benson in 1881, and established a small furniture business on the north side of the tracks. In 1888, he built the first section of this building. It was located on 13th Street South. Besides operating his furniture business, Mr. Hoiland was also a professional photographer and undertaker.

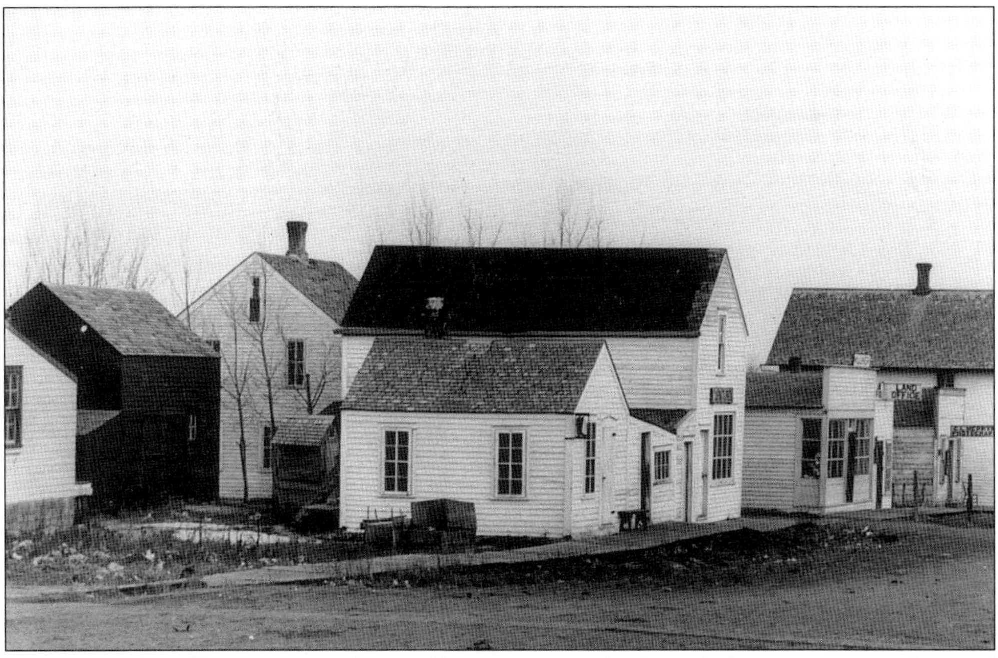

A photography gallery was opened in Kerkhoven in 1892, by C. Lincoln Merryman, professional photographer. Merryman worked in a tent for several months before he opened his studio in the small building on the right.

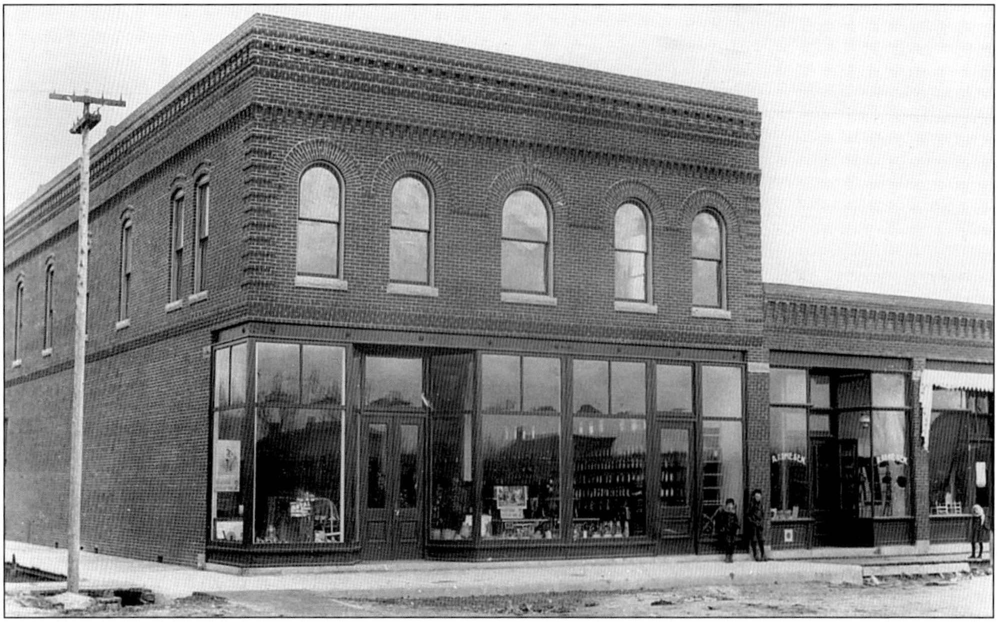

Olson and Pederson Hardware opened for business in a frame building in Benson in 1890. In 1897, a fire destroyed the building and all of the stock. Even though the owners had no insurance, they immediately began construction on a new brick building on Atlantic Avenue and 13th Street North. Mr. Pederson died in 1902, and the store's name was changed to Olson Hardware Company.

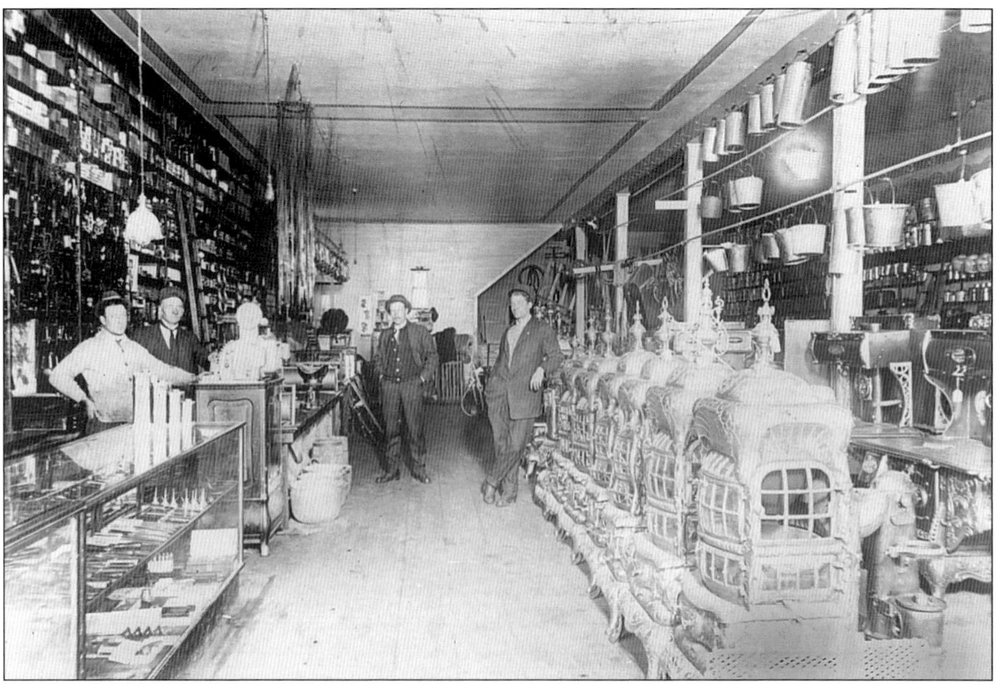

This c. 1912 photo is of the interior of Olson Hardware Company in Benson. On the left is Rudolph Johnson, clerk. Next to him is the owner, Adam Olson. The two customers are unidentified.

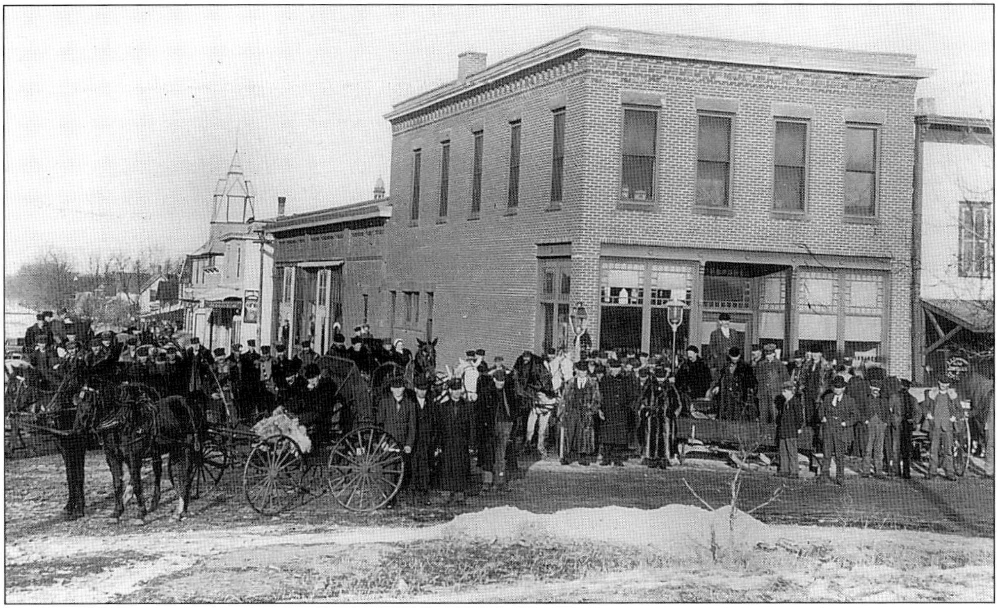

William Merryman opened his first hardware business in Kerkhoven in 1886. It was located in a two-story frame building on Ninth and Atlantic Avenues. He built this brick building on the corner of 11th Street and Atlantic Avenue in 1902. The building had maple floors and an elevator to the basement.

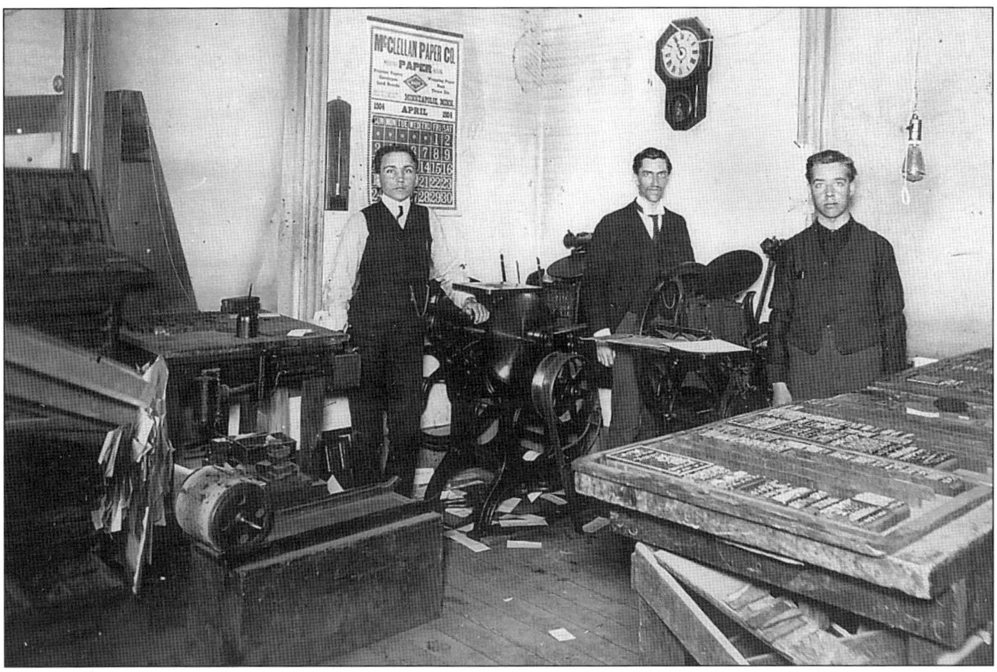

Besides reporting what was happening on the local scene, newspapers were the only source of national and state news. Of the eight incorporated villages in Swift County, Clontarf is the only one that did not have its own paper. Appleton, Benson, and Kerkhoven have published newspapers since 1880. This is the *Swift County Monitor* in Benson, which began publication in 1886. The photo was taken in 1904.

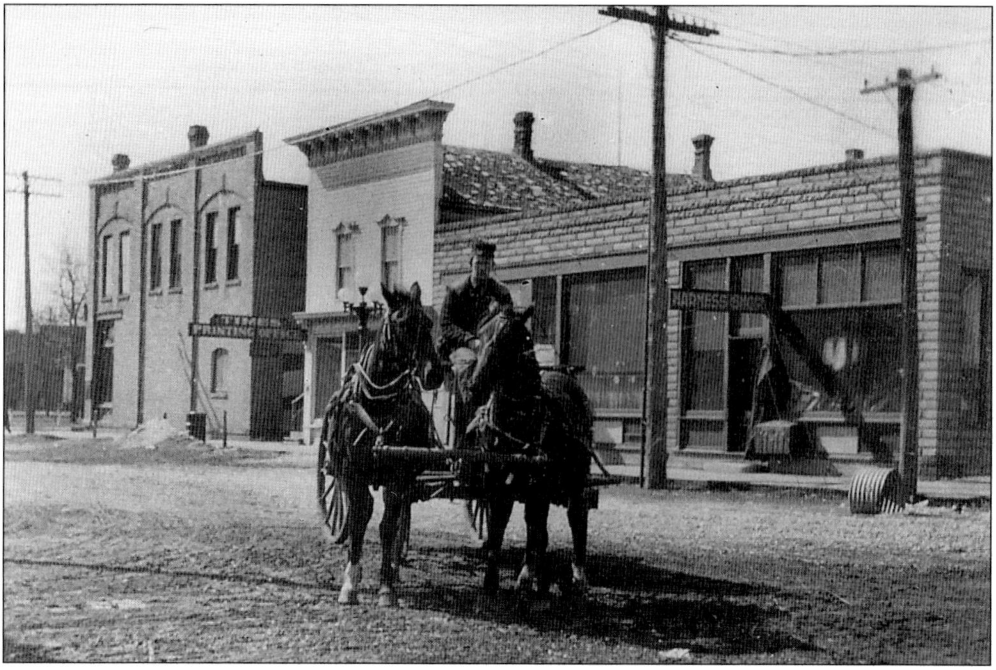

This photo was taken on 13th Street North, Benson. The building to the left is the Abstract Block, built in 1891. Next to it is the Times Printing Office, which printed newspapers in Benson from 1876 to 1912. On the right is the harness shop of Frank O'Brien.

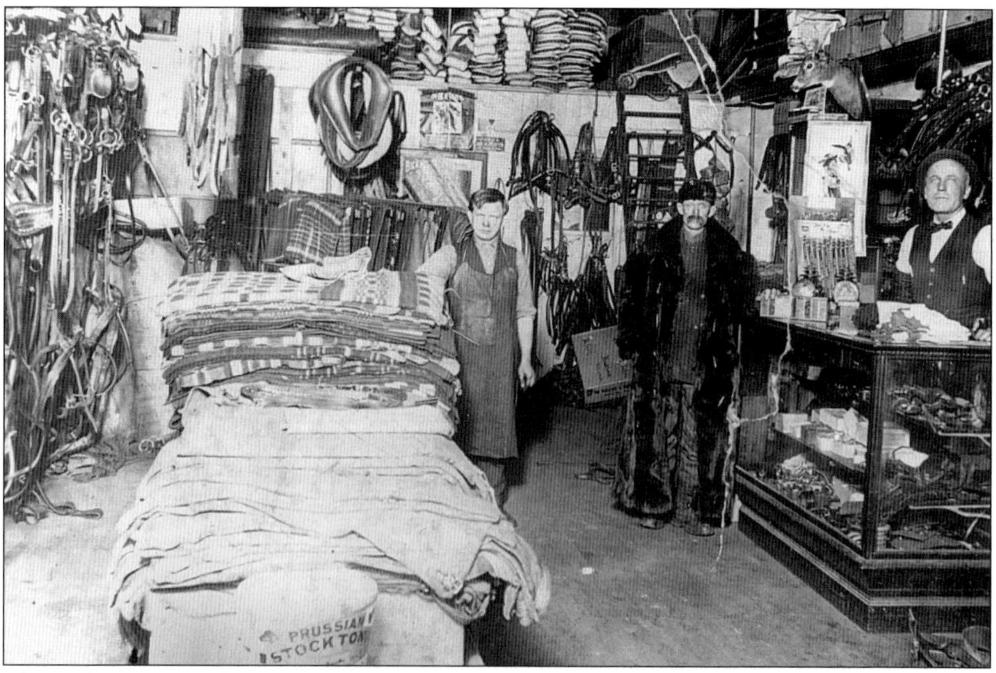

This is the interior of O'Brien's harness shop. Frank O'Brien established his harness business in Benson in 1897. When automobiles became popular, he diversified to include selling trunks, baggage, tires, repair, and sale of auto tops and upholstering. In 1923, he added a shoe shop that included shoe repair. Mr. O'Brien is the man on the right.

Two

A Place to Stay

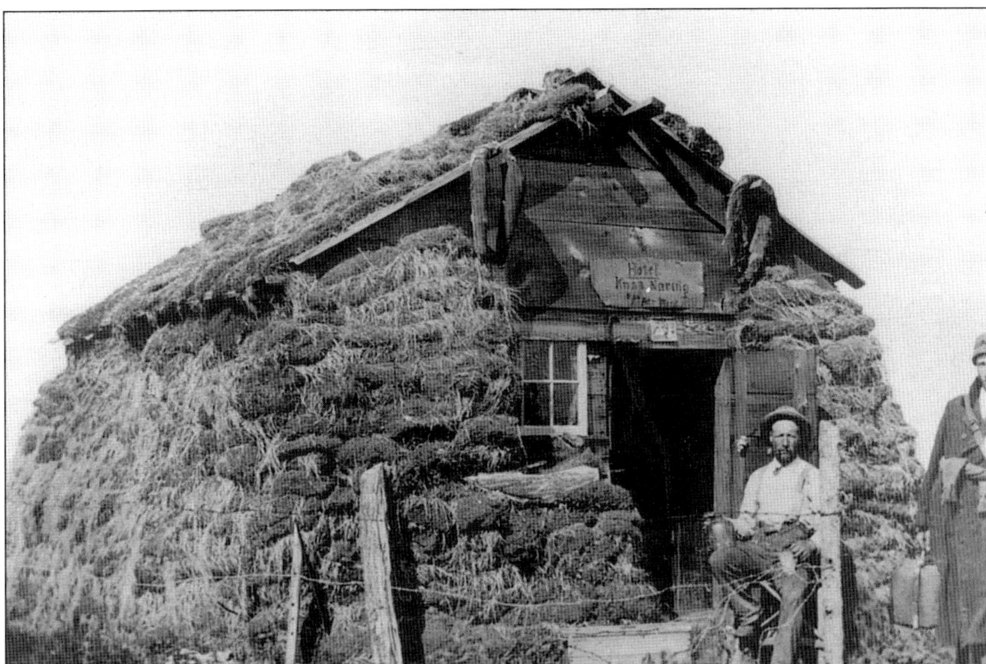

This sod house was located in the country close to Appleton. The sign above the door says "Hotel" and is believed to be a joke. Pioneers seeking a claim on the open prairie would spend an evening or more in the home of an earlier settler if they were lucky enough to find one. Some of the established settlers may have felt like their home had been turned into a hotel. Hotels were in great demand in the early trading centers. They were some of the first businesses to be established, since people always needed a place to stay.

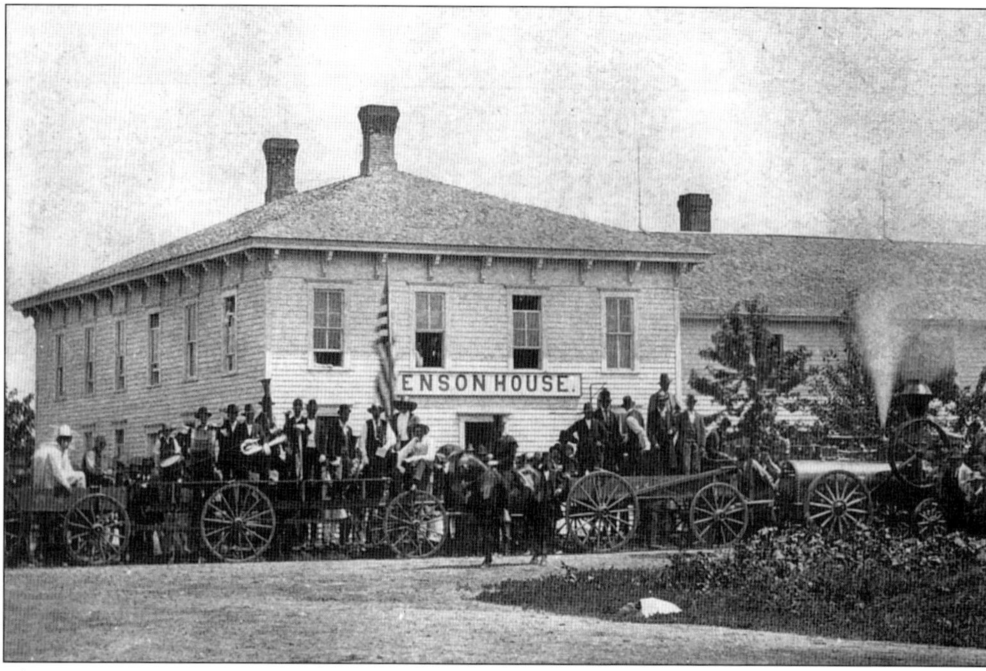

The Benson House Hotel, built in 1871 or 1872, was one of the first hotels in Benson. It was located on the business block of Atlantic Avenue that was destroyed by the fire of 1880.

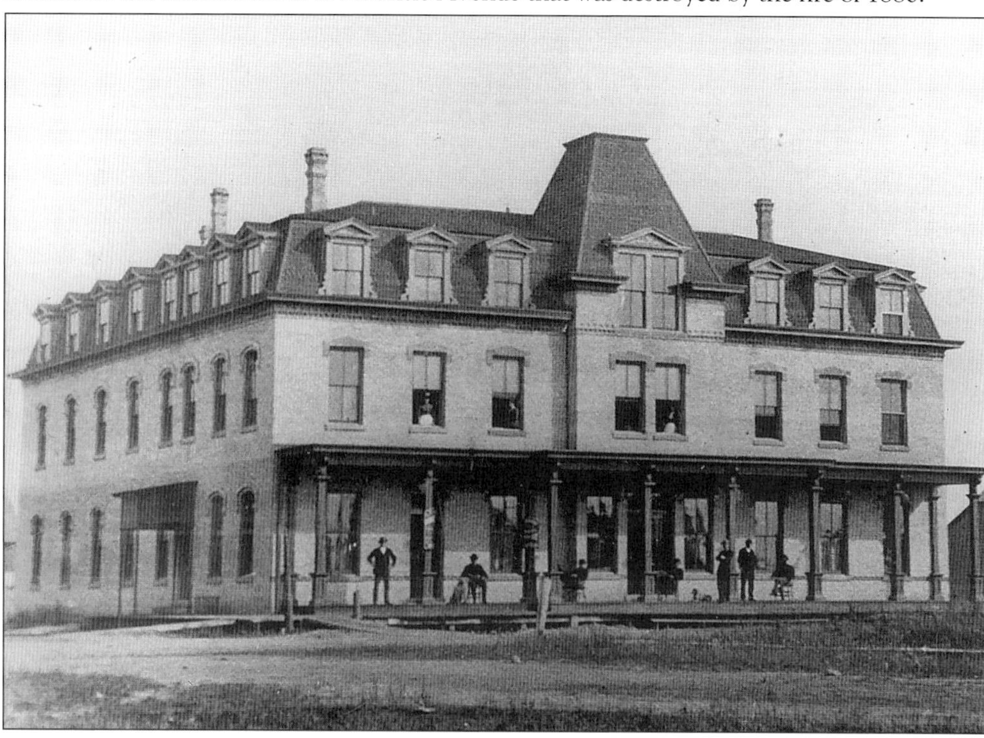

After the 1880 fire, construction began immediately on a new hotel on the same location as the Benson House. The new brick building was named the Aldrich House after its owners. This hotel building was destroyed by fire in the 1930s.

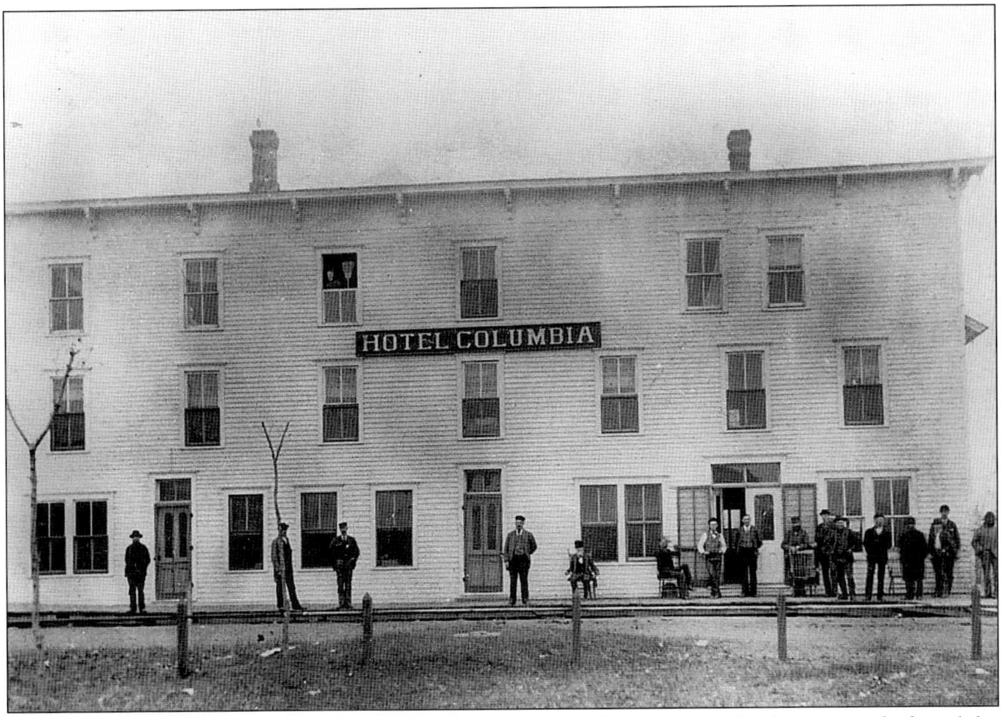

The corner of 14th Street South and Pacific Avenue in Benson was the location of a hotel for more than a century. During the first 30 years, the hotel went by the names of Pacific, West, and Columbia. In 1900, the Hotel Columbia was cut in two sections, the dividing line being just to the east of the middle door. The section on the right was moved by horses one block to the southwest.

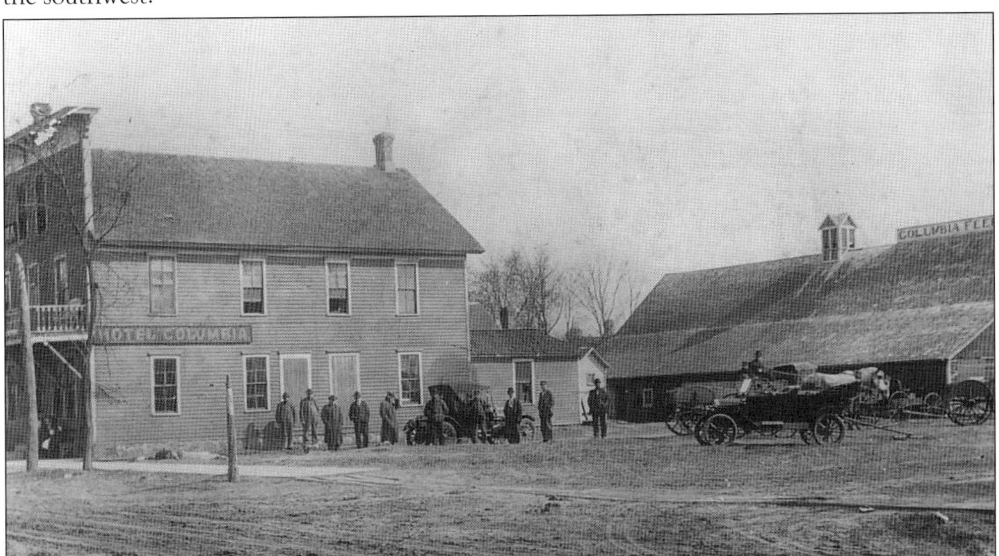

This is the Hotel Columbia in its new location. The sign on the large building on the right says Columbia Feed. When the hotel was moved in 1900, this barn would have been used as a livery for hotel guests' horses. Automobiles seemed to be the common mode of transportation when this photo was taken.

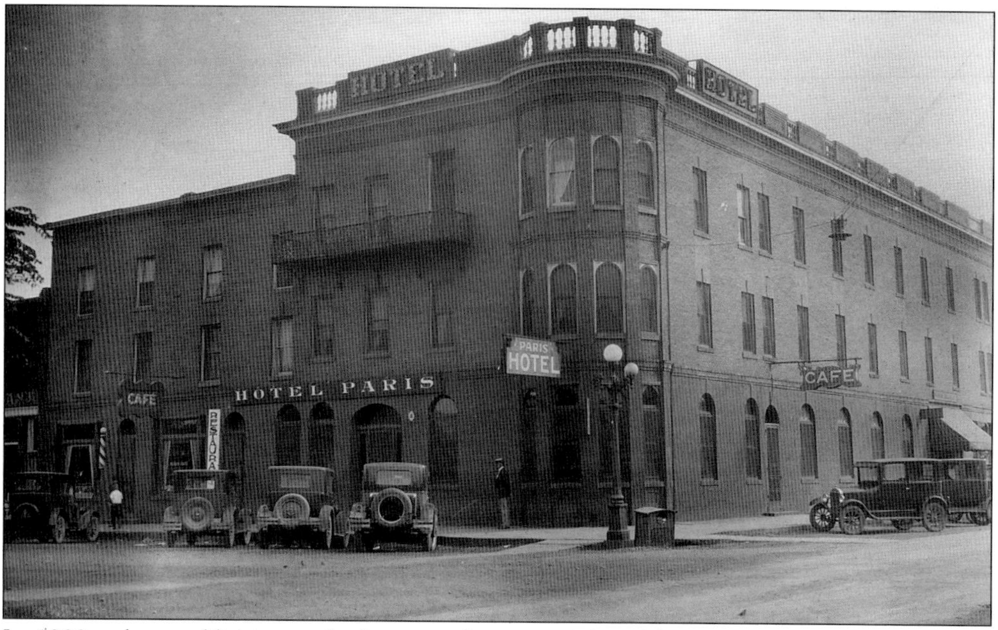

In 1900, a large addition was built on to the part of the old Hotel Columbia that was not moved from its original location. The new hotel in Benson was called the Hotel Paris. With the furnishings and the heating plant, the Paris cost $25,000, and boasted such luxuries as steam heat, electric lights, hot and cold water, baths, call bells, and telephones.

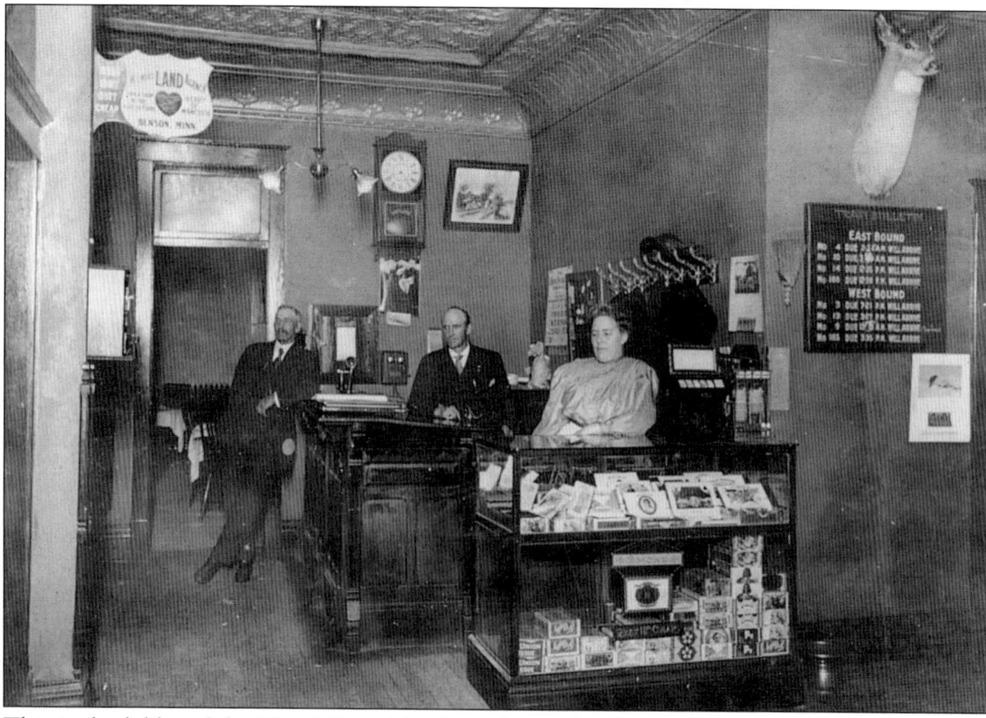

This is the lobby of the Hotel Paris. To the right, under the deer head, is the train schedule. Since the majority of hotel guests traveled by train, it was important that schedules be accessible to the guests.

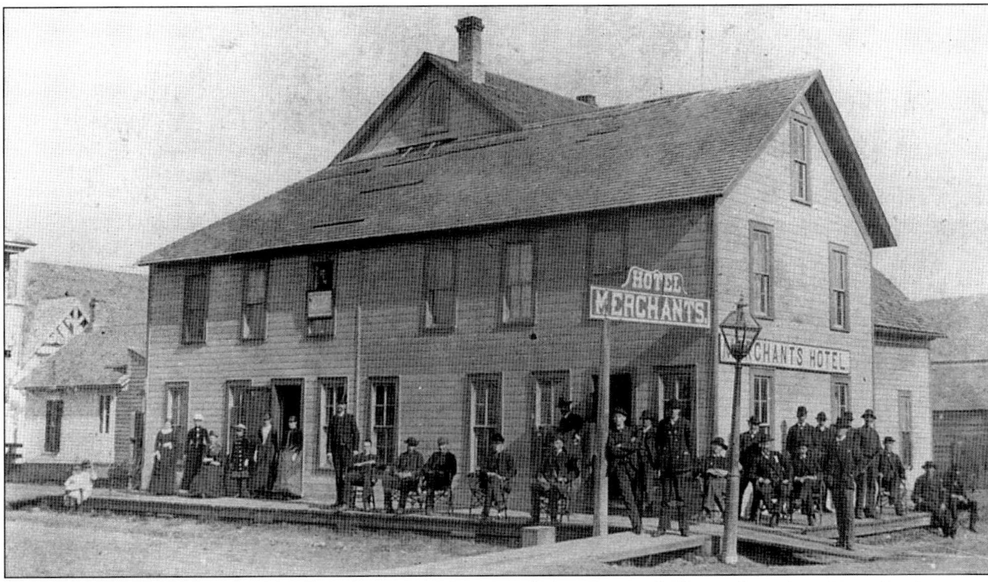

Ole Thorson arrived in Benson in 1872 and opened the Central House hotel on Pacific Avenue. By 1879, he had sold the Central House and constructed the Merchants Hotel one block north of Atlantic Avenue. Fire damaged the wood-frame Merchants beyond repair in 1906.

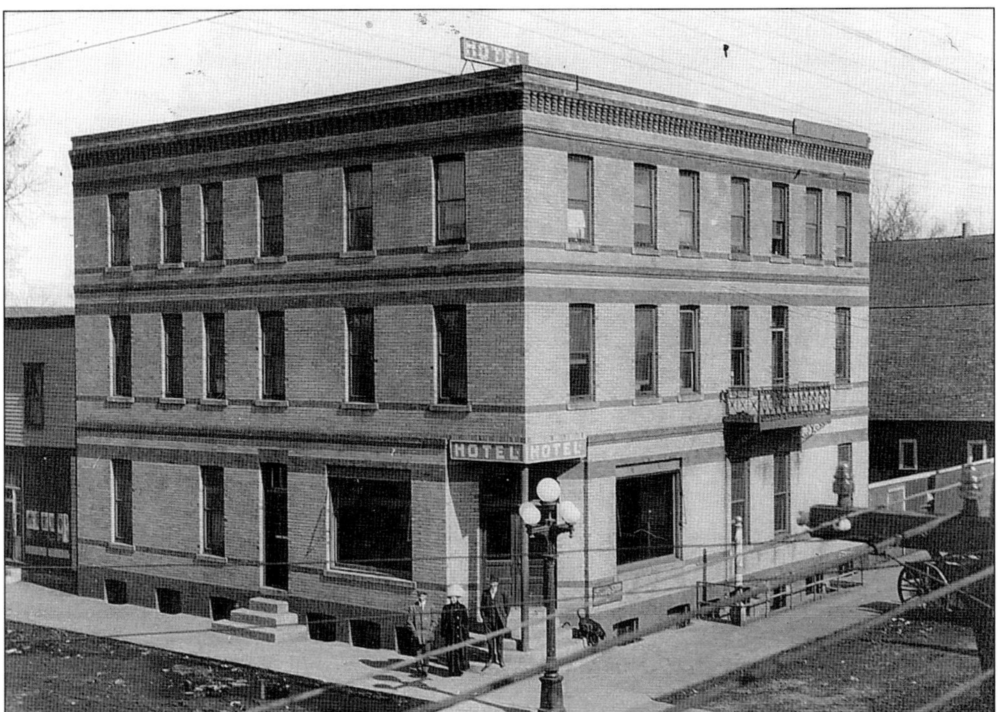

The new brick Merchants Hotel was completed in 1907. It consisted of three floors with a full concrete basement. The Merchants provided 35 bedrooms that rented at $1 to $1.50 a day. Besides the office, kitchen, and dining room, there were two writing rooms, public washroom, a special entrance for the ladies, rooms for the help, and the owner's apartment.

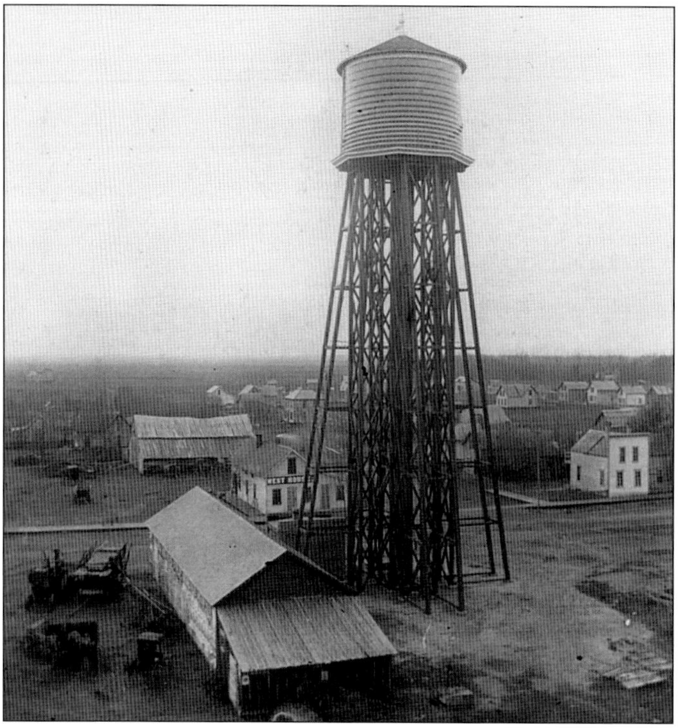

Not every hotel in Benson was as elaborate as the Aldrich, Paris, or Merchants. Because there was such a great need for a place to stay in the early days of Swift County, even the smallest of buildings were used for a hotel. The small house behind the water tower was erected in 1872 as a hotel.

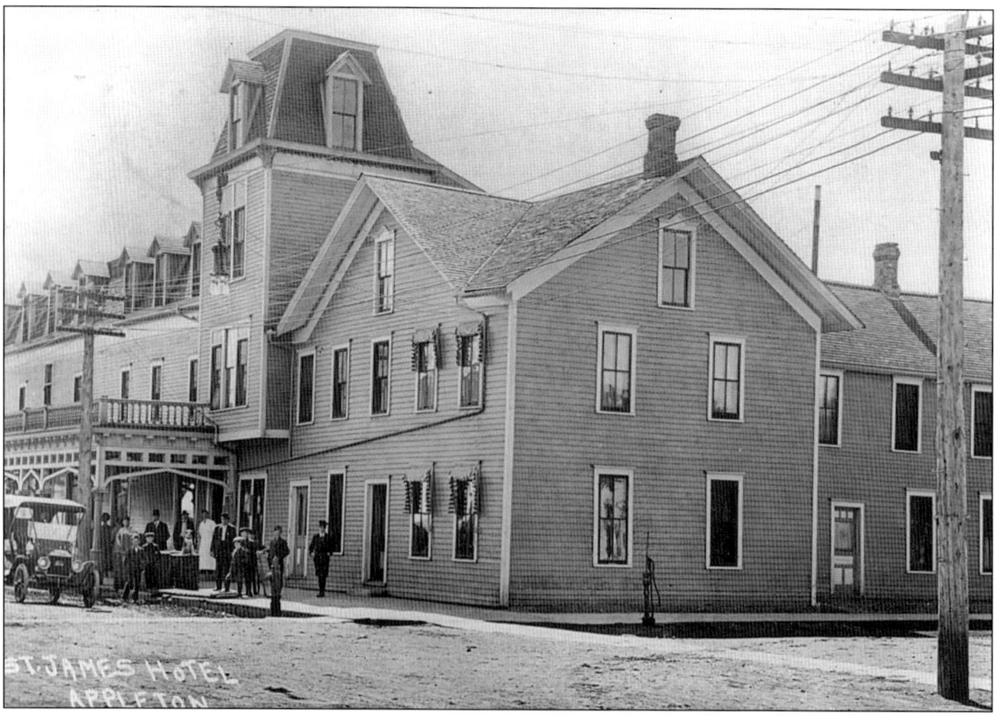

In 1892, Appleton had four large hotels to accommodate the traveling public. One of them was the St. James. Started by Thomas and William Mehegan, the building originated with the portion on the right in 1880. A three-story addition (on the left) was built in 1884.

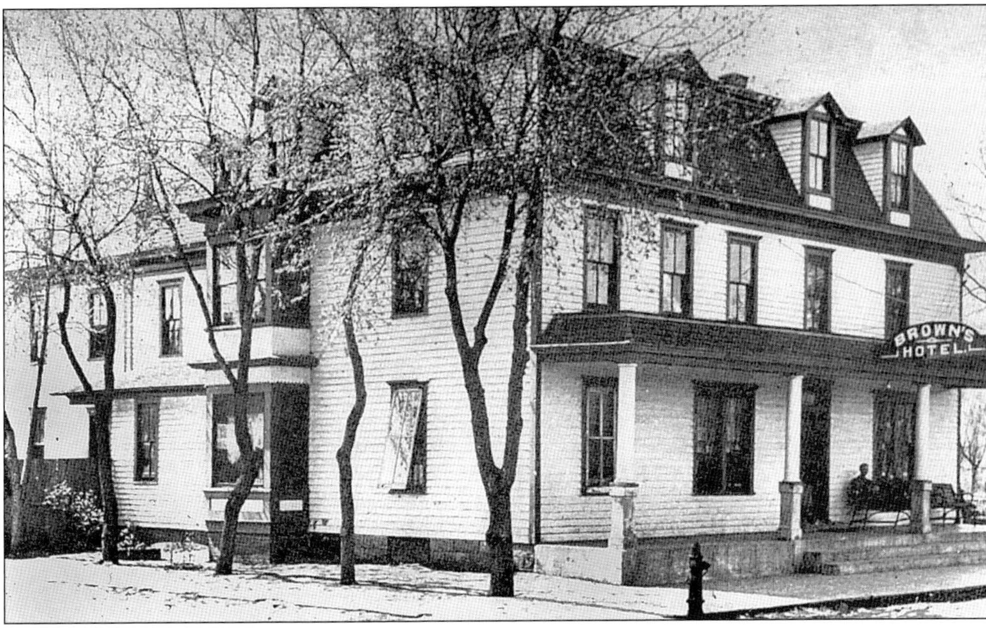

Ole Brown came to Appleton in the late 1870s and began the hotel business in a small way. This three-story hotel was constructed after Mr. Brown had built up his business by catering to the needs of farmers. He provided meals and lodging for them, as well as barn accommodations for their horses.

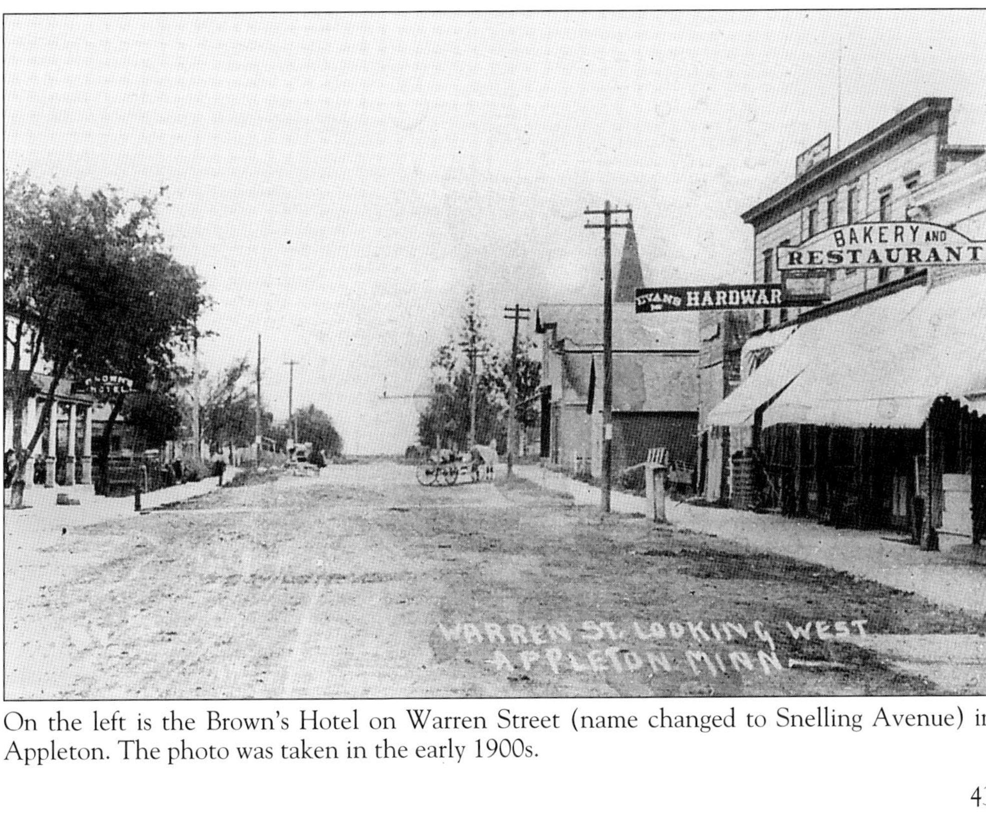

On the left is the Brown's Hotel on Warren Street (name changed to Snelling Avenue) in Appleton. The photo was taken in the early 1900s.

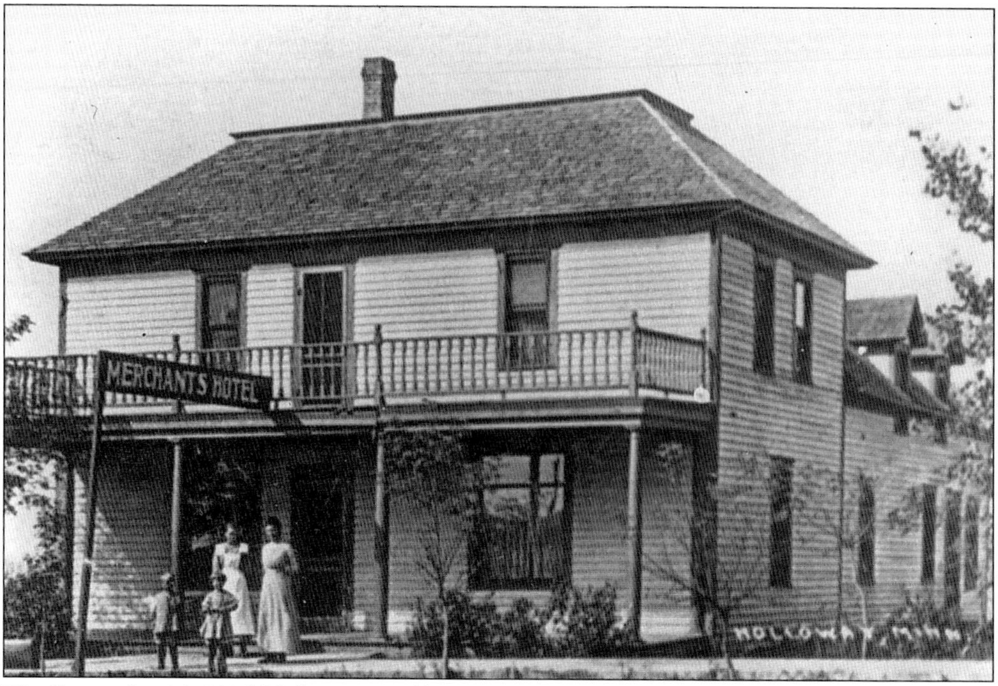

The September 14, 1916, *Holloway Herald* newspaper carried an article advertising the Merchants Hotel in Holloway for rent and all of its furnishings for sale. The hotel's proprietor was listed as S.A. Lewis.

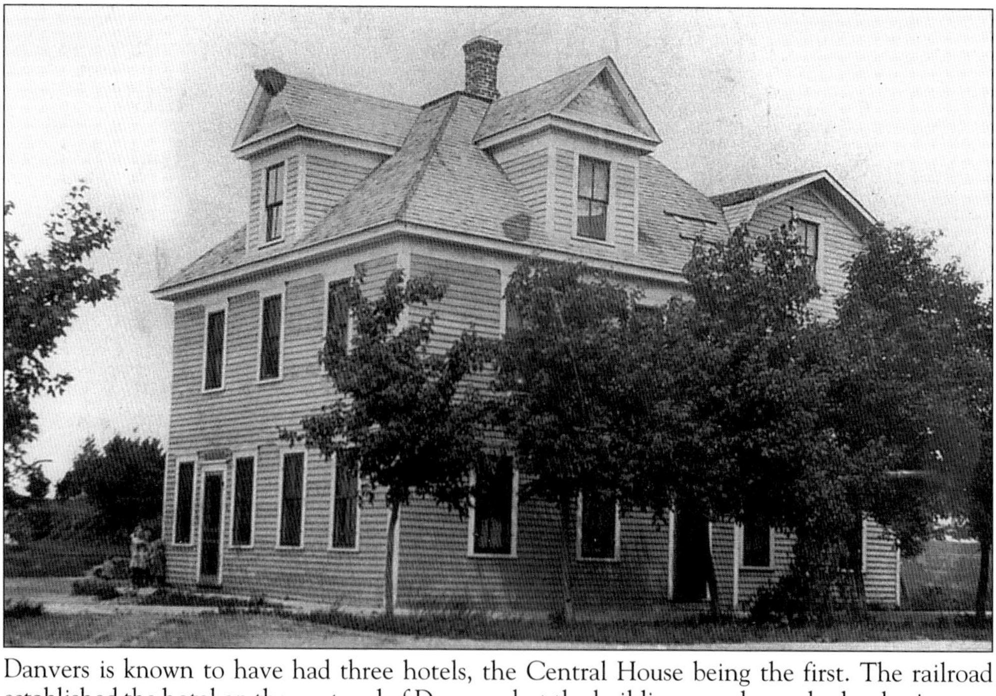

Danvers is known to have had three hotels, the Central House being the first. The railroad established the hotel on the west end of Danvers, but the building soon housed other businesses. The other two hotels were the West House, owned by Charles Dolan, and the East House, which is the hotel in this picture. The proprietor was a Mrs. Frederickson.

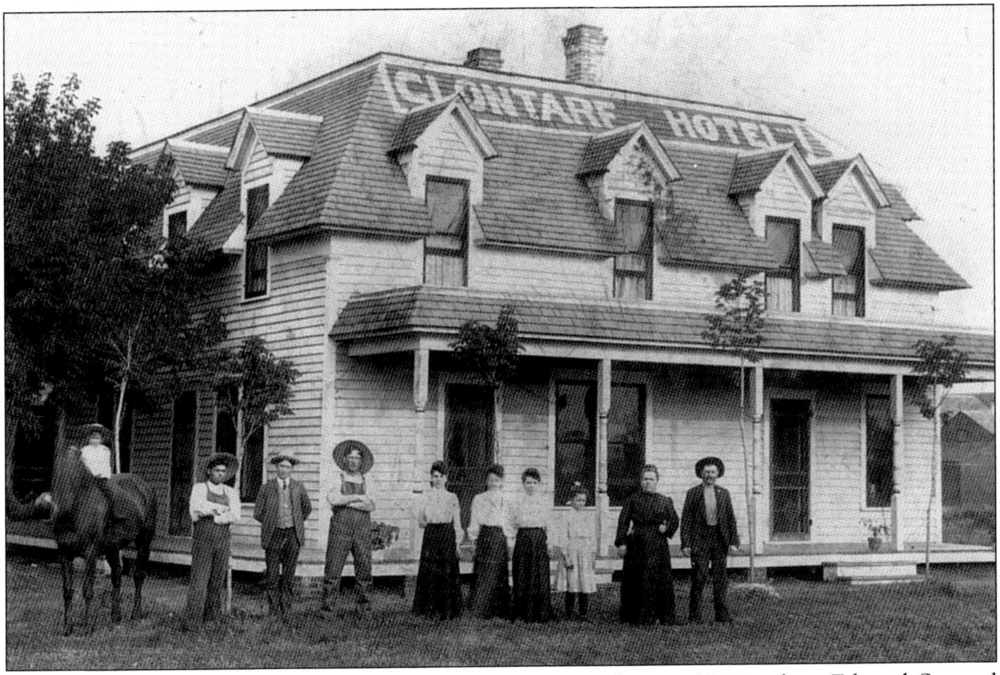

This hotel was located in Clontarf. This picture was taken *c.* 1900, when Edward Sr. and Belzimere Boutain operated the Clontarf Hotel. Their sons helped with the livery stable, and their daughters worked in the restaurant. The hotel was also managed by Jeremiah and Elizabeth Chamberlain.

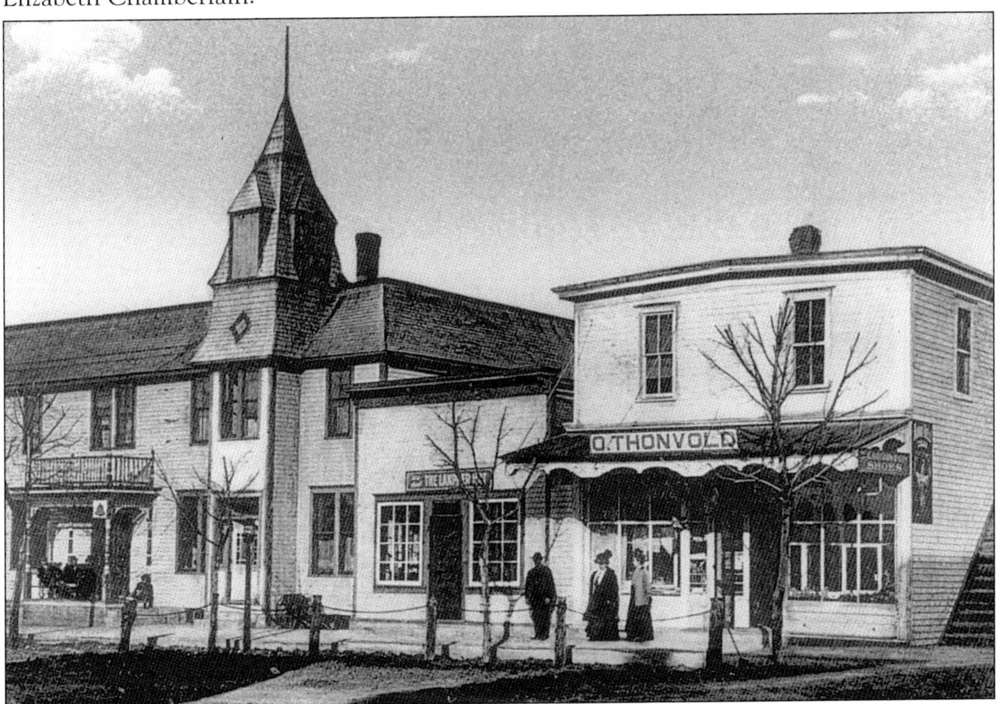

In 1903, the old school building in Kerkhoven was moved and remodeled into the Merchants Hotel, the building on the left. The Merchants Hotel was the fourth hotel in Kerkhoven.

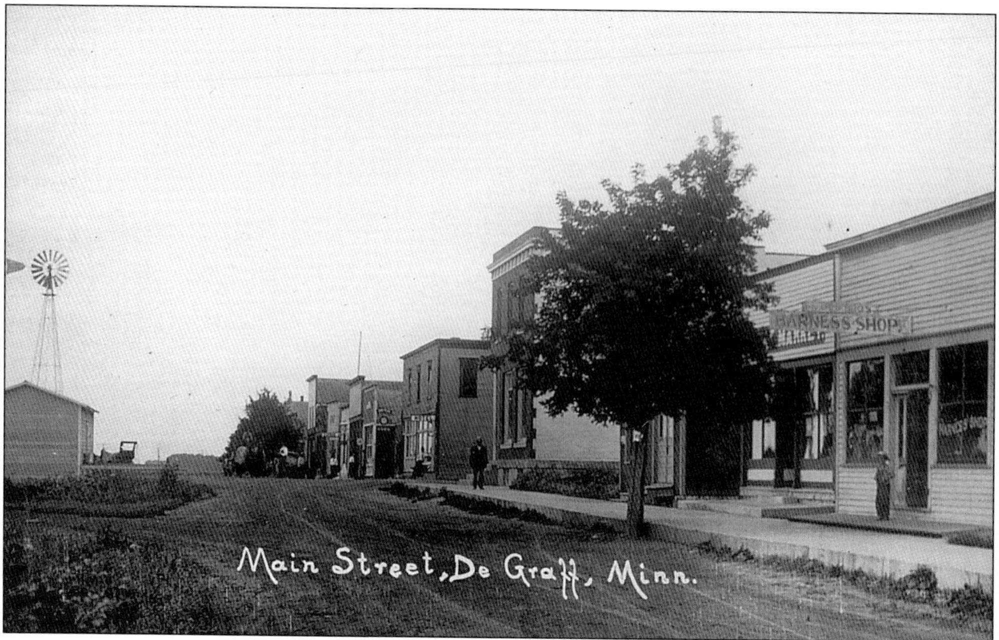

To the left of the tallest building in the photo is one of DeGraff's hotels. The 1879 newspaper reported that DeGraff contained three hotels at that time. Other records of DeGraff hotels include the Kielty Hotel in 1898, and an advertisement for the DeGraff Hotel with John L. Walsh as proprietor in 1925.

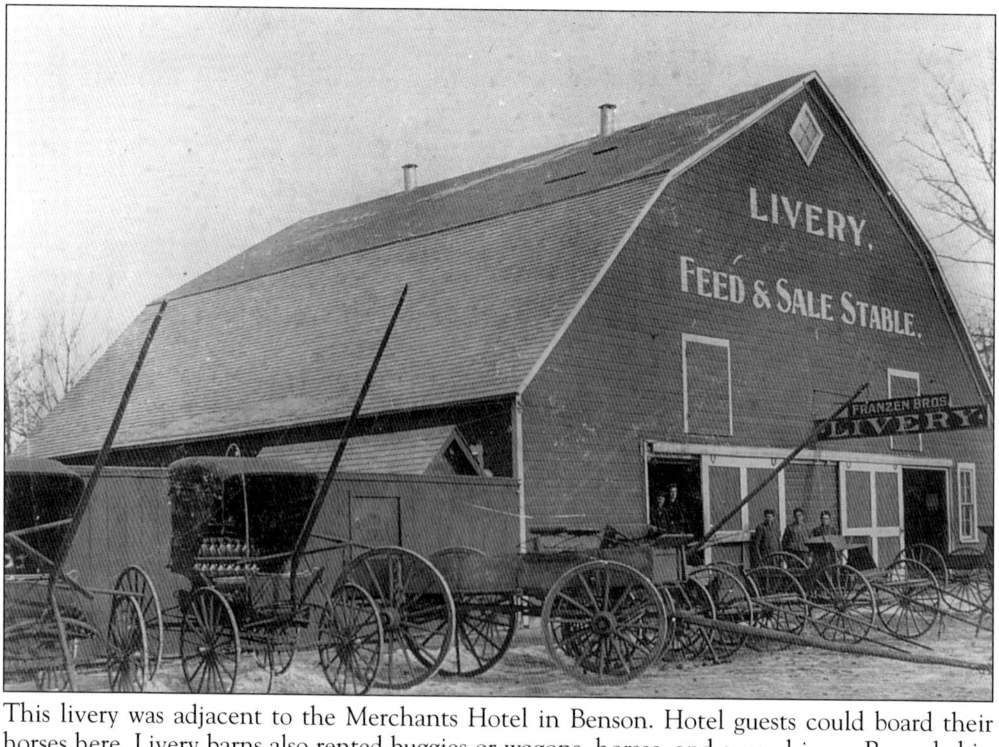

This livery was adjacent to the Merchants Hotel in Benson. Hotel guests could board their horses here. Livery barns also rented buggies or wagons, horses, and even drivers. Recorded in old livery ledgers are the names of doctors who regularly rented buggies, horses, and drivers.

Three

EARLY INDUSTRIES

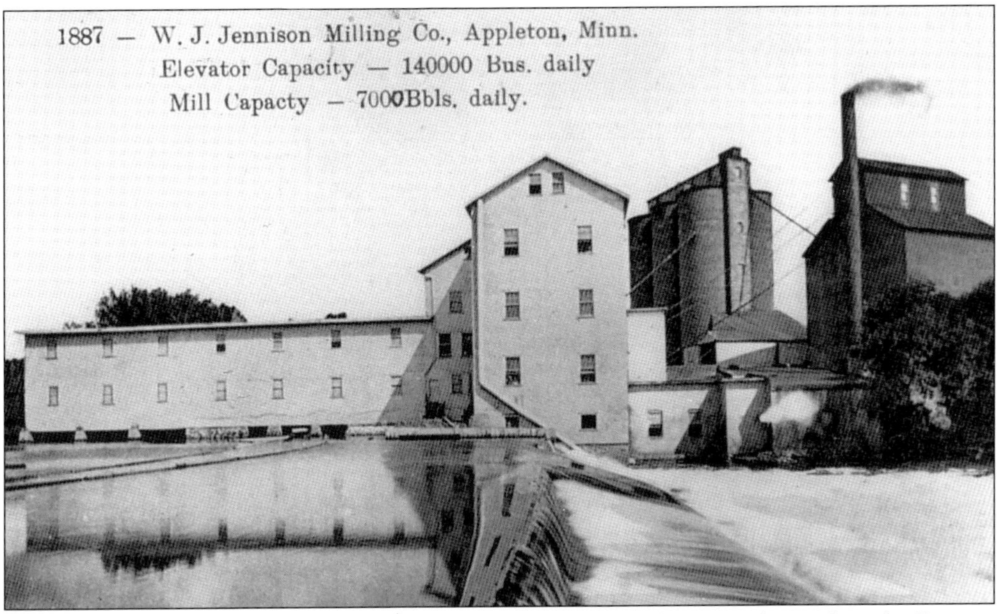

Flourmills were a vital industry in Swift County. Because Appleton was located on the Pomme de Terre River, which had three falls providing water power, it became the site of two flourmills. The Lathrop brothers completed construction of a mill by 1872. The Rosette Mill was built in 1878. Dams were built to enhance the power for the mills. C.W. Jennison, son-in-law of A.W. Lathrop, managed the mill started by the Lathrops. In 1895, W.J. Jennison purchased the mill. The W.J. Jennison Milling plant was reduced to ashes in a fire August 27, 1905. Work began immediately to rebuild the mill. After the completion of the new mill in 1906, work began on six huge grain tanks for storage of 100,000 bushels of wheat. The new mill and storage tanks can be seen in this 1910 photo.

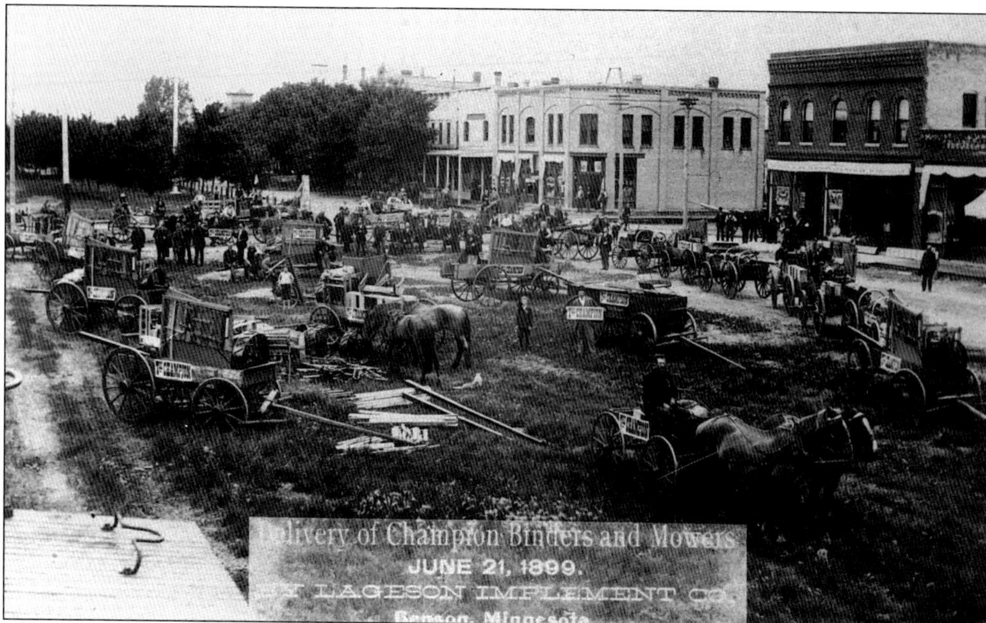

The population of Swift County in 1895 was 12,013, with an estimated 9,500 on farms. The acres in cropland also increased as soon as sources for marketing the crops became available in the county. The increase in farmers and cropland resulted in the need for farm machinery. This 1899 photo of a delivery of binders and mowers to Benson is evidence of the greater number of farmers and land becoming cultivated for crops.

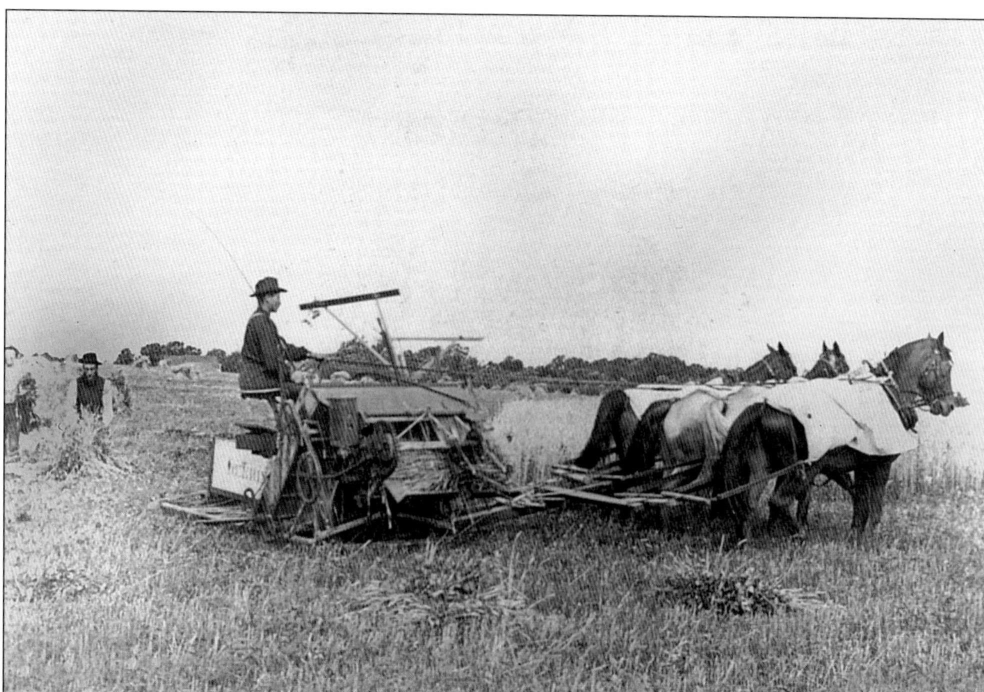

This photo was taken in 1890 on Captain Uytendahl's farm in Benson Township. M.A. Overlie is on the binder, which was used to cut the wheat and tie it into bundles.

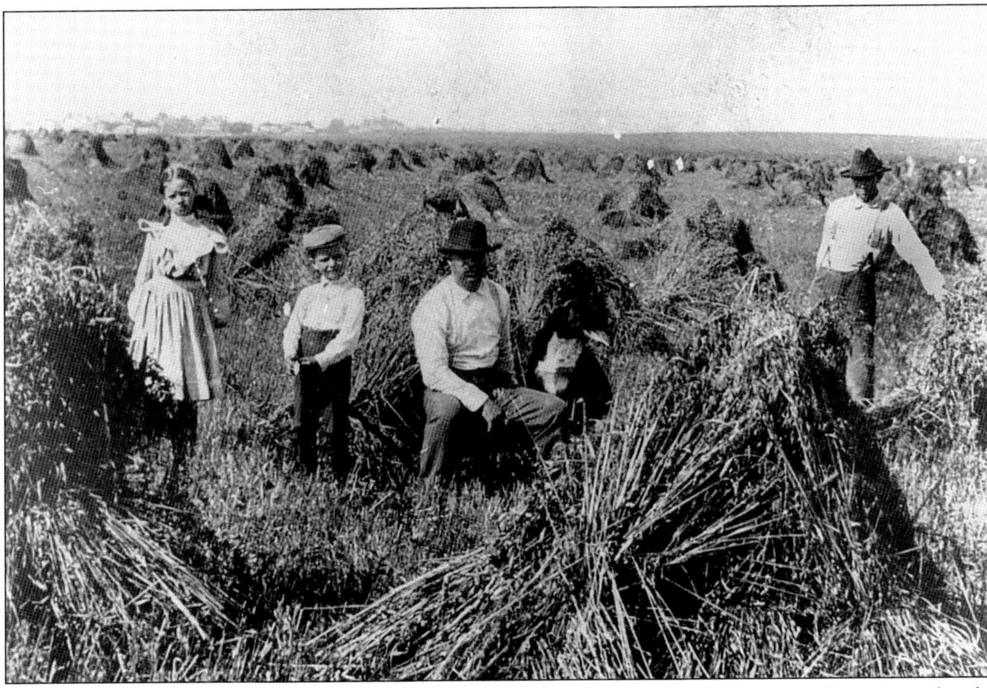

The farmer would prepare the bundles of wheat for threshing either by putting them into shocks as in this picture or piled in large grain stacks. This field of wheat shocks was located 1 mile south of Appleton, which appears as a haze in the background. The children are Muriel and Bernard. Their father, John McLaughlin, is sitting next to them, and the other man is believed to be a hired hand.

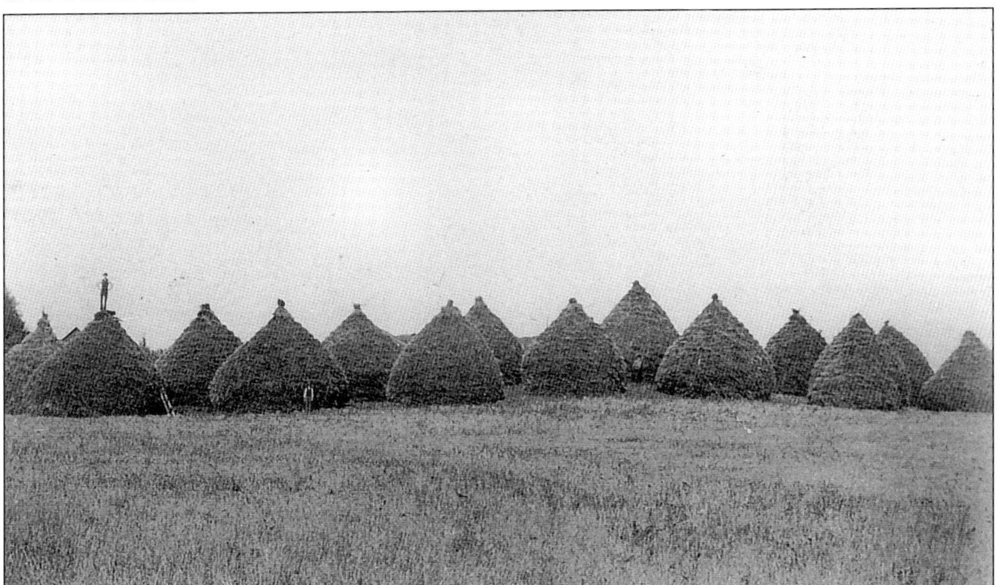

This field of grain stacks was in Benson Township. The size of each stack can be determined by the man, Editius Torgerson, standing on top of one of the stacks on the left. Wheat bundles were put into shocks or grain stacks because the wheat needed to be dried before it could be threshed.

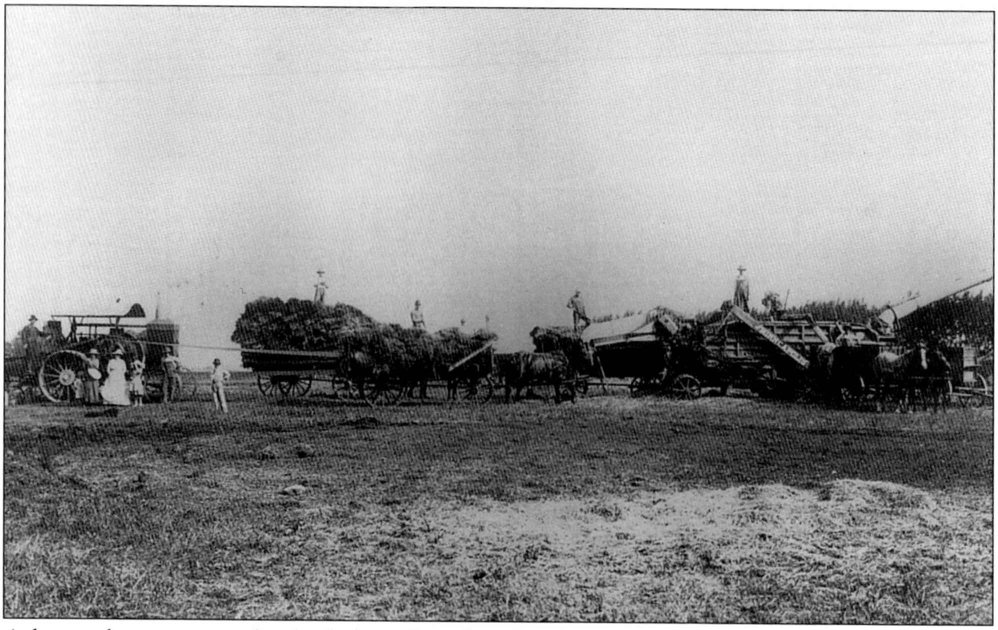

A horse-drawn wagon load of wheat bundles that had been in shocks has been hauled to the threshing machine. Threshing machines were pulled to grain stacks by horsepower, before the onset of tractors. Women were kept busy cooking meals and taking lunches to the threshing crews.

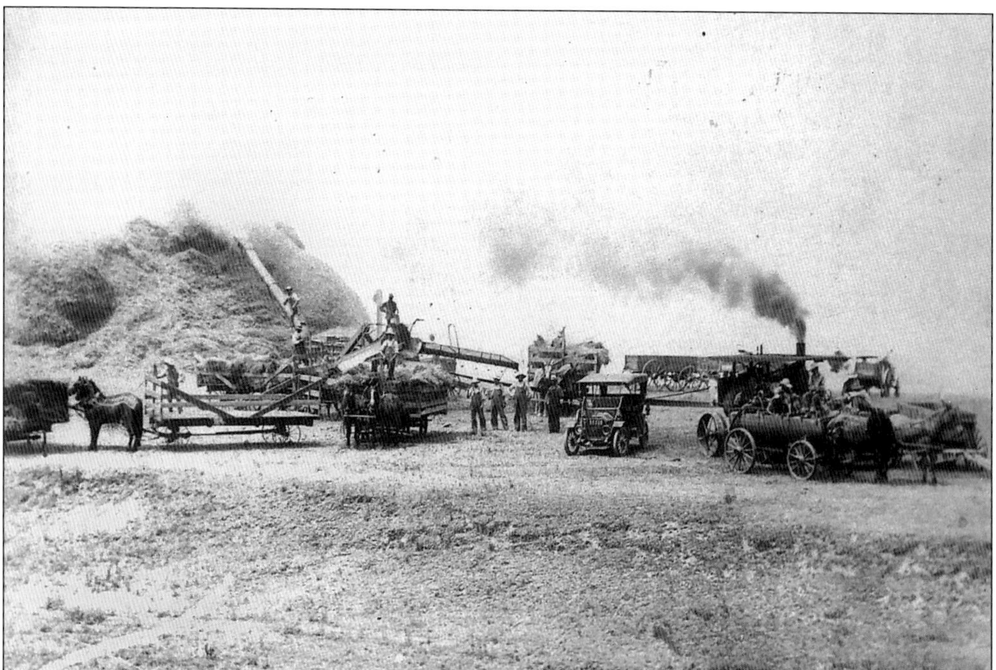

The bundles of wheat would be run through a threshing machine (also referred to as a separator) where the grain, chaff, and straw would be separated. The straw and chaff would be blown into a large pile to be used as bedding for farm animals. This photo was taken on the Robert Darling farm in West Bank Township, 1915.

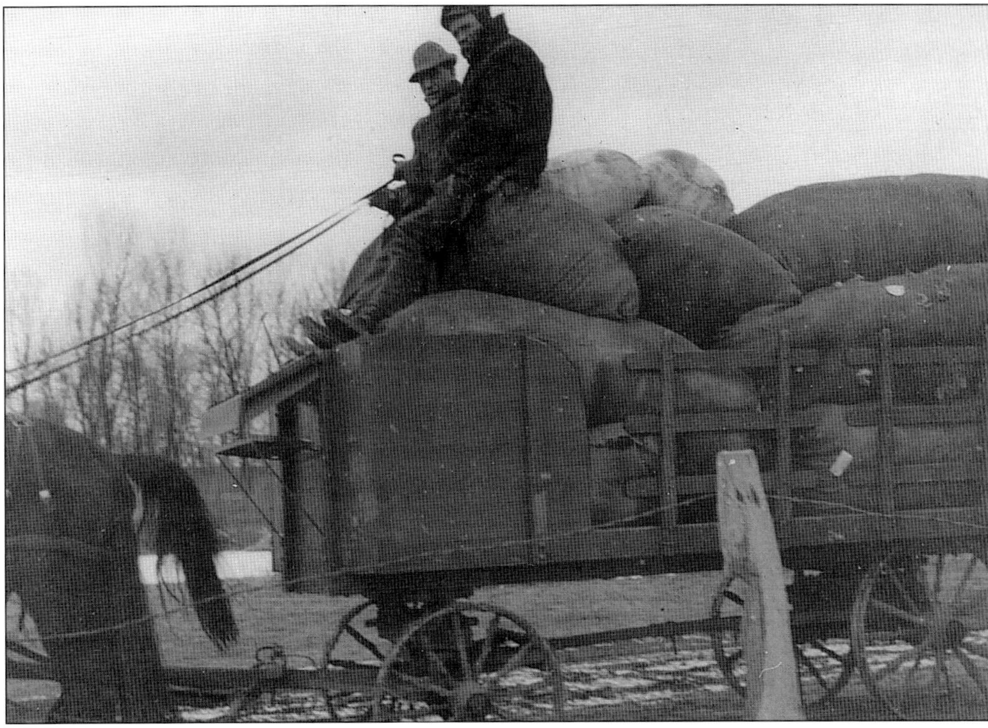

The light fall of snow on the ground makes it evident that the harvest season is over. These farmers are preparing for the long winter ahead by hauling a load of wheat to town. The wheat might have been made into flour at one of Swift County's mills. All of the trading centers had grain elevators where it could have been taken and sold.

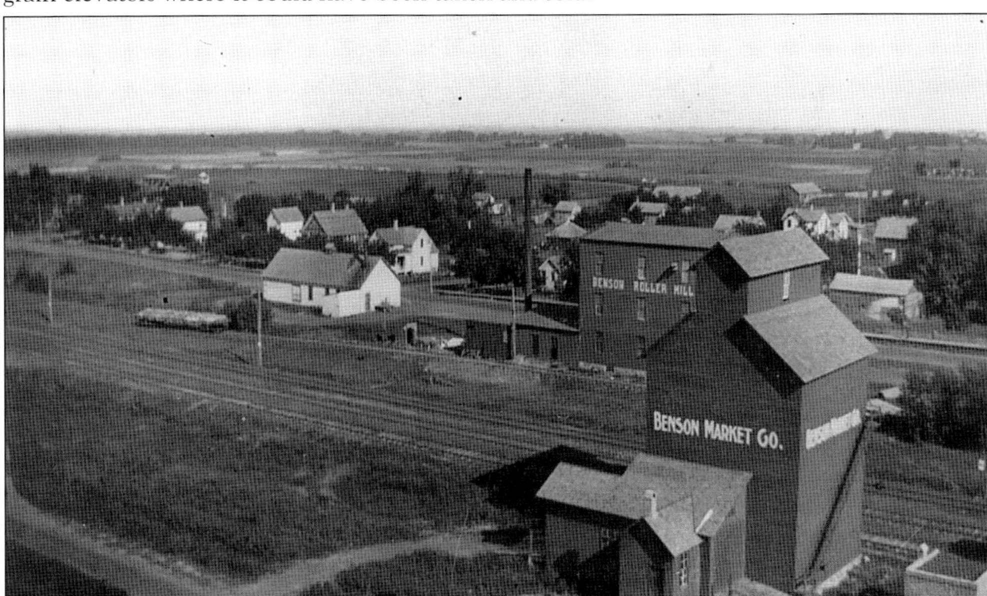

The Benson Market Company was organized and built in 1898 on the south side of the railroad tracks on the west end of the business district in Benson. It had a capacity of 20,000 bushels. North of the tracks was the Benson Roller Mill.

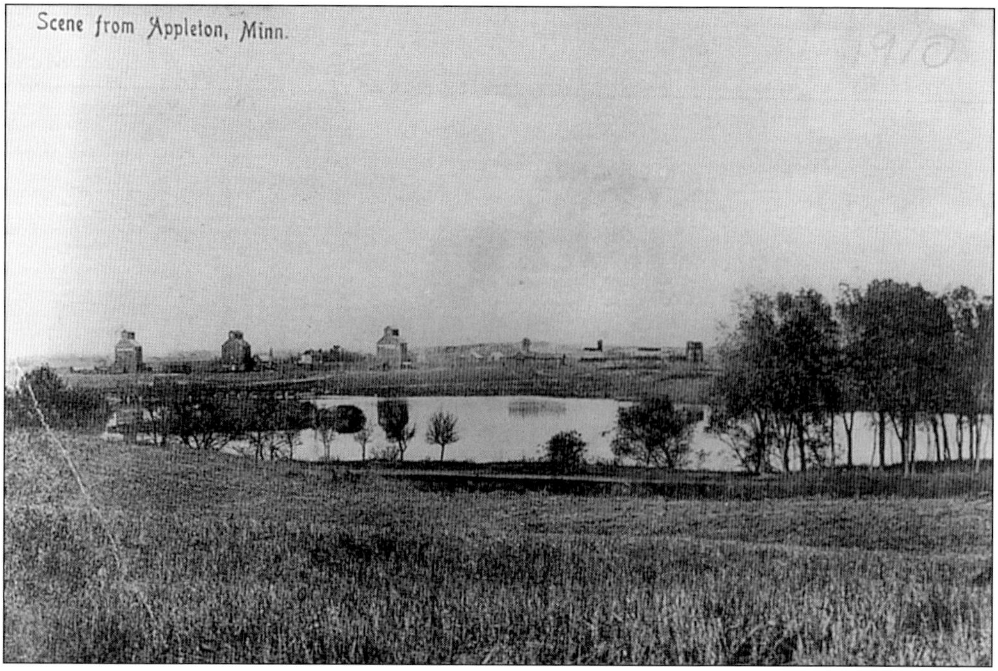

The Pomme de Terre River reflects the grain elevators at Appleton. In 1880, the majority of the grain raised in Swift County was wheat, with a total of 44,394 acres, compared to a total of 10,731 in other grains. By 1925, the number of acres tilled had increased greatly with 97,988 acres of oats and 84,696 acres of corn planted. Wheat acres had dropped to 29,429 acres.

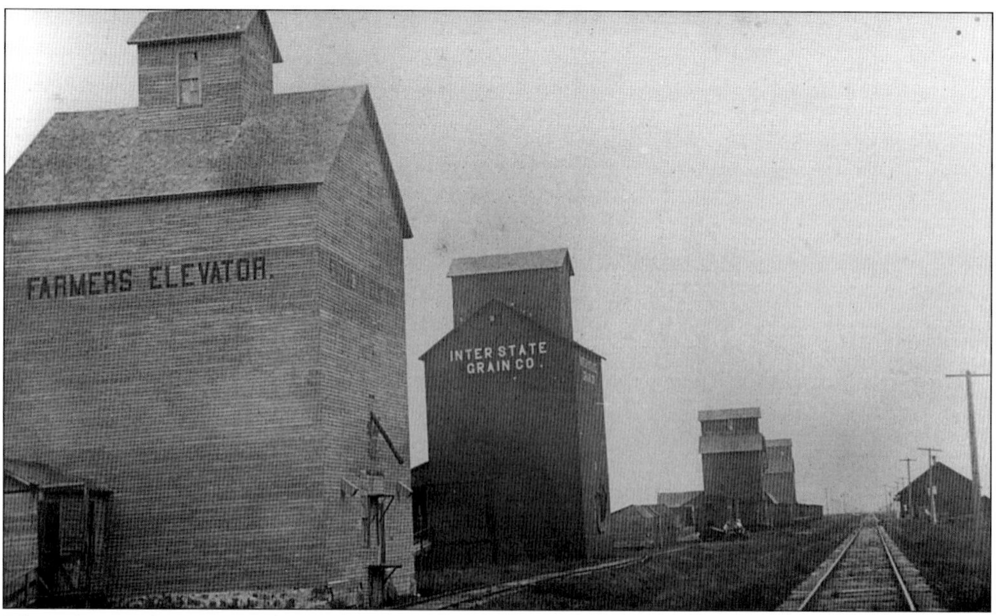

This photo of Danvers shows four grain elevators. The first elevator in Danvers was the Northwestern Elevator Company started shortly after Danvers was plotted in 1887. Elevators were constructed close to the railroad tracts for convenience of shipping.

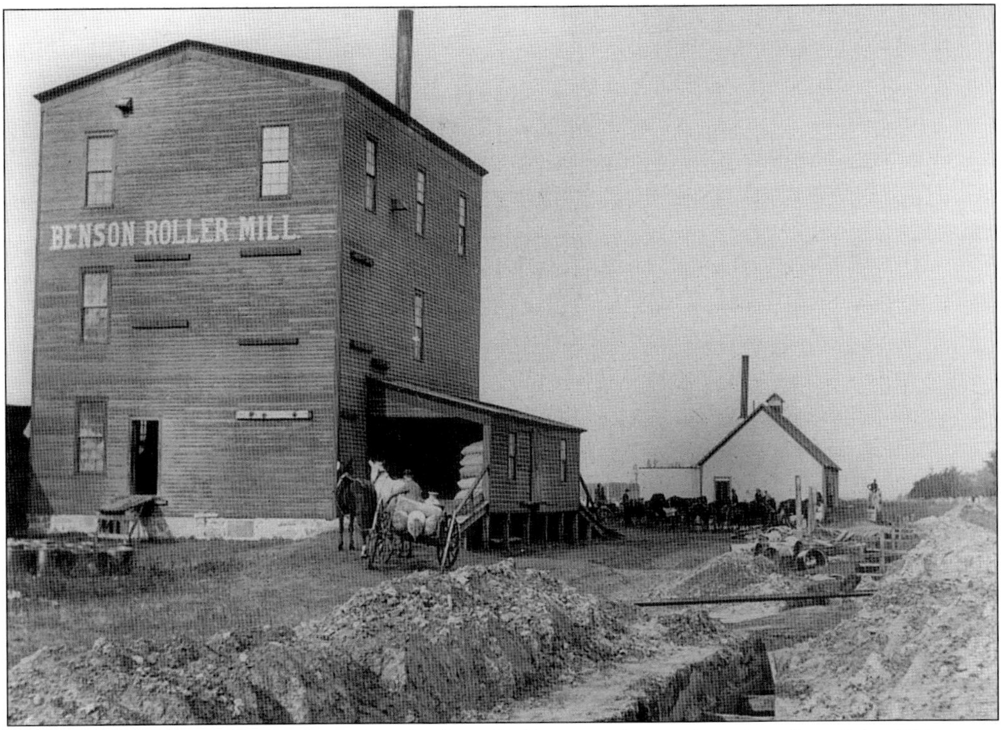

When the Benson Roller Mill was first built in 1881, it was located on the edge of the Chippewa River. Each day 100 barrels of flour would be hauled to the depot and a cord of wood hauled back to be burned for power. About ten years later, it burned to the ground. This building was constructed in the downtown business district closer to the depot.

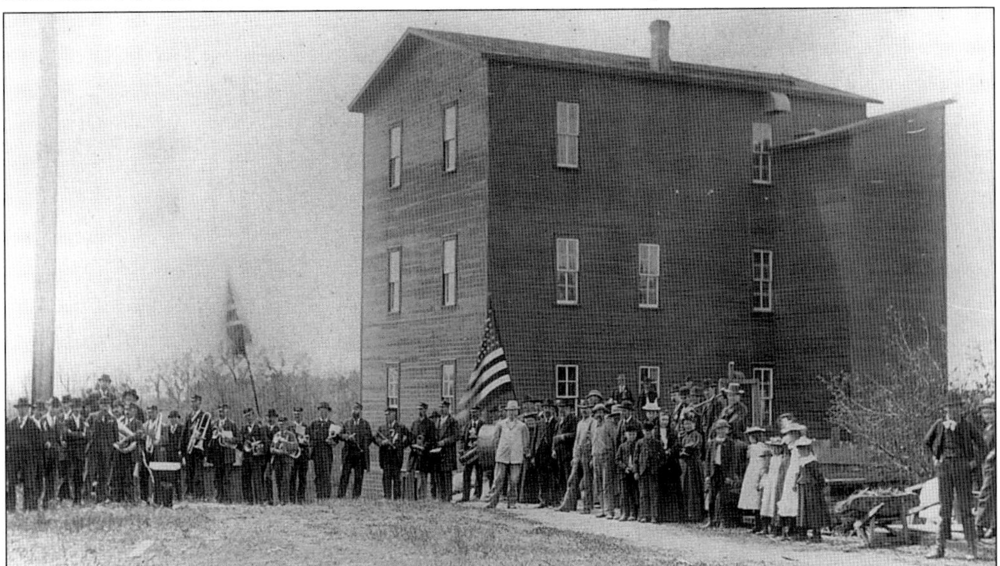

The first flourmill at Swift Falls was built north of the waterfalls. In order to obtain more waterpower, another mill was constructed south of it. In 1895, the boiler exploded and it was destroyed, but a new mill was erected the same year. On May 17, 1895, people gathered for its dedication.

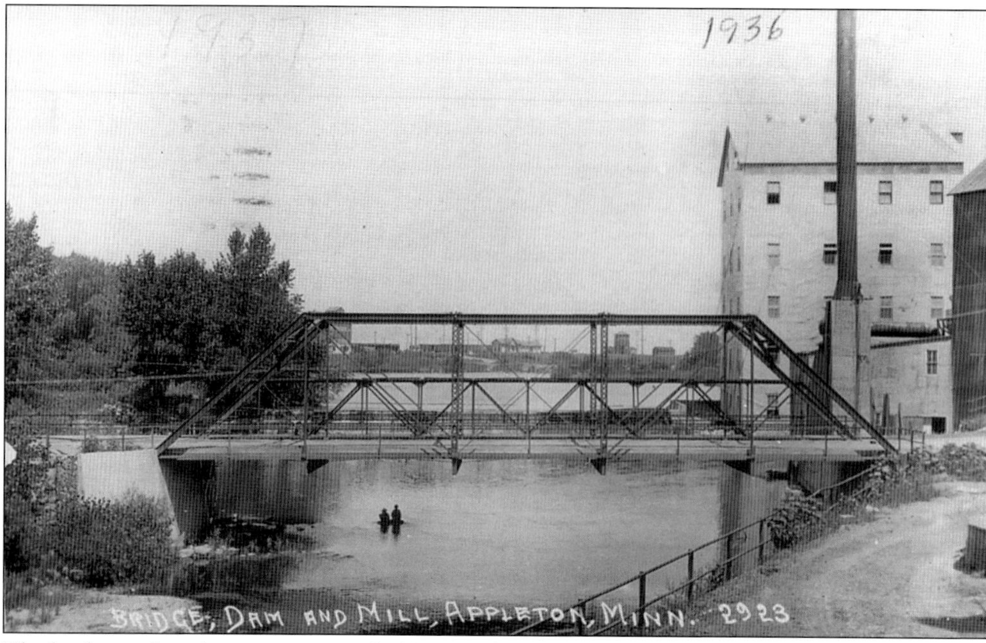

The bridge in this photo was across the Pomme de Terre River at Appleton. The Great Northern Depot can be seen as you look through the center portion of the bridge. Grain elevators, on both sides of the depot, provided a market for the farmers' crops. The Jennison Milling Company, on the right, was a source for selling wheat and having it ground into flour.

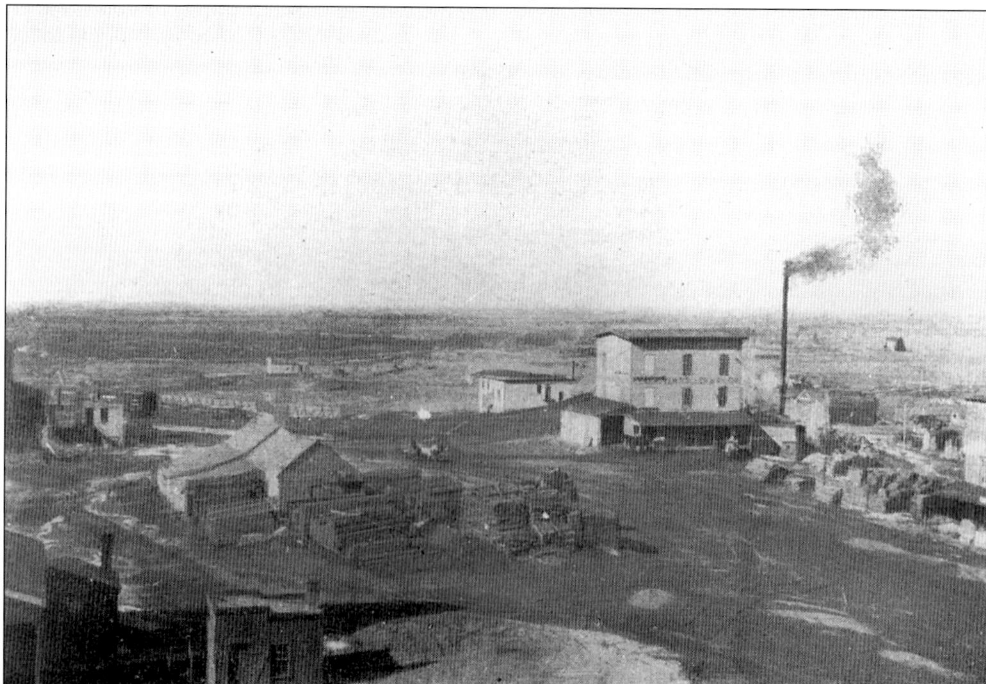

The Kerkhoven city council made a contract with L. Nyquist to construct a roller mill capable of producing 75 barrels of flour a day. The Kerkhoven Roller Mill was built in 1889, and ceased operations in the 1920s. The mill is the large building next to the smoke stack.

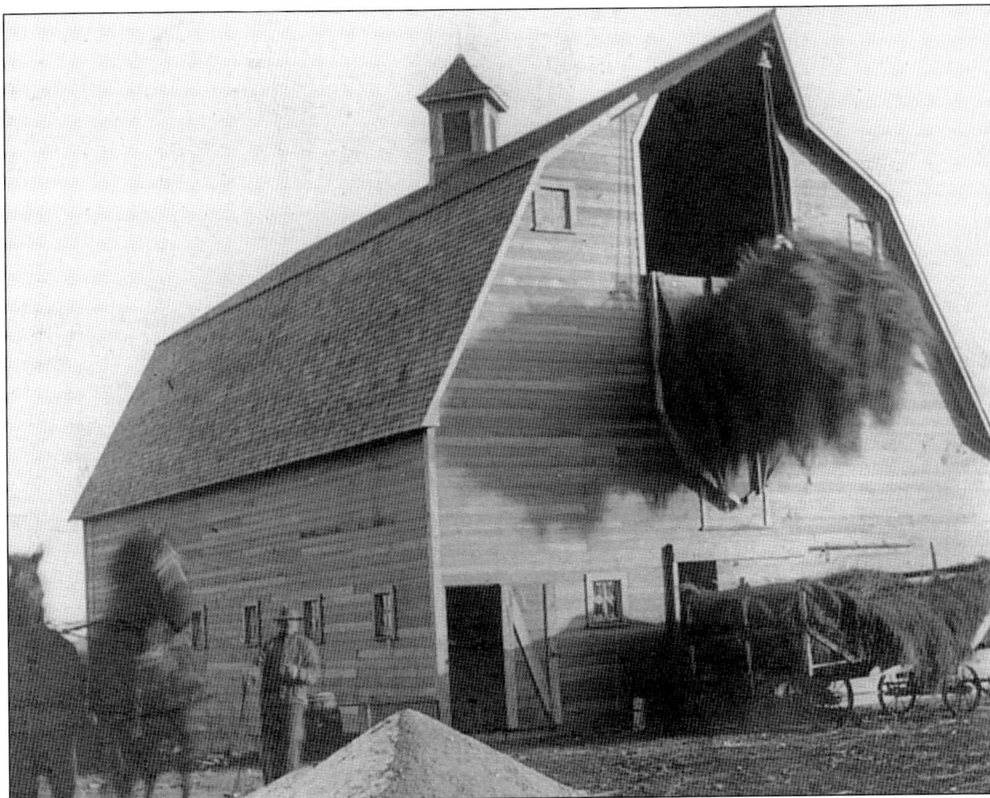

Geography textbooks used in the schools during the 1910s and 1920s referred to Clontarf as the "Hay Capital of the World." In the early 1900s, the Chicago Fire Department relied on Clontarf hay to feed horses used in pulling fire-fighting equipment. Hay was stored in barns for feed, which was especially needed during the winter months.

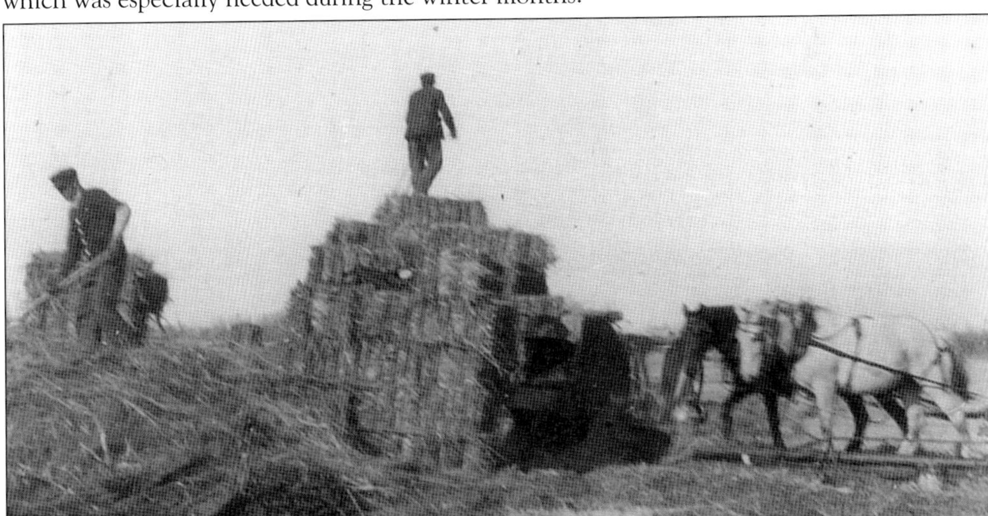

Hay was put through a baling machine to compress it. When the compressed hay came out of the machine, men used wire to bind the hay into bales. The baler operated through a system of gears, shafts, and pulleys that were powered by horses.

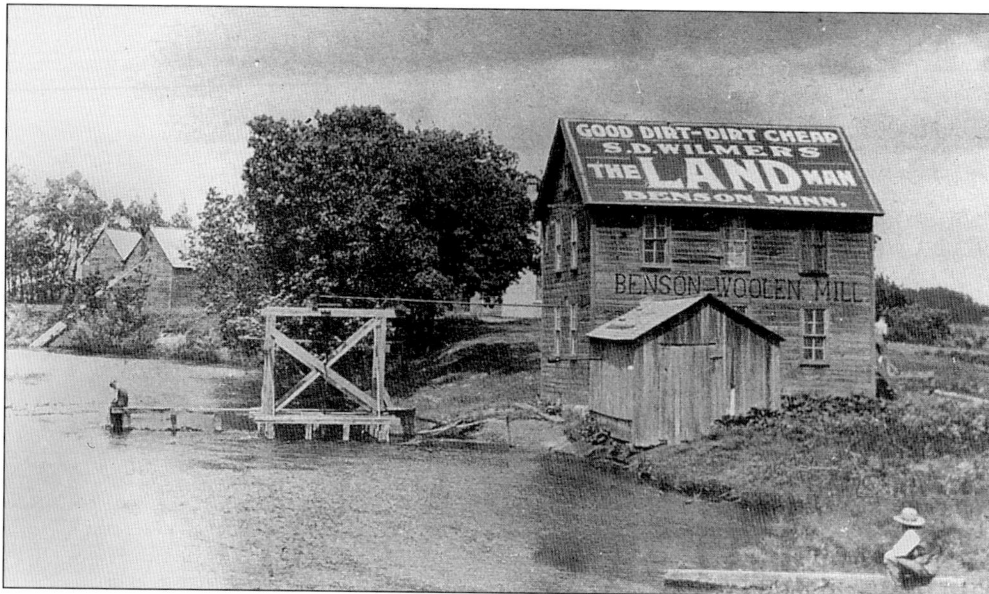

On May 21, 1880, the *Benson Times* reported that Jens T. Jensen, the proprietor of the carding mill at Benson, "intends to have his mill running in about a month. He intends this season to devote his time principally to carding, but next season will put in looms and all other necessary machinery for the manufacture of cloth." The woolen mill was located next to the Chippewa River, which was used as a power source.

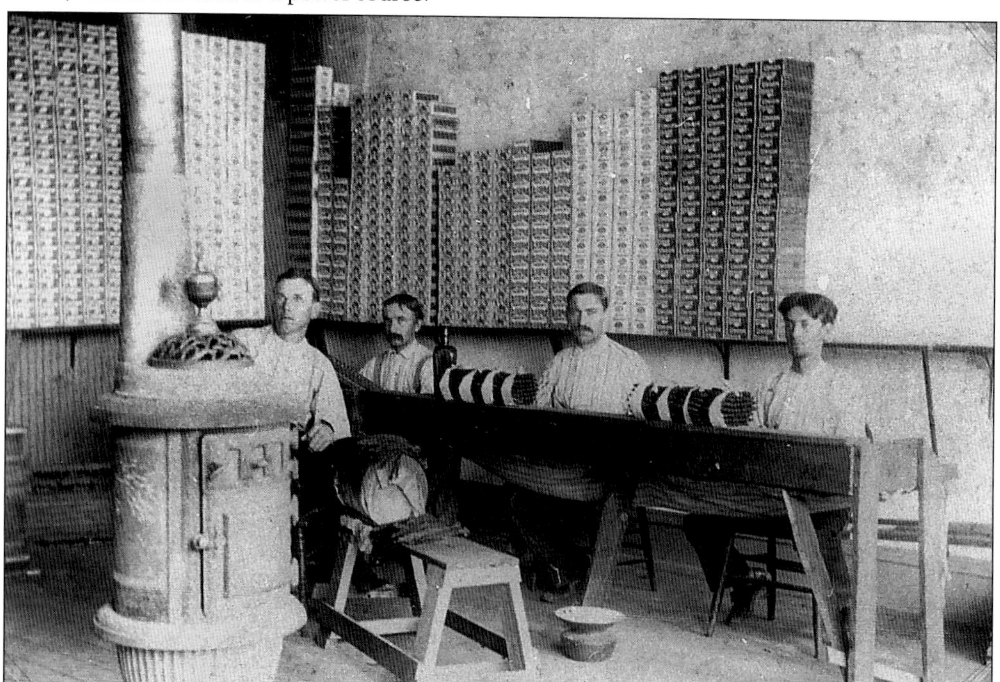

In 1904, Samuel Fargo came to Benson and opened a cigar factory. At its peak business operation, he had six cigar rollers or makers and two strippers whose job was to strip the main, coarse, center stem from the tobacco leaf. In 1912, when Minnesota was voted dry, the bottom dropped out of the hand-made cigar business.

Four

GOVERNING

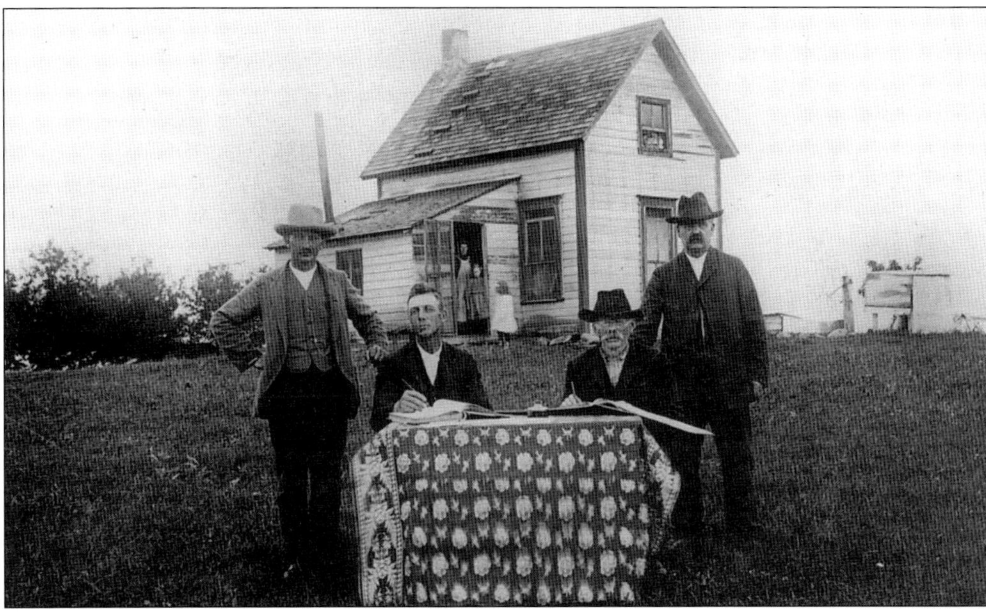

By 1879, Swift County had three tiers of seven townships in each. The top tier of townships (left to right) are Hegbert, Fairfield, Tara, Clontarf, Benson, Camp Lake, Kerkhoven; middle tier are (left to right) Shible, Moyer, Marysland, Six Mile Grove, Torning, Kildare, Hayes; bottom tier (left to right) are Appleton, Edison, West Bank, Swenoda, Cashel, Dublin, and Pillsbury. Township government officials included a chairman, supervisors, clerks, treasurer, assessor, justices, constables, and pound masters. Besides being in charge of caring for the poor, they saw to the needs of families quarantined with contagious diseases and assisted the mortician with burials if the disease resulted in death. This is a photo of the Six Mile Grove Township Board in 1906.

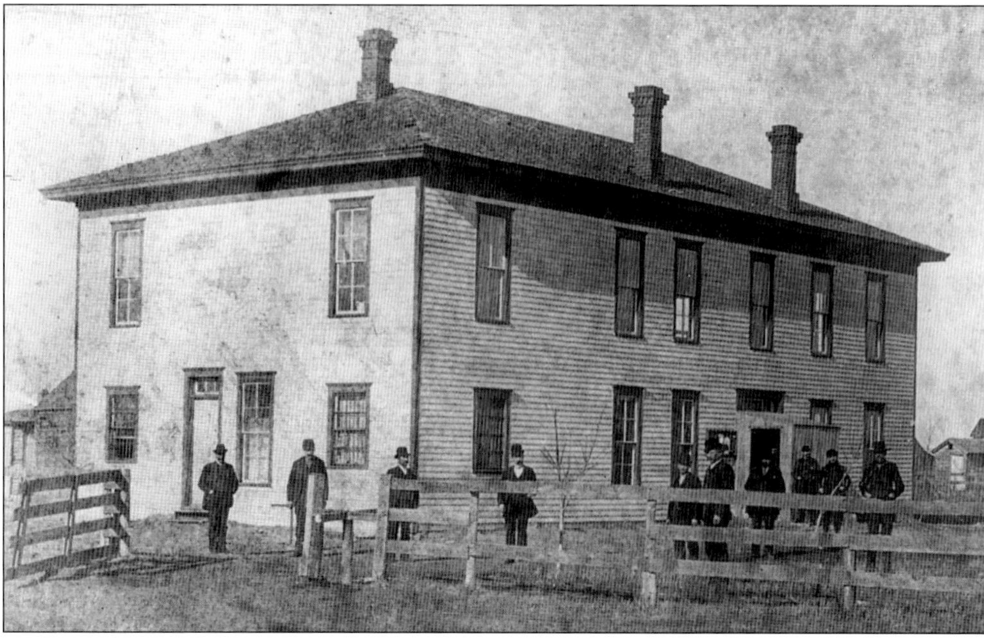

In 1876, the legislature authorized the construction of a courthouse in Benson for $3,000, which became available when the people voted 244 to 104 to accept the proposal. Plans and specifications for this frame building were established for $2,600, with another $439 spent on additional flooring and improvements.

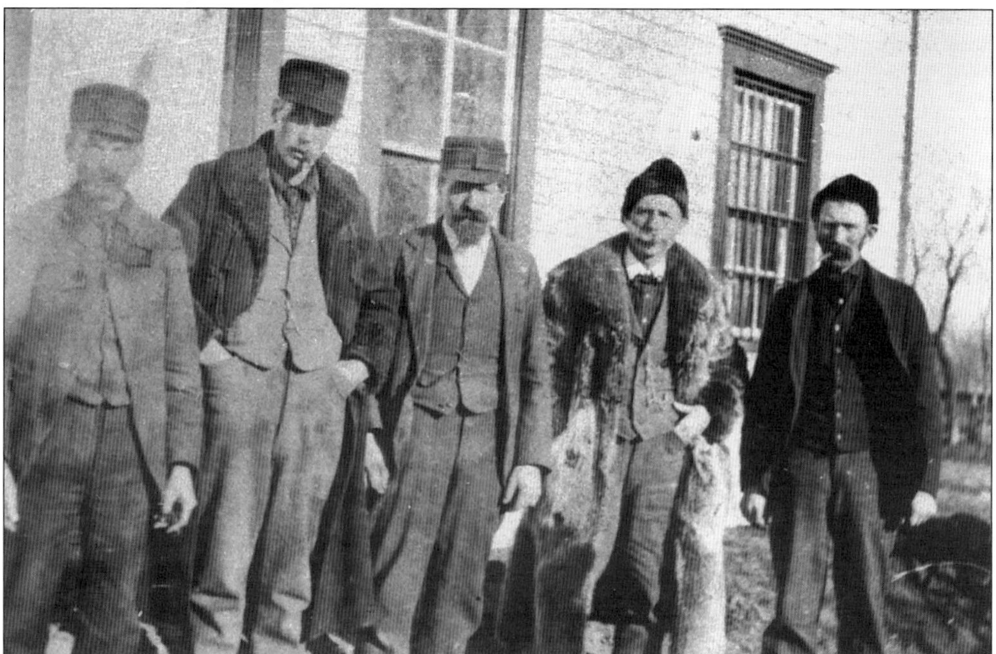

In 1889, legislature authorized a one-mill annual levy for a new courthouse, as the 1876 courthouse proved to be too small to meet the needs of the county. The county commissioners in 1897 voted to advertise for the construction of a new courthouse. From left to right are Commissioners Joseph Cannon, C.R. Alsaker, Leonard Bergstrom, P.M. Scott, and John Beyer.

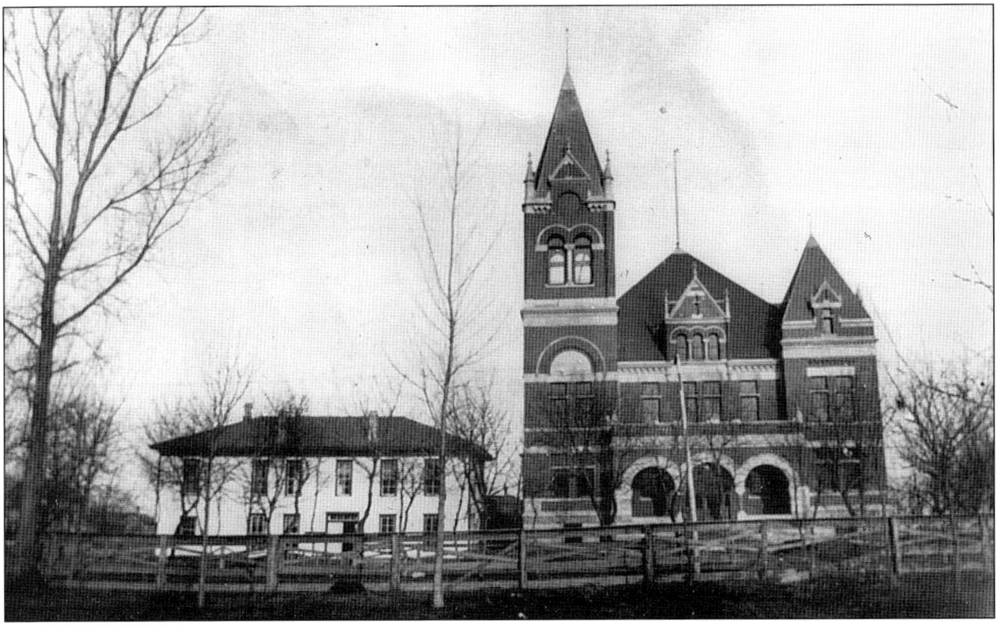

This photo of Swift County's first and second courthouse was taken in 1898, after the construction was completed on the second and present courthouse. The old courthouse was then moved one block to the west and converted into an apartment building.

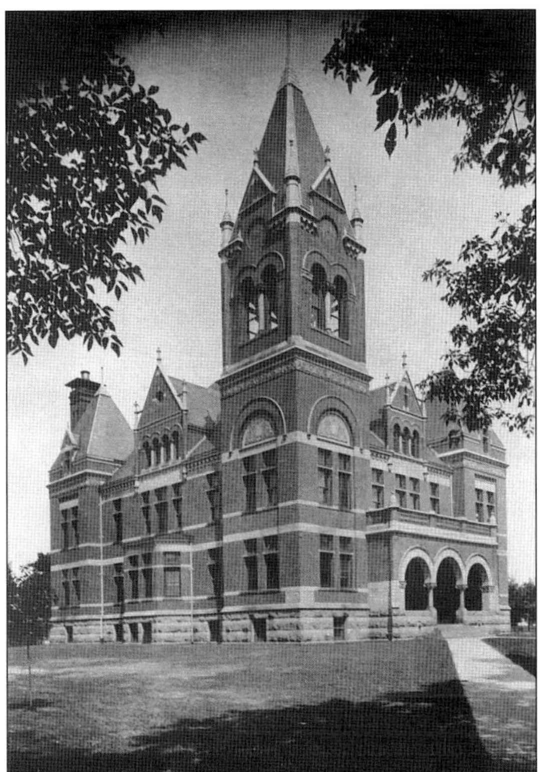

The cornerstone of Swift County's courthouse was laid in Benson on September 28, 1897. The construction plans included all the modern conveniences, specifically plumbing and electricity. County officials moved into their new offices in May of 1898. Total cost with furniture and steel vaults was approximately $45,534.

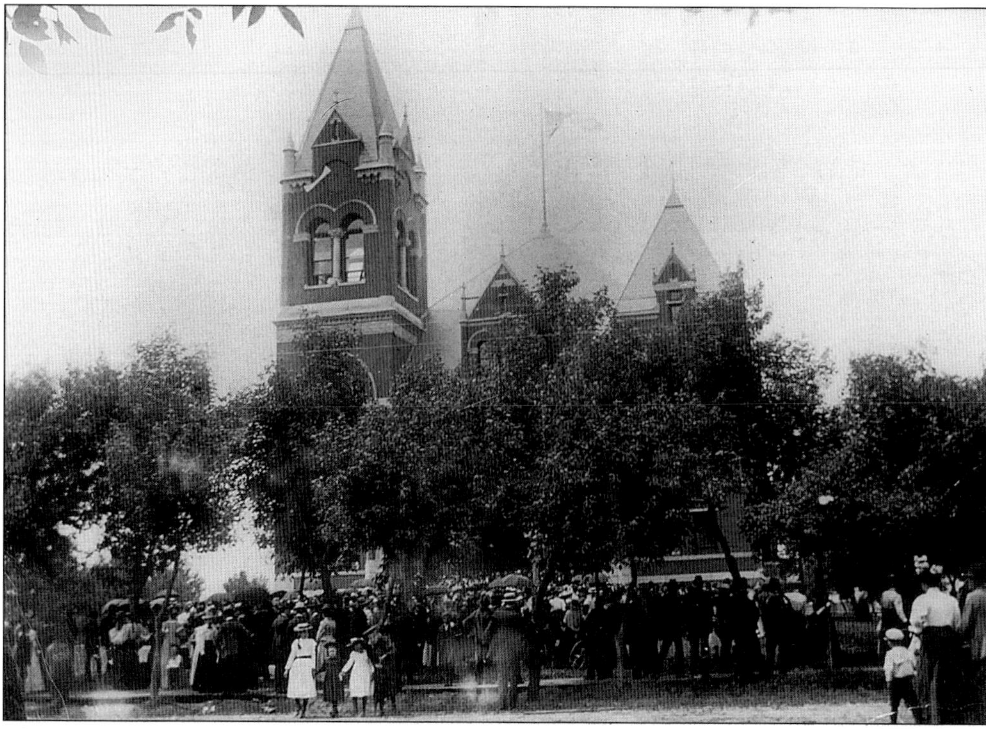

The new brick Swift County courthouse was dedicated on June 11, 1898, with an estimated crowd of 4,500. One of the highlights of the celebration came in the evening when all the electric lights in the courthouse were turned on.

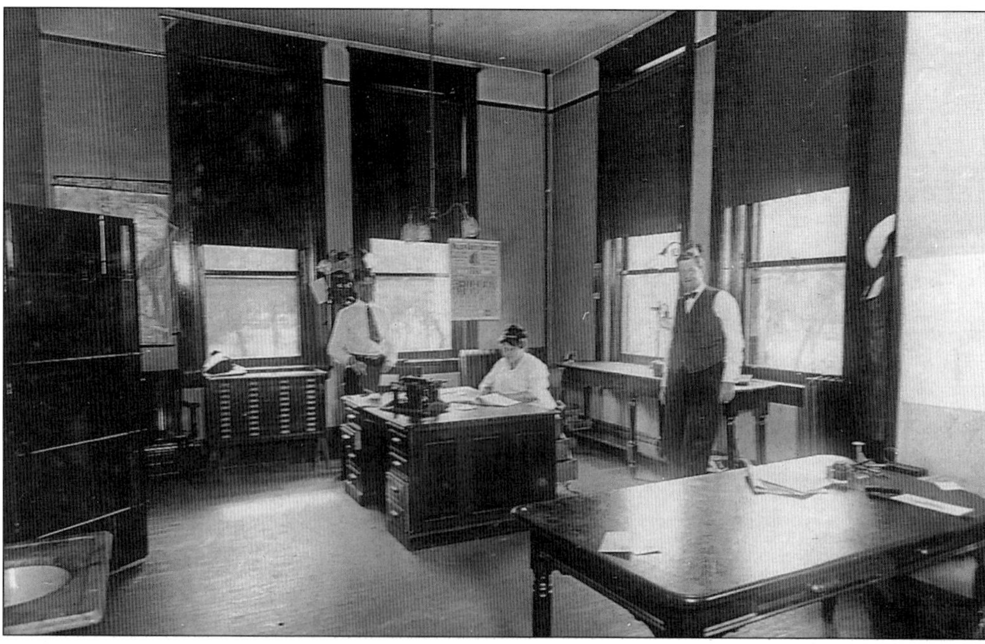

A photo was taken of the interior of one of the courthouse offices shortly after its construction in 1898. On the left is a sink surrounded by a marble countertop. The door opens to one of the steel vaults. All the wood furnishings for the courthouse were made of oak at a cost of $2,700.

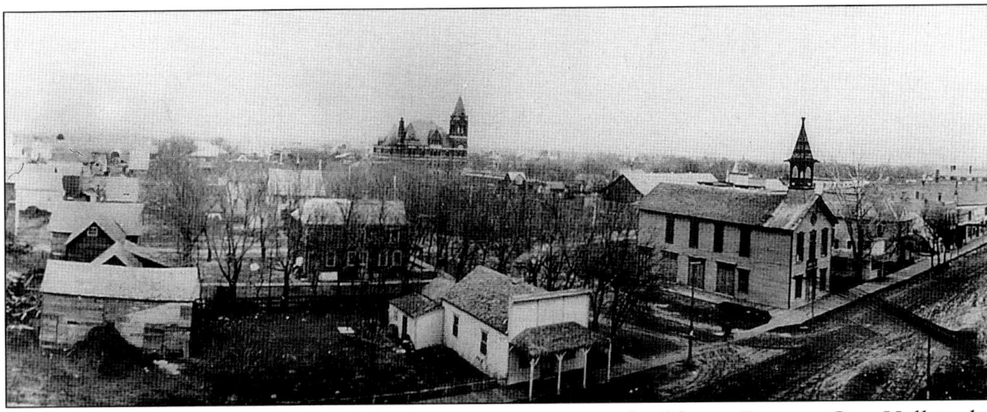

This panoramic view of Benson takes in two government buildings. Benson City Hall is the building on the right with the bell tower. The tower of the Swift County Courthouse can be seen in the background.

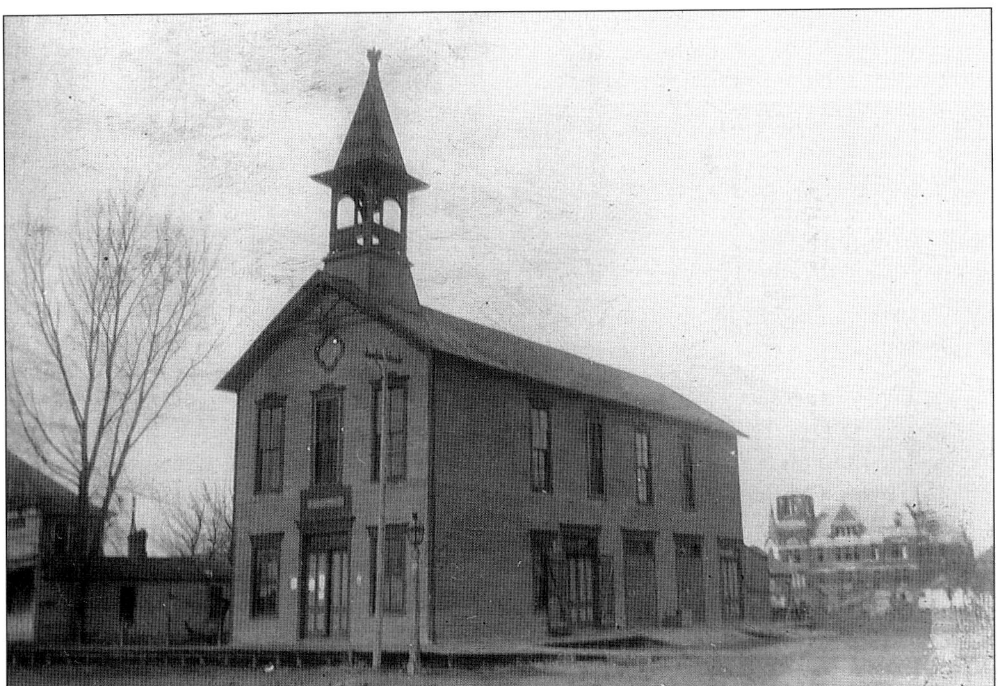

Benson's first city hall was constructed in 1881. The fire of 1880, which wiped out an entire city block, found Benson without a fire department. One purpose for the city hall was to provide space for fire fighting equipment. This photo was taken during construction of the second courthouse.

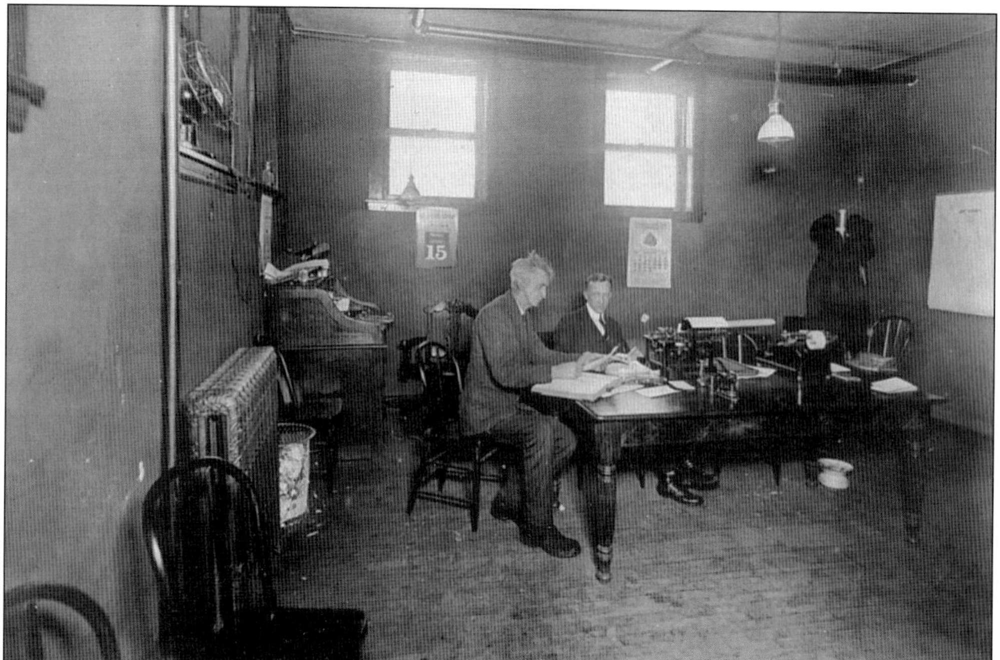

This photo of the office of the city clerk in Benson was taken between the years of 1915 and 1918, when L.M. Pederson, on the right, served as clerk. The gentlemen on the left is D.W. Hume, the mayor of Benson at the time. The city clerk's office was located in the basement of the Carnigie Library built in 1911.

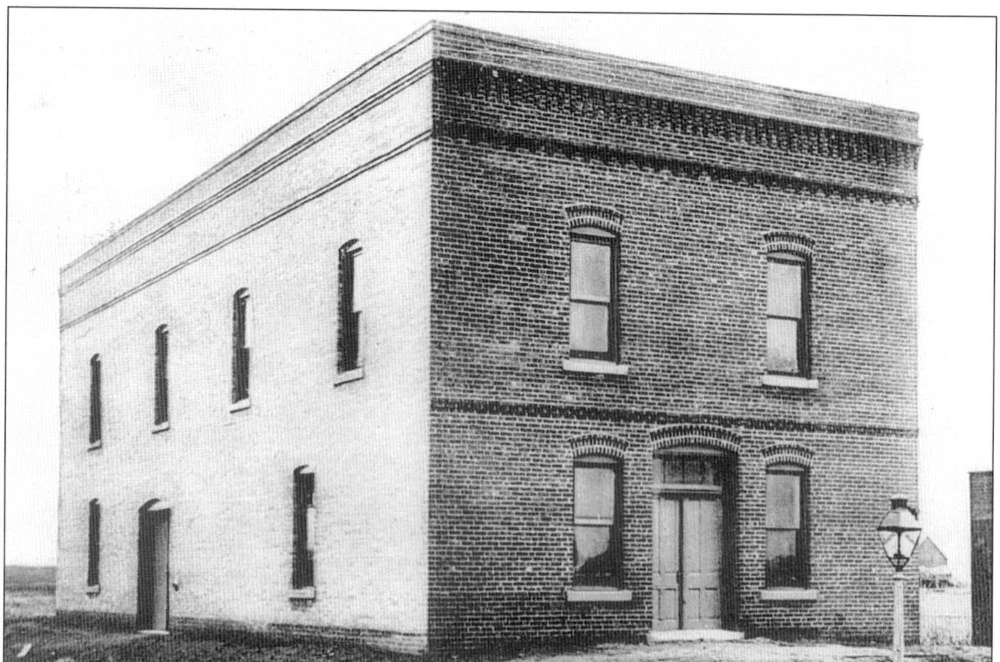

The city hall in Holloway was built in 1907. It was a two-story brick structure. The bottom floor housed the council rooms and fire hall as well as the jail. The second floor was where all the community activities were held, such as vaudeville shows and dances.

The first city hall in Murdock was a two-story building erected by the 1890s. For many years it was used for medicine shows, elections, school programs, church festivals, and public dances. During the 1917–1918 school term, it served as Murdock's high school while a new school was being built.

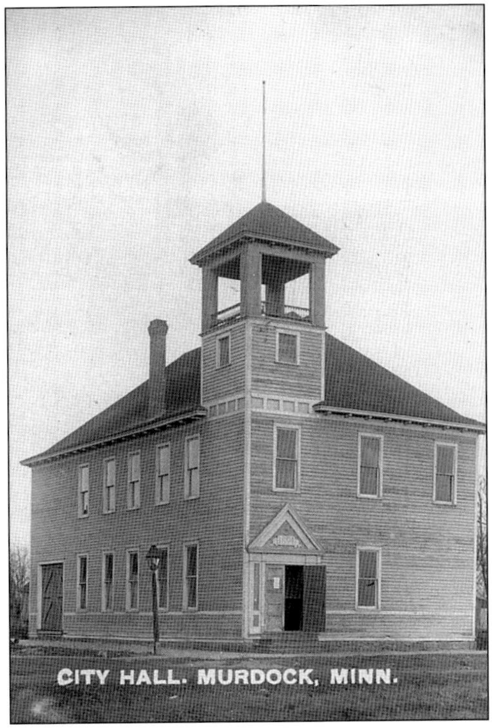

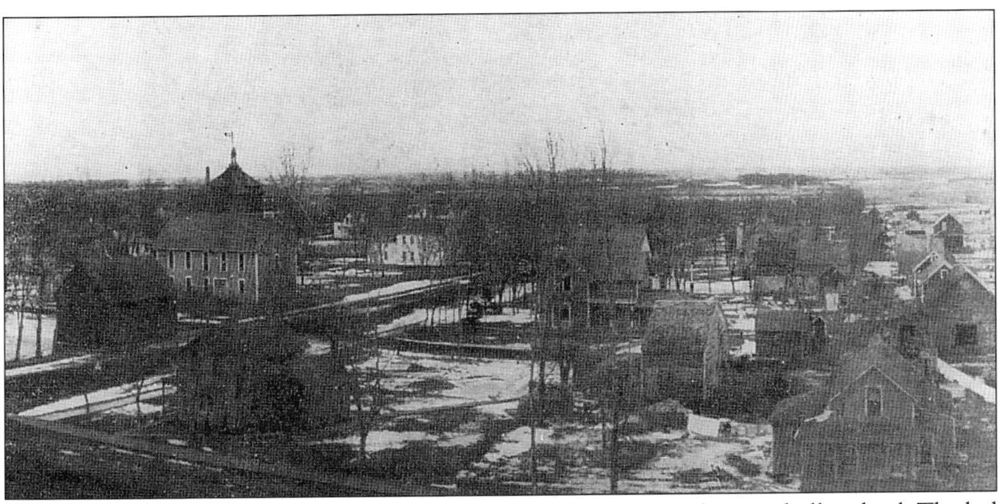

In 1882, the Kerkhoven town council called for the construction of a town hall and jail. The bid for a 22-by-44-foot town hall was allowed in 1883. Over the years, several improvements in the hall were made. The town hall is the two-story building with five windows on the top floor.

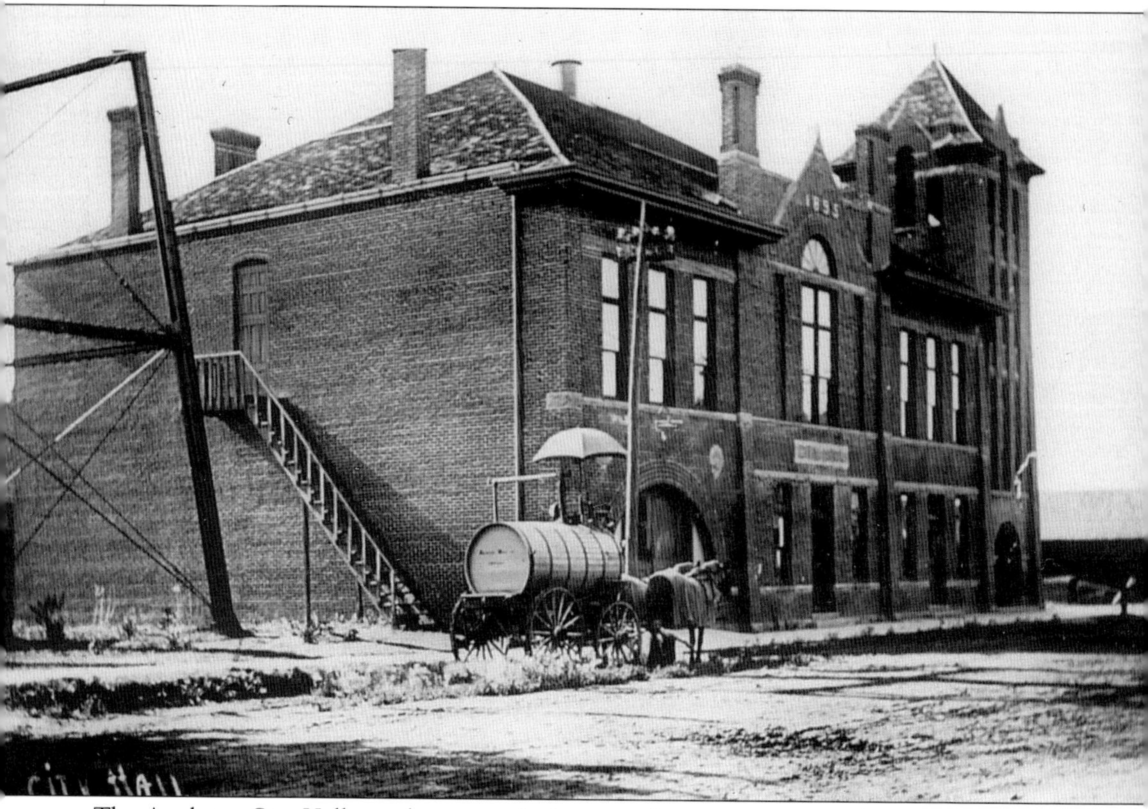

The Appleton City Hall was the cause of a long-standing controversy before it was even built. The village council purchased a site for a public building and called a special election to provide bonds to finance it in 1893. The proposal was rejected then, and a number of times following that. In the spring election of 1895, a proposal to sell $8,000 of village bonds to build a city hall passed. In June, a contract was let for $7,867. It was formally opened on December 3, 1895. The building included an auditorium with a 600-person seating capacity. On the occasion of the opening, a home talent cast presented the play *Damon and Pythias*, which received more news coverage than the new city hall.

Five

THE THREE RS

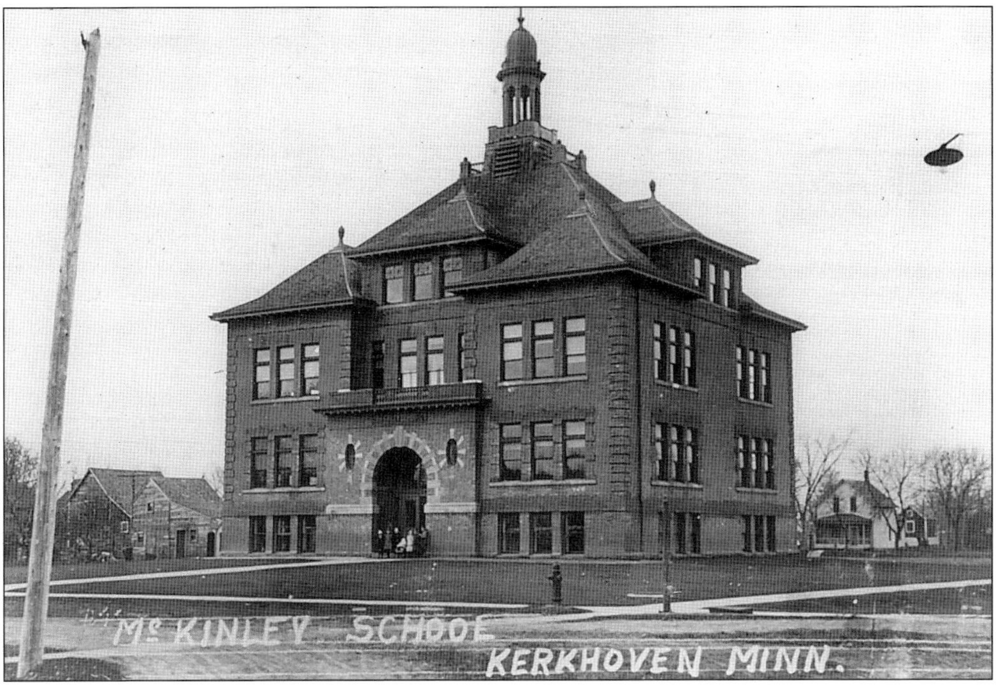

The first settlers of Swift County realized the importance of education. In 1874, the first school in Kerkhoven was built. The one-room school did not provide the space needed, as enrollment in first through seventh grades totaled more than 70 students. A two-room school was built in 1890, with an additional two rooms added later. By 1903, students numbered 177 in a school with a capacity of 160. This spacious three-story building with attic was built in 1904. The basement had a 23-by-26-foot gym. The building was dedicated in 1905 and named the McKinley School.

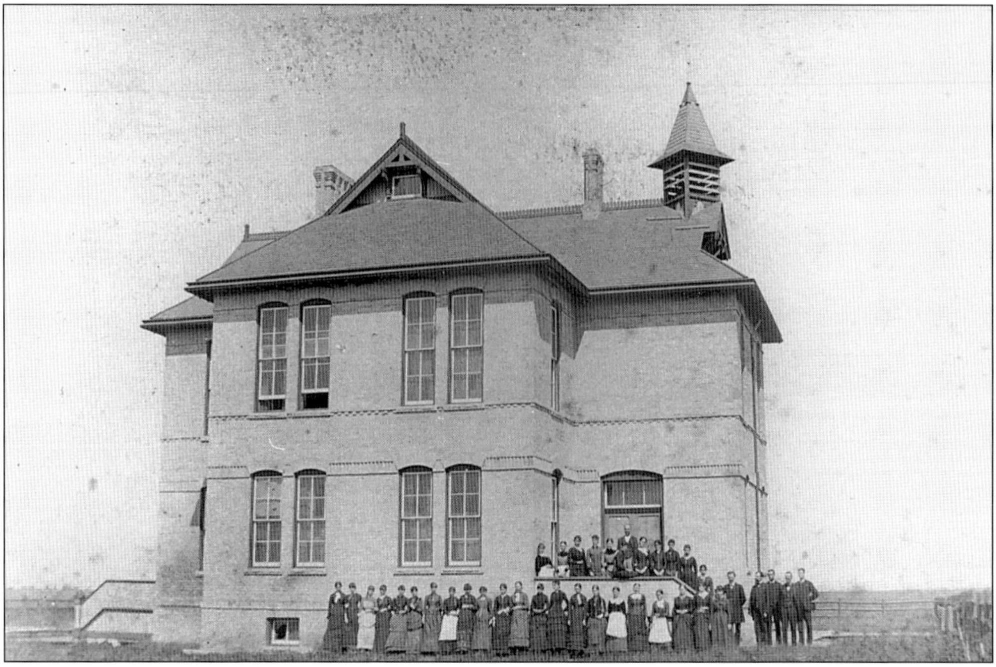

The first school in Benson was a one-room school, built in 1871, on the same block that the courthouse would later stand. In 1879, the Benson School District decided to build a new brick school on 13th Street North. In the 1890s, teachers attending the Teacher's Institute in Benson posed for a picture in front of the 1879 school. The school was demolished in 1905.

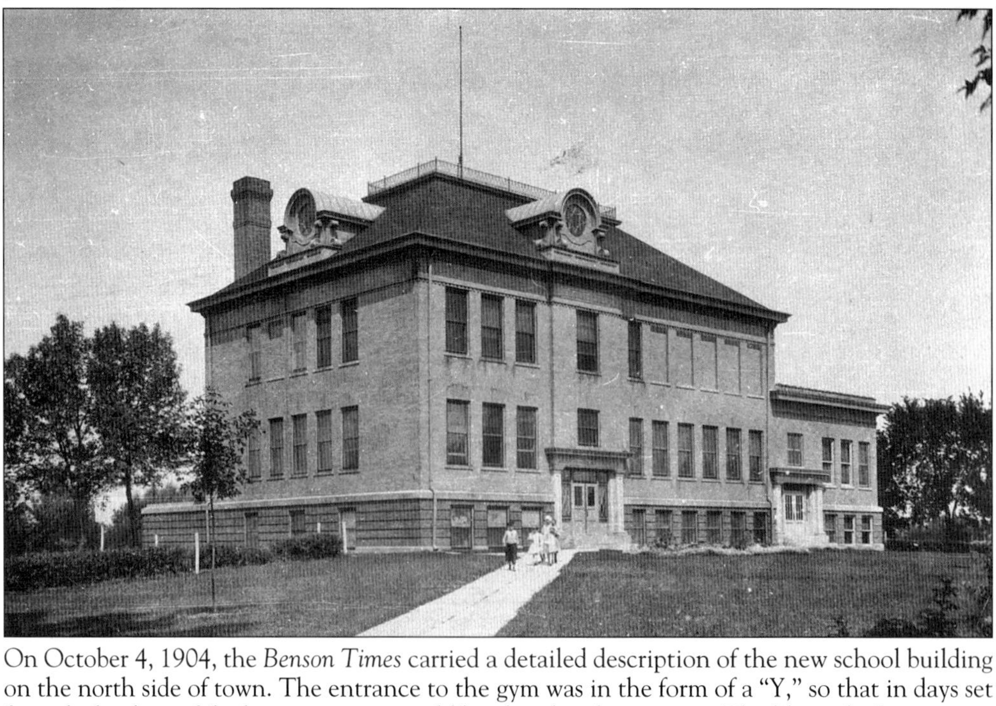

On October 4, 1904, the *Benson Times* carried a detailed description of the new school building on the north side of town. The entrance to the gym was in the form of a "Y," so that in days set for girls the door of the boys entrance would be closed and vice versa. The library had a capacity for five thousand volumes.

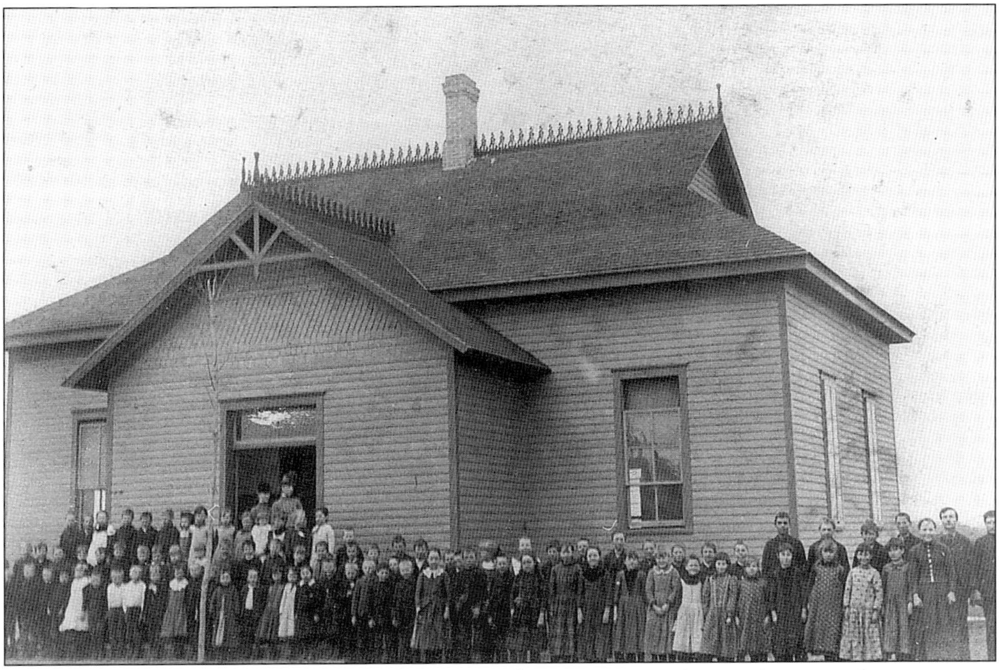

This two-room school was constructed in 1888, after a vote was taken and approved to construct a school on the south side of Benson, since the north side school was becoming overcrowded. In 1891, the structure was raised and a one-room, the size of the two rooms in this photo, was built below. Seven years later two more rooms, one on top of the other, were added.

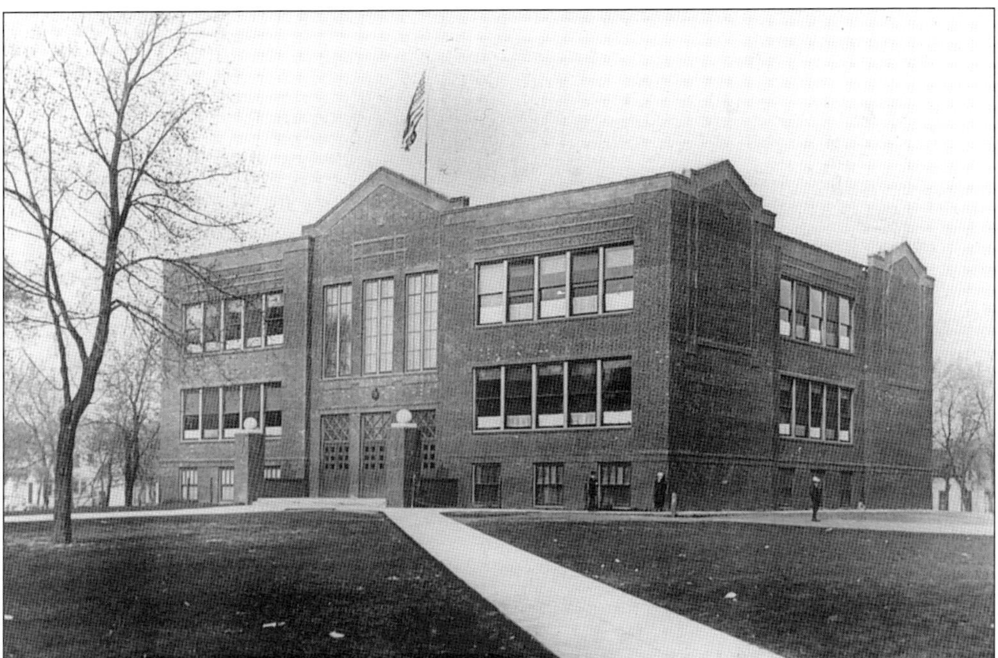

Benson's brick south side school was built in 1913 at a cost of $36,689. Elementary-aged students attended this school. The south side wood-frame school was torn down.

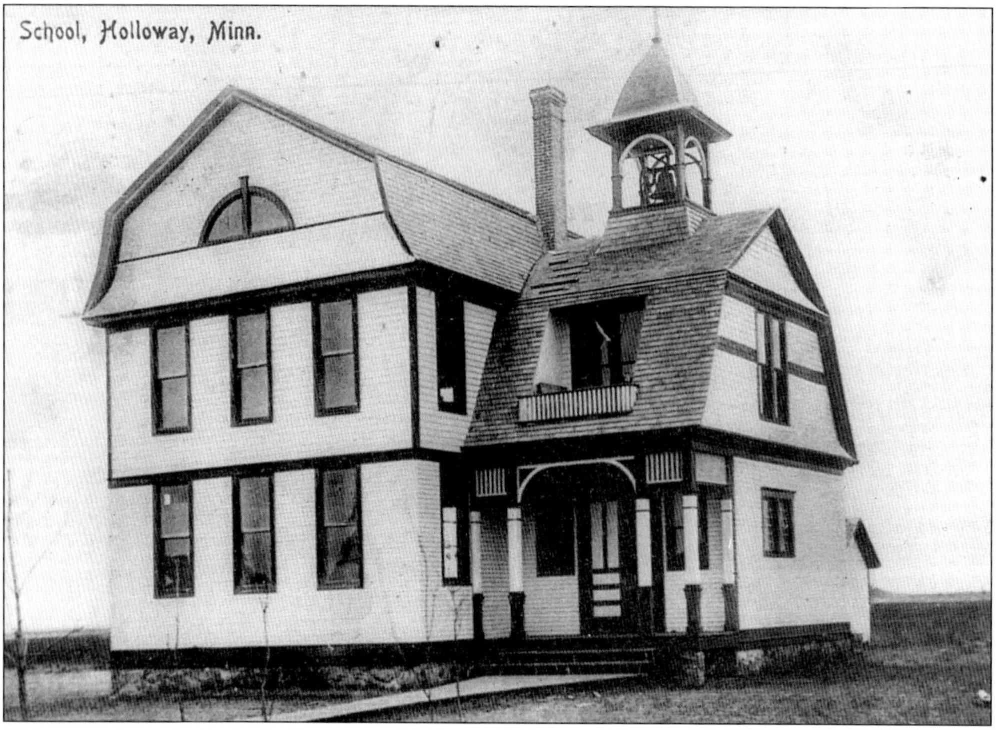

This school was built in Holloway in 1898. In 1900, an addition was constructed to match the architectural design of the left portion of the building.

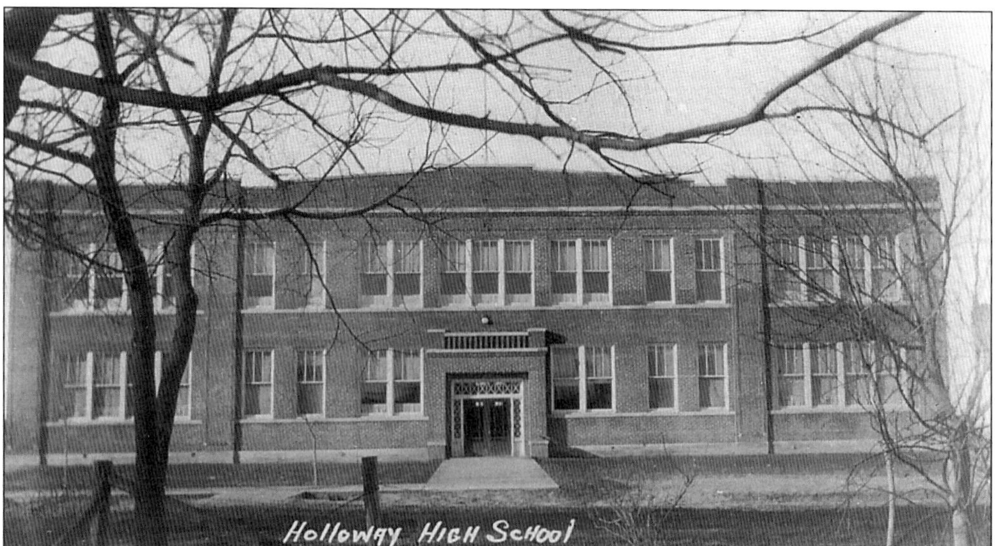

On July 26, 1918, the *Holloway Herald* reported that a meeting was held to vote on the erection of a new and up-to-date school building. Personal accounts state that this building was open for classes to students through grade 12 in 1920.

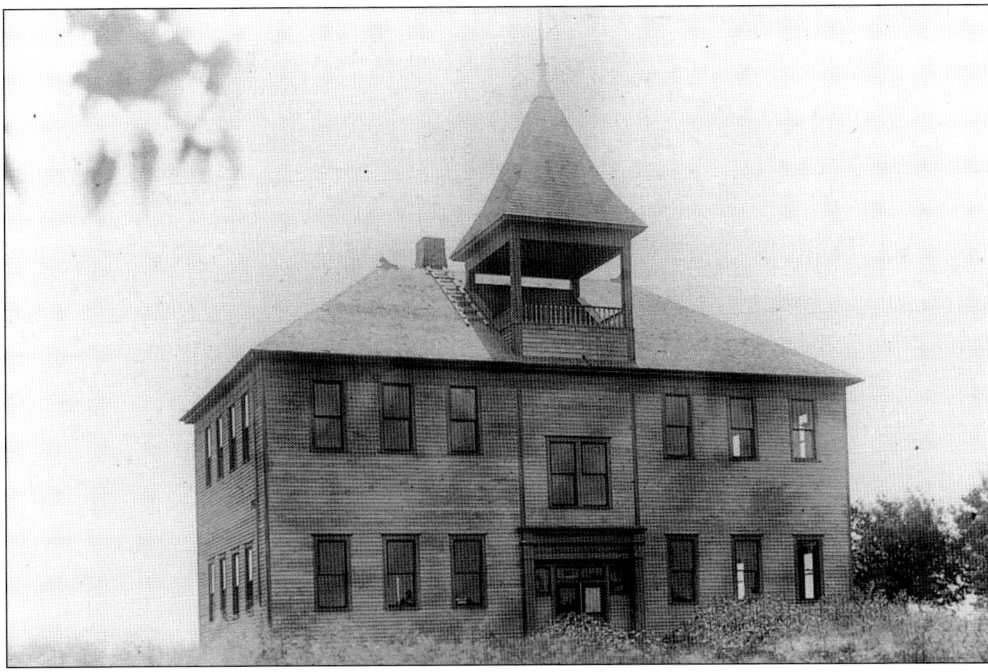

Little history is known about the early schools of Murdock. The November 1904 newspaper stated that a 40-by-60-foot school was completed with furnishings of the most modern desks and seats. Each room was lighted with ten windows.

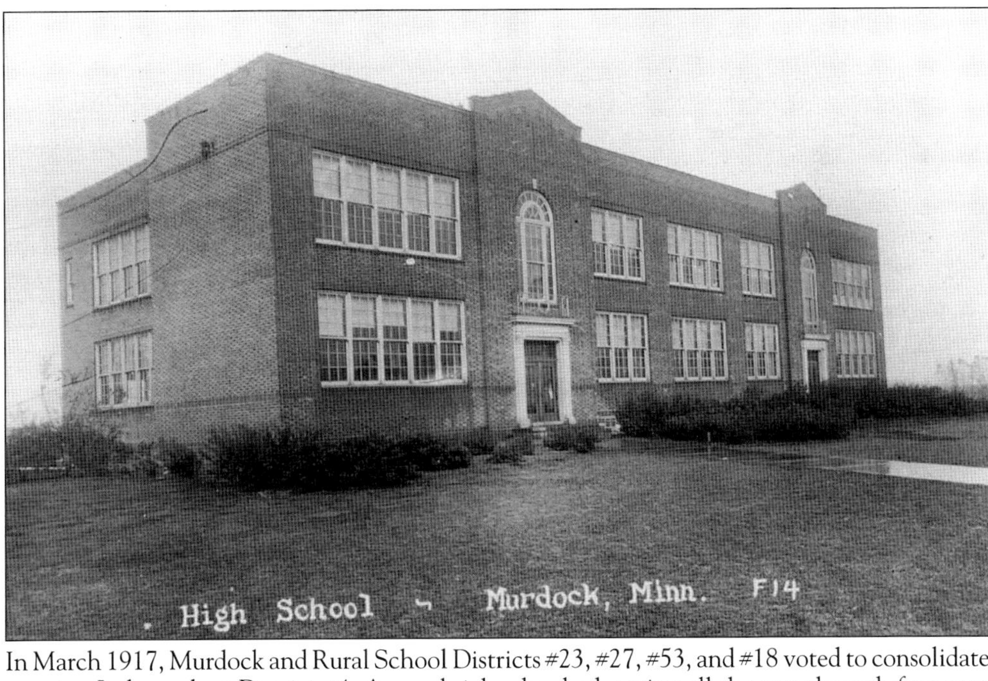

In March 1917, Murdock and Rural School Districts #23, #27, #53, and #18 voted to consolidate, creating Independent District #4. A new brick school educating all the way through four years of high school was built in Murdock. Five Studebaker buses were purchased to transport students to and from school.

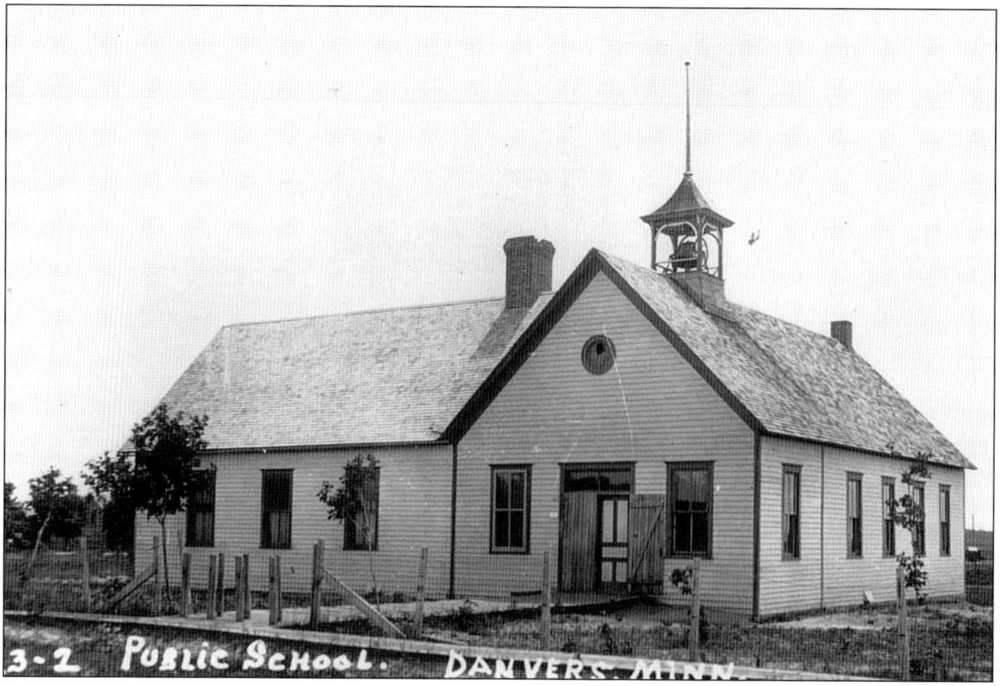

A school district in Danvers was organized in 1899. The village hall was remodeled for the first one-room school. An increase in enrollment made it necessary to add another room in 1904. This school was used until 1920, when a brick building for grades one through ten was constructed.

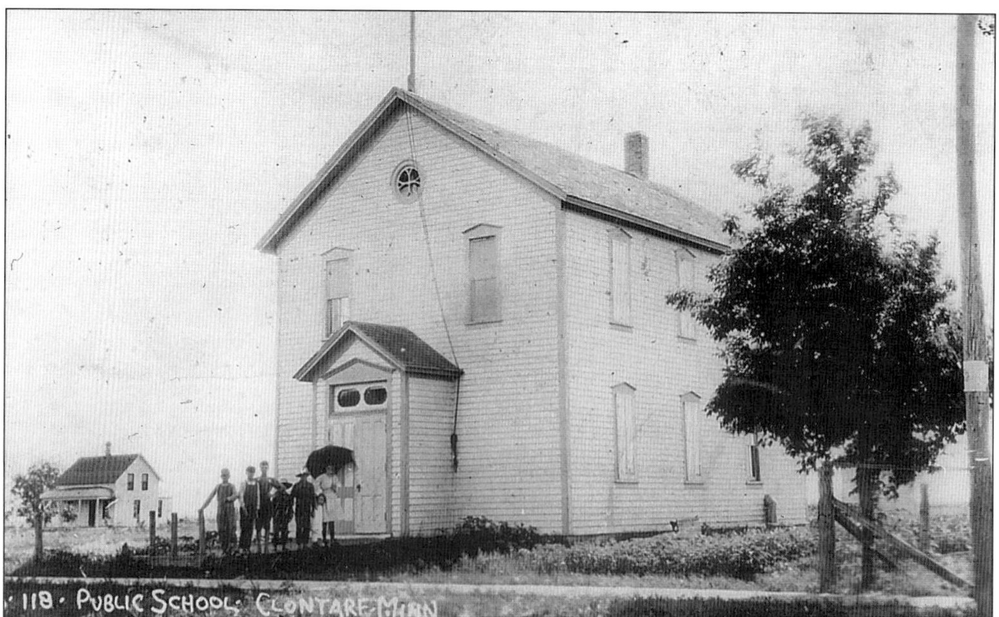

Clontarf School District #25 was organized in 1878. Classes were held in the Catholic church until this two-room school was built in 1880. It was replaced in 1917, with a brick structure at a cost of $60,000.

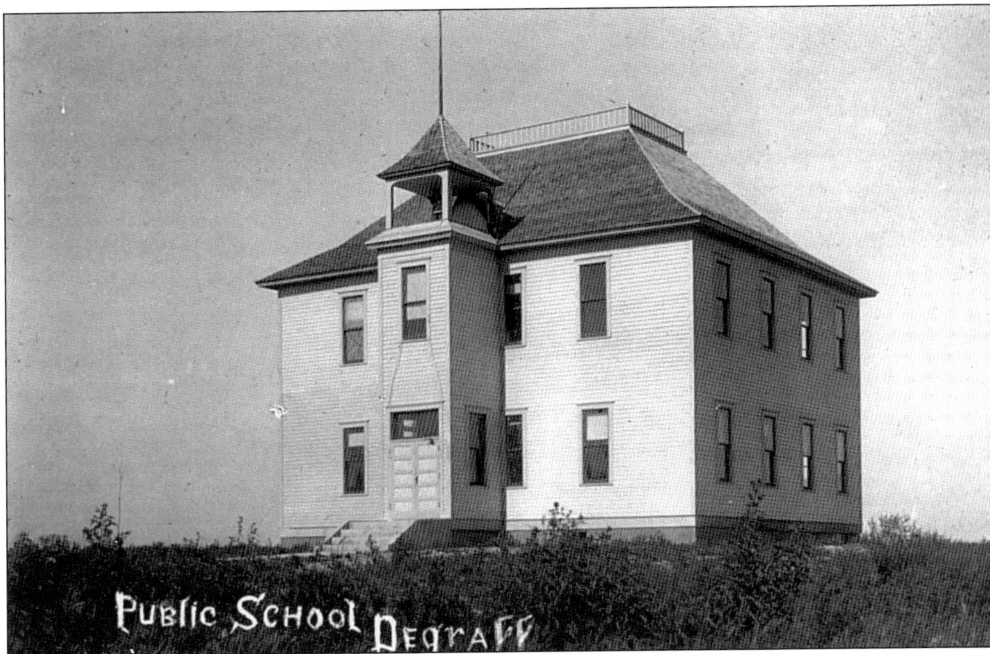

District #17 of DeGraff was organized in 1876. Before the first school was built in 1878, classes were held in the depot. The school was added onto in 1910. High school students were transported to Benson or Murdock in 1939.

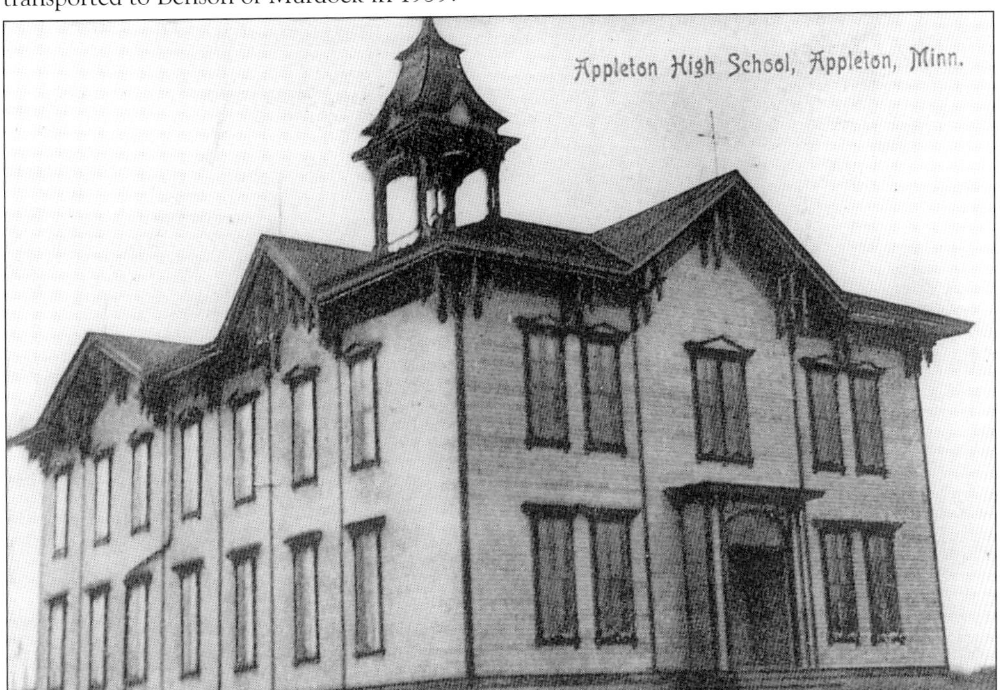

In 1880, Independent District #1 was organized at Appleton, and a new school was constructed. This photo is of the school after an addition was built in 1892. The building was razed in 1916 to make room for a new high school.

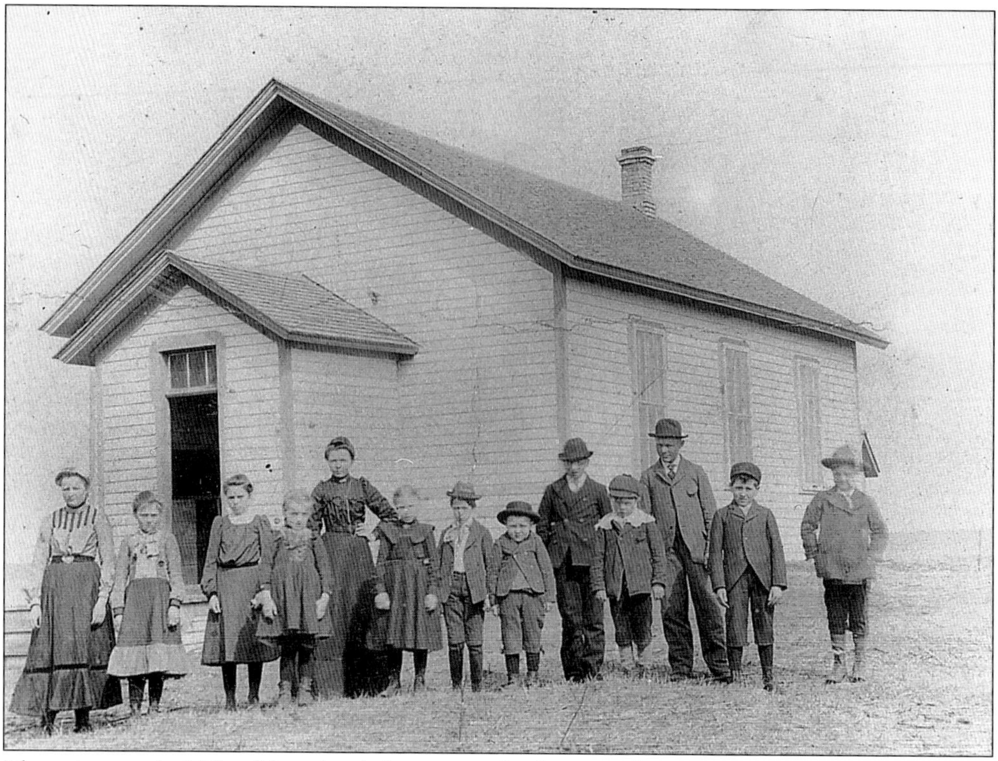

There is a total of 99 public school districts in the history of Swift County. All but eight were located outside the trading centers. Those in the rural areas were known as Common School Districts. This photo was taken about 1903 in front of District #7 in Six Mile Grove Township. It was organized in 1871.

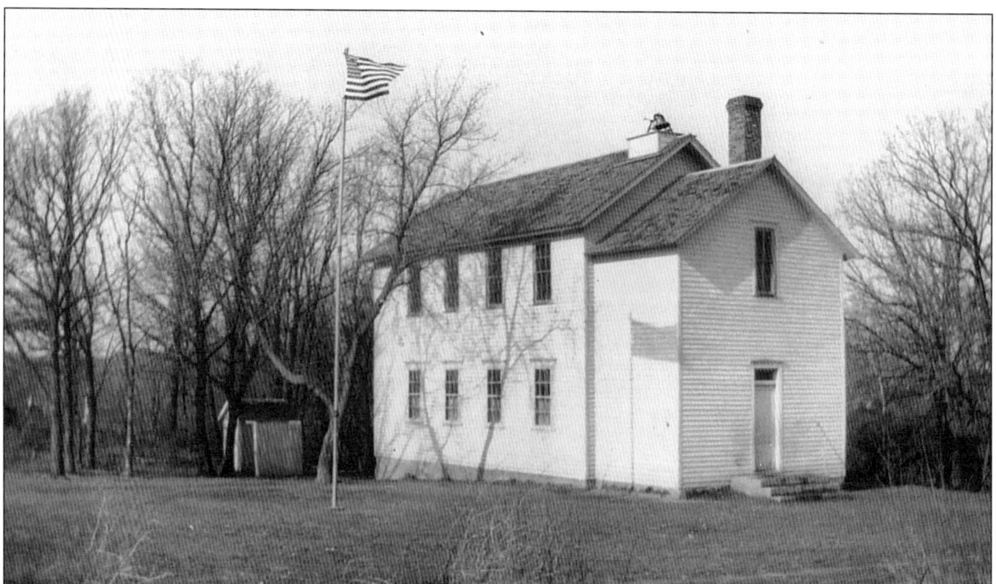

Classes for District #13 at Swift Falls were taught in homes until a school was built in 1878. Another room was built below the original structure in 1892. This building was used until 1941.

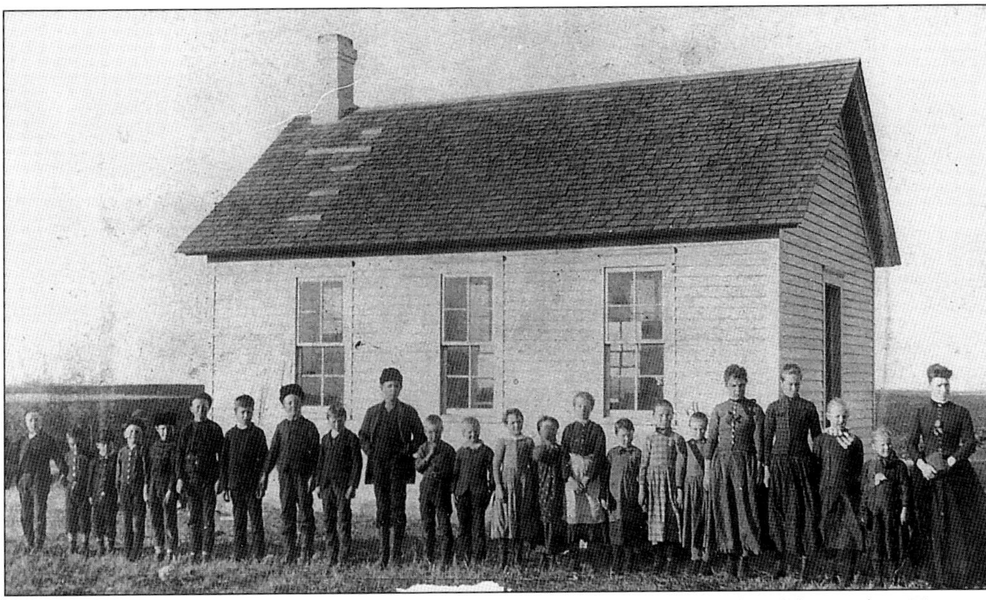

These students and teacher are standing in front of the one-room school located in Torning Township. The District organized as #16 in 1887. By the spring of 1888, the school building was completed, and Ena Nelson was chosen to teach a two-month school term.

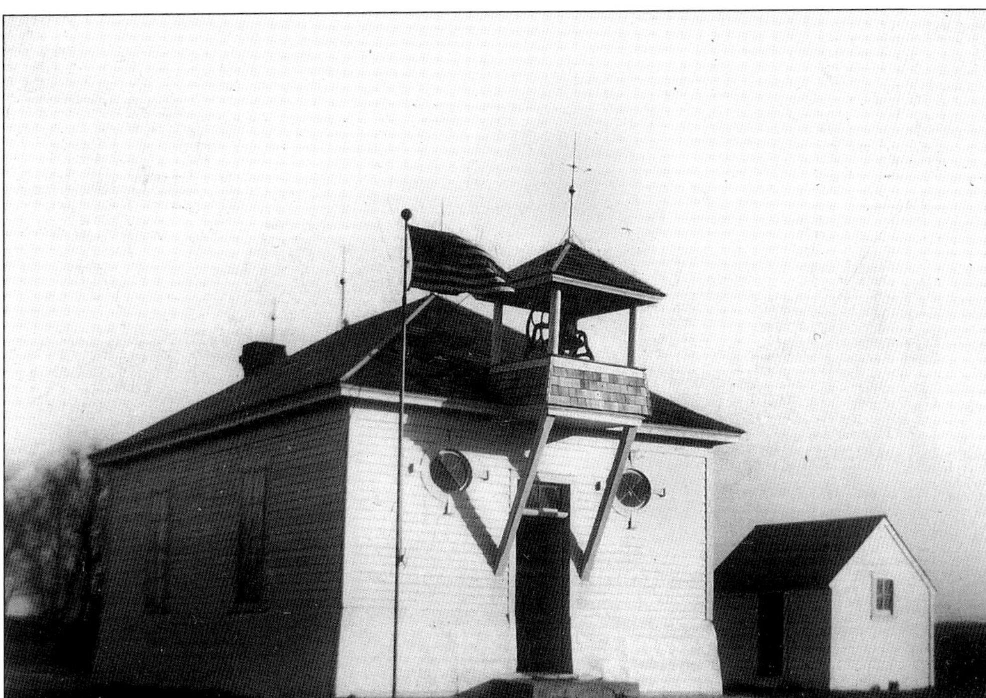

Common School District #86 was organized in May of 1901. That same summer, a school was built in Section 10 of Hayes Township. During the first three years, the school term was three months. This was typical of rural schools, as students were needed to help with the farm work. This photo of District #86 was taken in the 1930s.

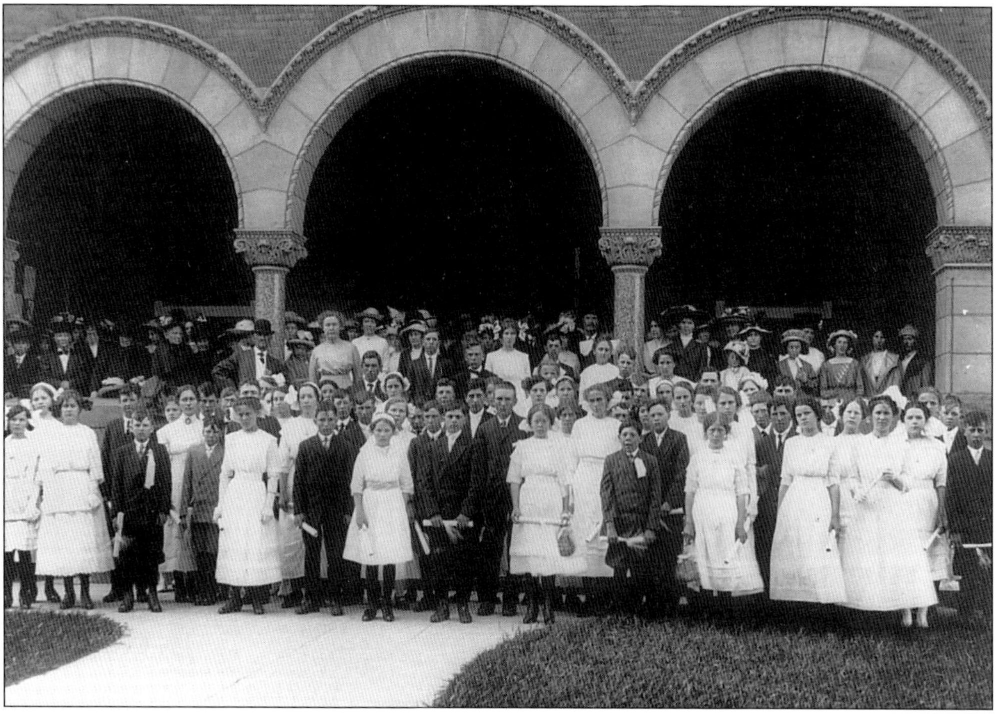

These youth are students from Swift County who graduated from eighth grade in 1912. In the early history of Swift County, students participated in eighth grade commencements, which were often held at the Swift County Courthouse in Benson.

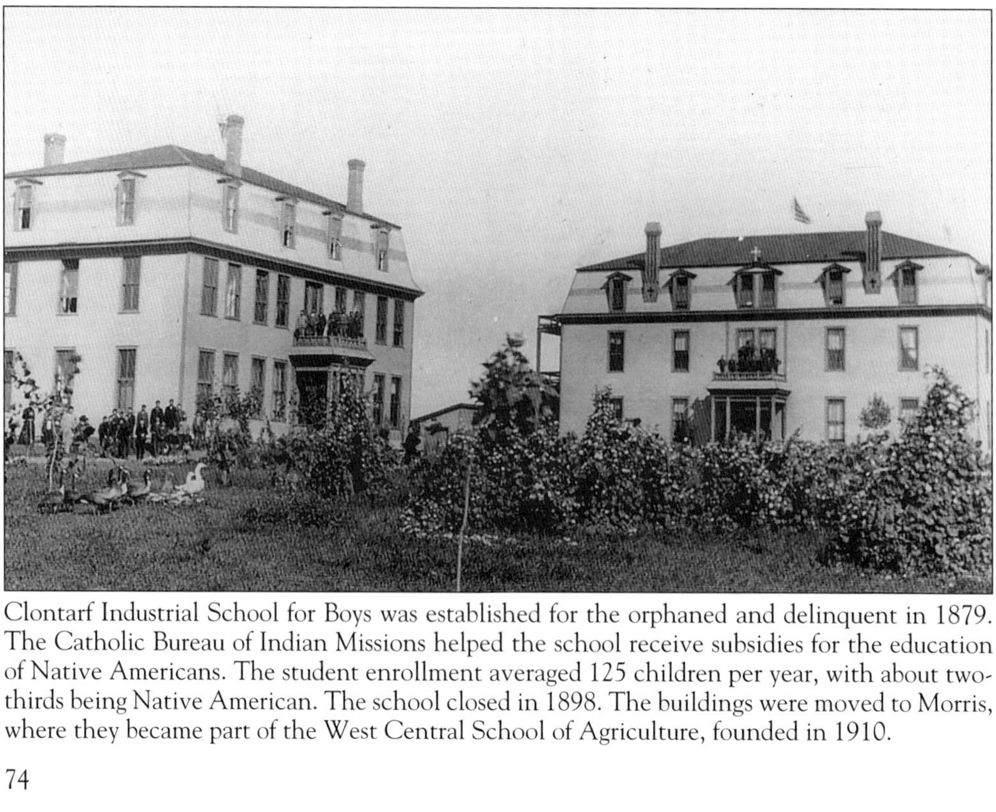

Clontarf Industrial School for Boys was established for the orphaned and delinquent in 1879. The Catholic Bureau of Indian Missions helped the school receive subsidies for the education of Native Americans. The student enrollment averaged 125 children per year, with about two-thirds being Native American. The school closed in 1898. The buildings were moved to Morris, where they became part of the West Central School of Agriculture, founded in 1910.

Six

Giving Thanks

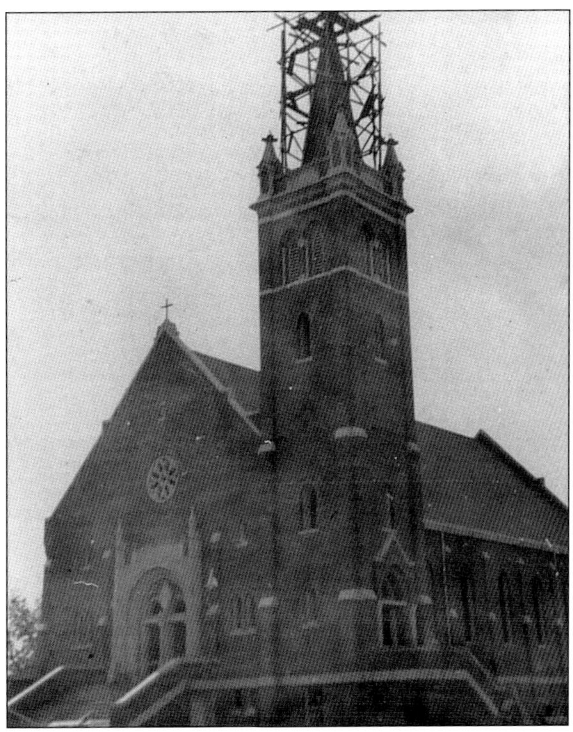

Father Valentine Stemler, a brother of Mrs. Joseph Schaff, went to the Schaff farm in April of 1880 to say Mass, and continued to say Mass monthly for the 37 Catholic families in the Murdock area. It was apparent that Murdock needed its own church. The first church for the Sacred Heart Catholic congregation became a reality in 1894. In 1924, bids were let on a new church, at right. The church was a Gothic structure, built of Springfield brick and trimmed with Bedford stone from the Indiana quarries. The art glass used in the windows was from England and Germany. The total cost of the building was a little over $90,000—$65,000 of which was raised at the time of construction. The first service held in this church was midnight Mass on Christmas of 1925.

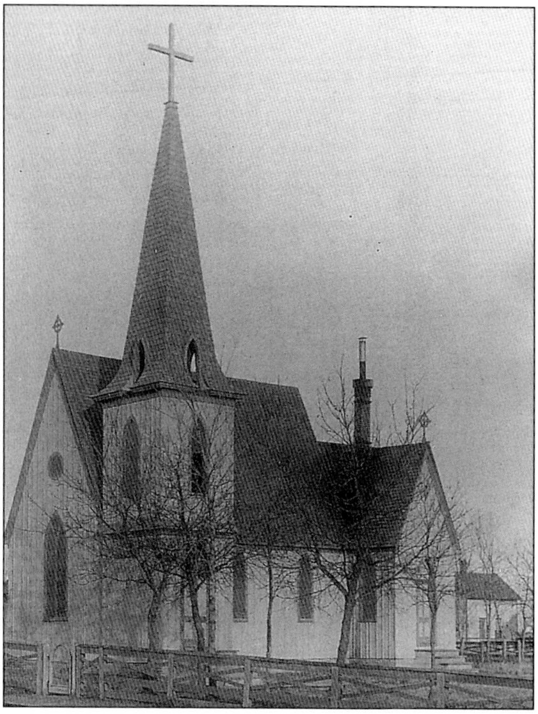

On December 4, 1876, Bishop B.H. Whipple gave his consent to the organization of the Christ Episcopal Church in Benson. The church building was completed in 1879 on the southwest corner of Idaho and 13th Streets.

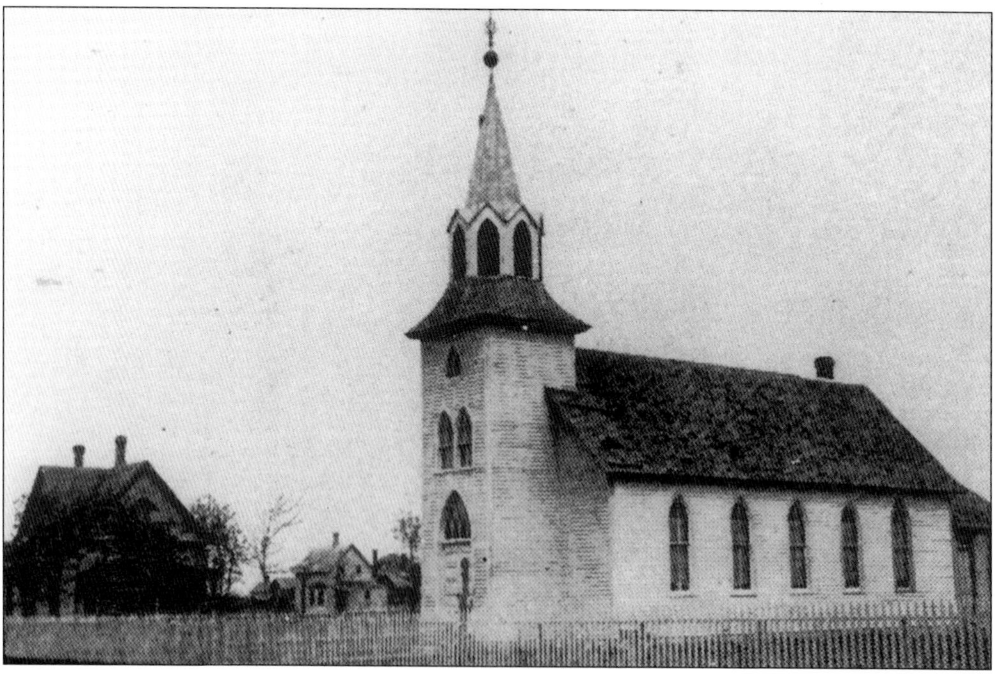

In 1872, a missionary pastor stepped off the train at Benson and asked a young boy if there were any Swedish settlers in the area. The pastor was guided to the dugout home of the boy's parents. Two years later, the Swedish Trinity Church was organized, with services held in homes. The first church edifice was completed in 1890.

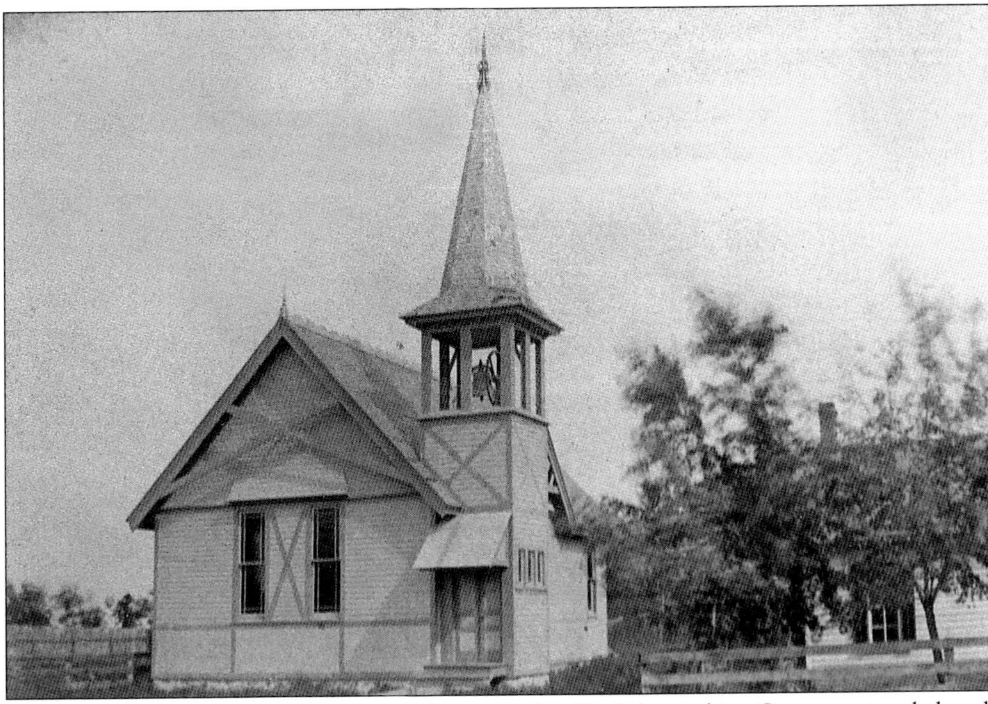

Rev. Richard Hall came to Benson in 1871 to see if an English-speaking Congregational church could be built in Benson. Services were held in the Immigrant House Hotel until the first church was built in 1876. This is the second church of the Pilgrim Congregational in Benson, built in 1883 at a cost of $2,100.

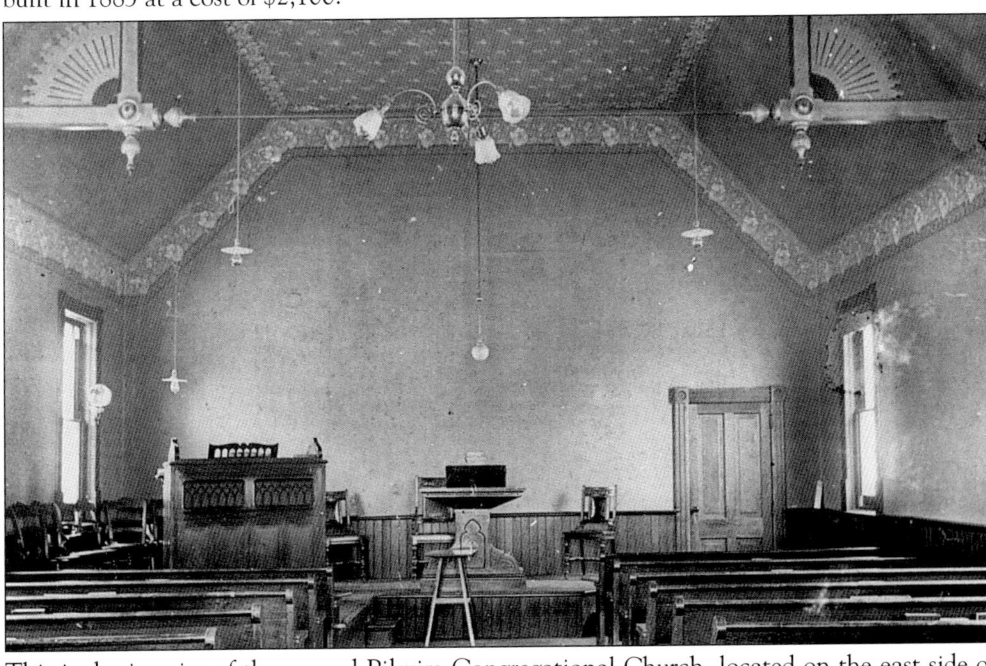

This is the interior of the second Pilgrim Congregational Church, located on the east side of 13th Street North in Benson. As the congregation outgrew the building, plans for financing a new building began in 1913, with the cornerstone not being laid until 1923.

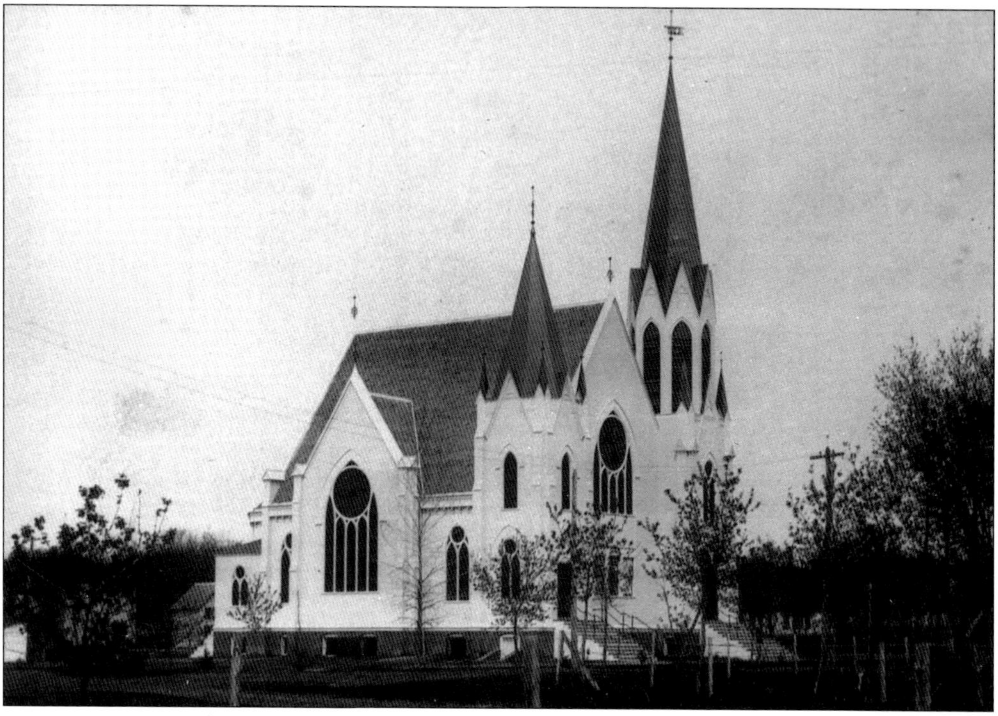

In 1870, concerned Norwegian settlers formed the Norwegian Evangelical Lutheran Trinity Church of Swift County. It later was divided into two districts, with the northern becoming Our Savior's Norwegian Evangelical Congregation in Benson. A new church was dedicated in 1903.

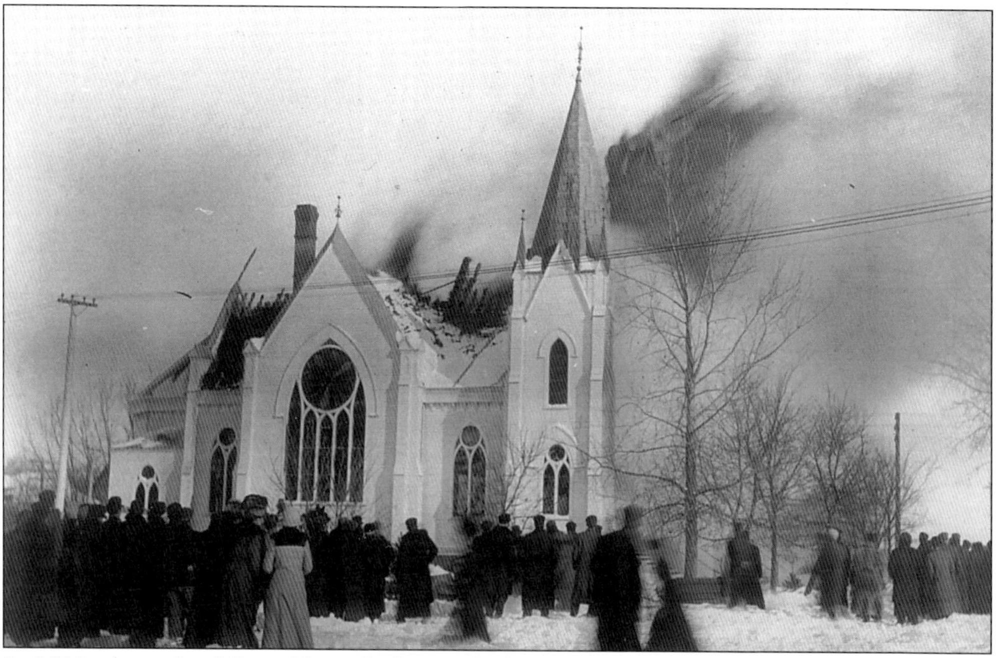

In 1911, the wife of Rev. Christ Pederson died. As the funeral procession was leaving Our Savior's Lutheran Church of Benson, a fire broke out and completely destroyed the church.

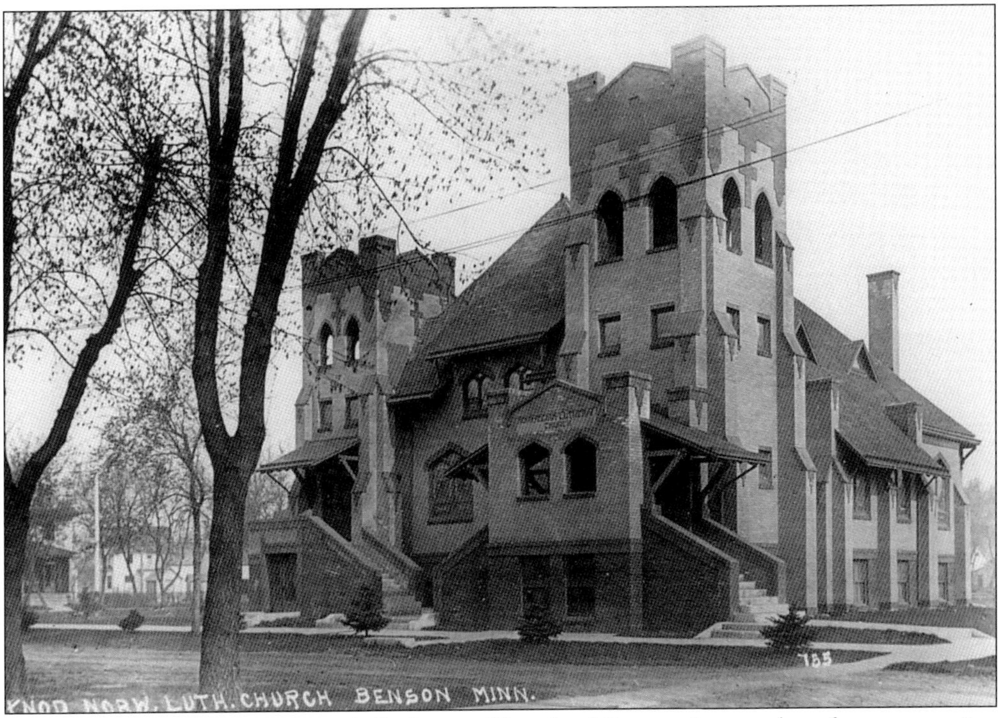

The congregation of Our Savior's Lutheran Church of Benson began plans for construction of a new edifice immediately after the 1911 fire. It was completed in time to use for services Christmas Day, 1912.

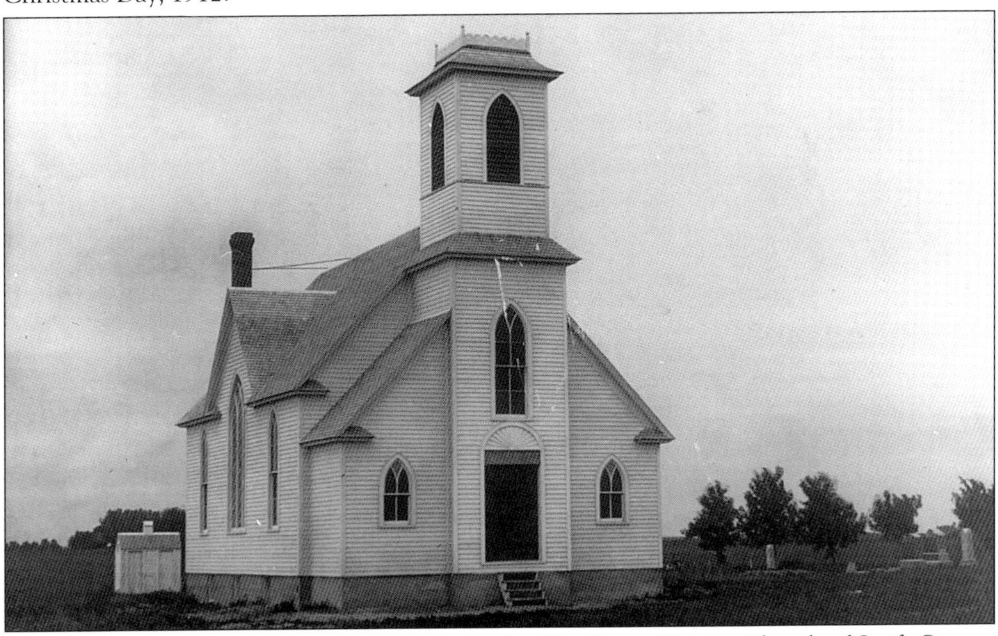

The southern district of the Norwegian Evangelical Lutheran Trinity Church of Swift County was located in Swenoda Township and became known as the Swenoda church. The first church, built in 1901, was struck by lightning and burned to the ground in 1910. Pictured is the second church, built in 1911.

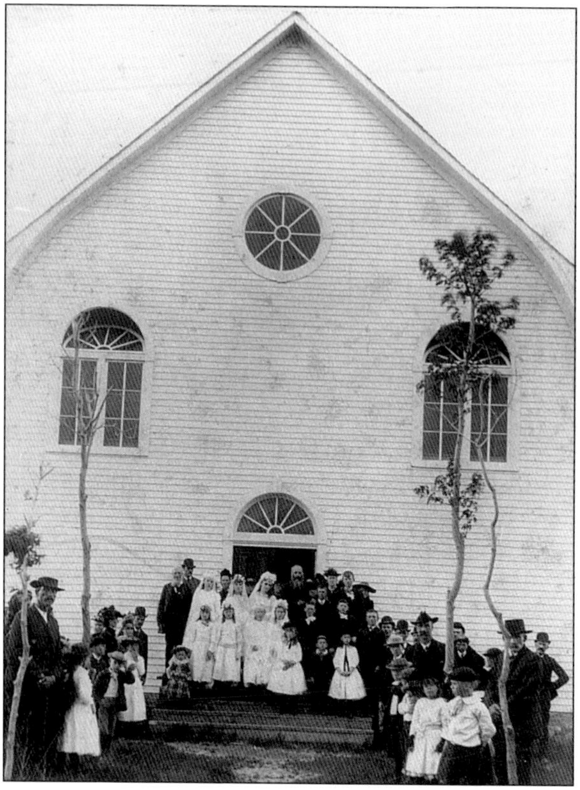

In the spring of 1882, work began on St. Francis Xavier Catholic Church in Benson. The majority of the construction was done during the winter months when the people, mostly farmers, could put in more time. Pictured on the steps of St. Francis Xavier is the 1891 confirmation class.

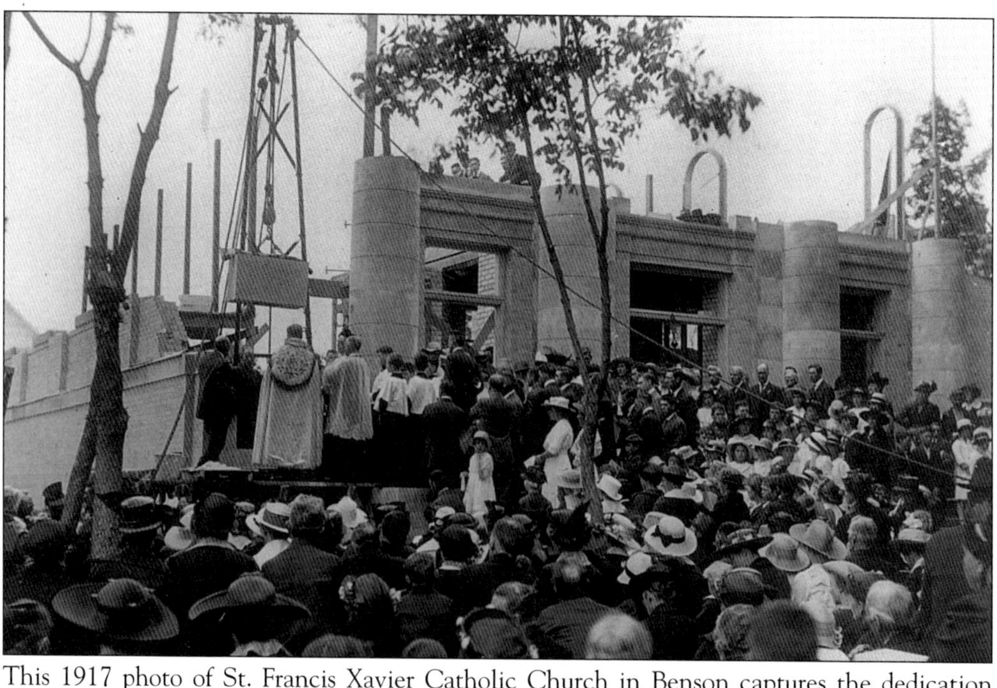

This 1917 photo of St. Francis Xavier Catholic Church in Benson captures the dedication ceremony of laying the cornerstone for its new church. In the process of building the church, a young man working as a mason fell off a scaffold and died.

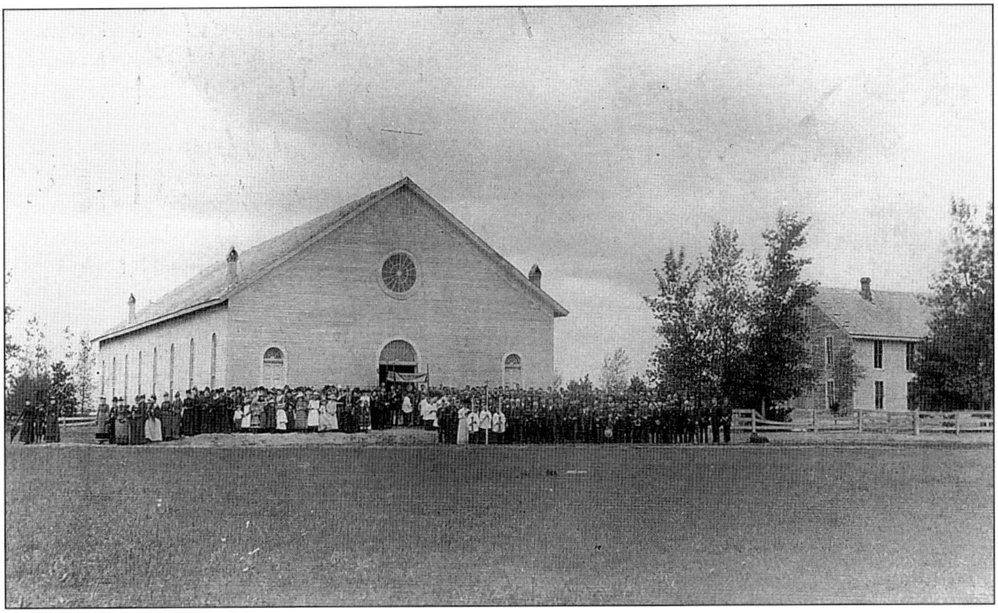

Father Francis Swift was assigned to DeGraff to serve the growing numbers of Catholics who were settling in the area due to the Catholic Bureau of Colonization. Before he left in 1879, the first church had been built and dedicated to Our Lady of Kildare. Later it became St. Bridget's. This photo was dated 1891.

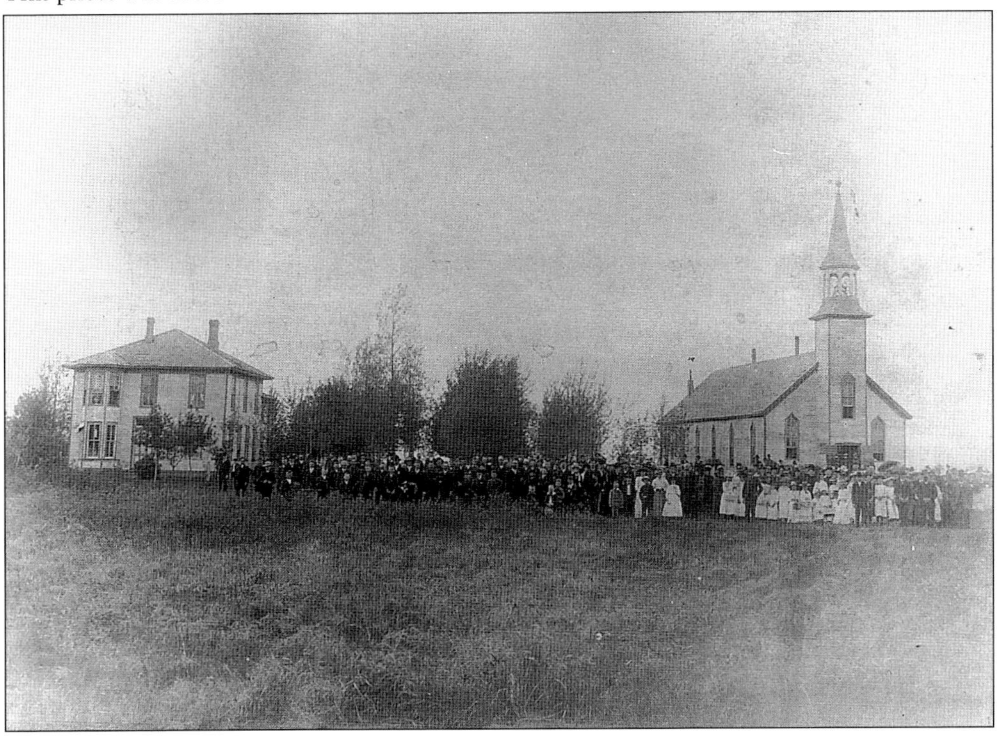

Clontarf had been planned as a colony by the Catholic Bureau of Colonization in 1876. Many of the settlers were French-Canadian. In 1877, a French priest began construction of the first church in Clontarf, St. Malachy, with the rectory being built in 1878. This photo is dated 1890.

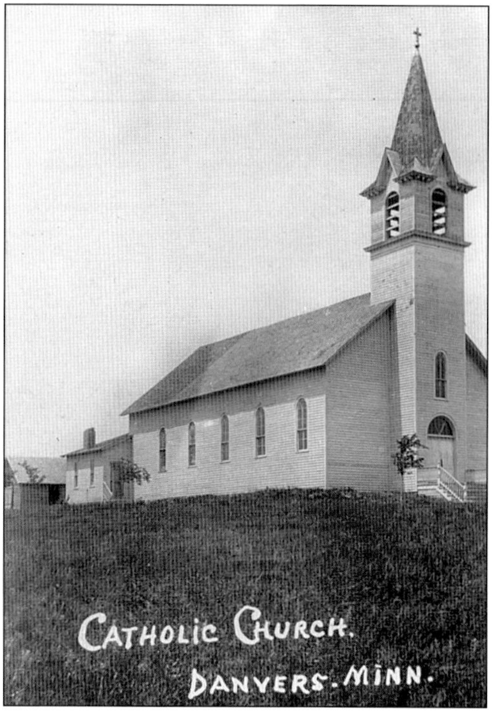

The first edifice for the Catholic Church of the Visitation in Danvers was built in 1892. On April 7, 1931, a fire, originated from burning grass on the church grounds, got out of control and completely destroyed the wood-frame structure and its contents.

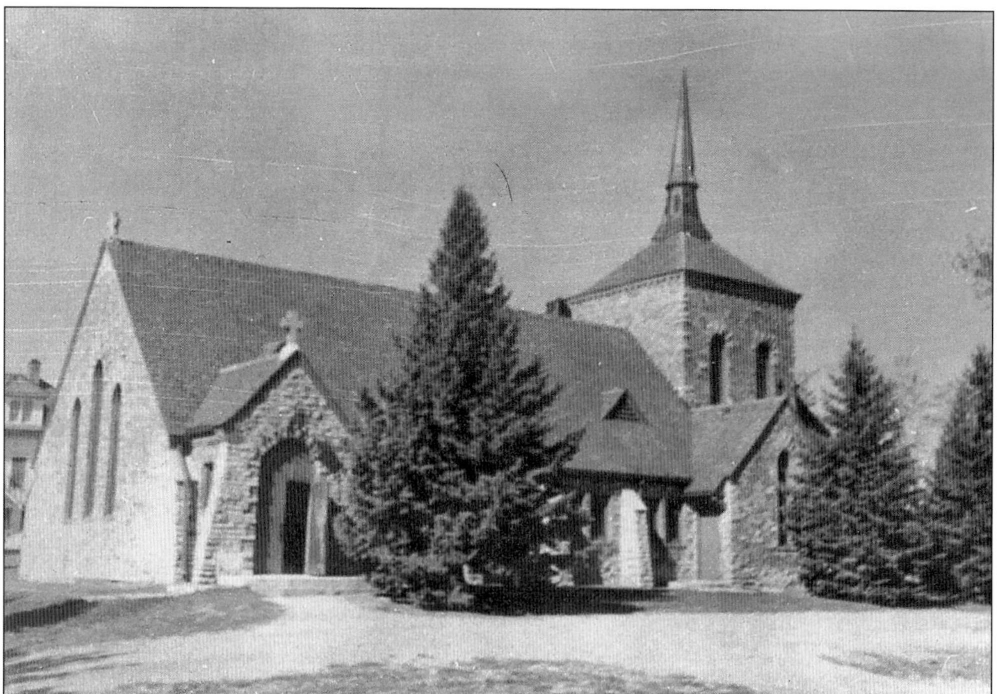

The Church of the Visitation erected a new structure in the French Normandy architectural style of stone and brick, tile roof, and copper steeple for a cost of $30,000. First Mass was celebrated in the new church on Christmas Eve, 1931.

On March 21, 1909, a meeting was held at the home of August Hoppe Jr. to form the Immanuel Lutheran Church of Holloway. In the spring of 1912, the plans for the church building were completed, and it was officially dedicated on September 29, 1912. Church services alternated between English and German languages.

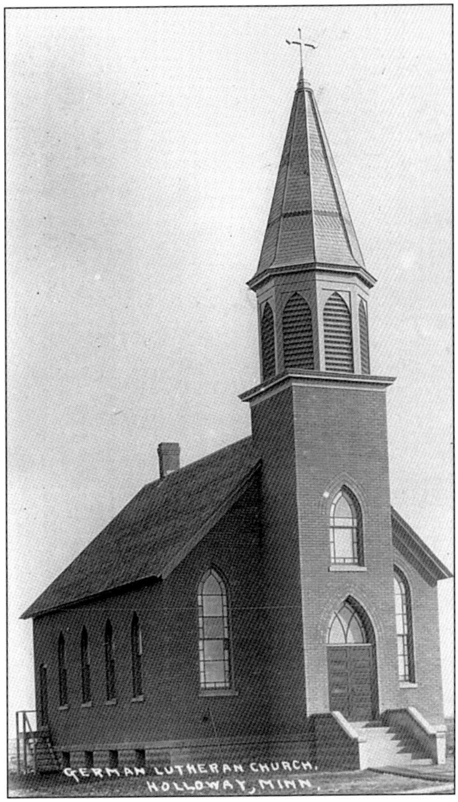

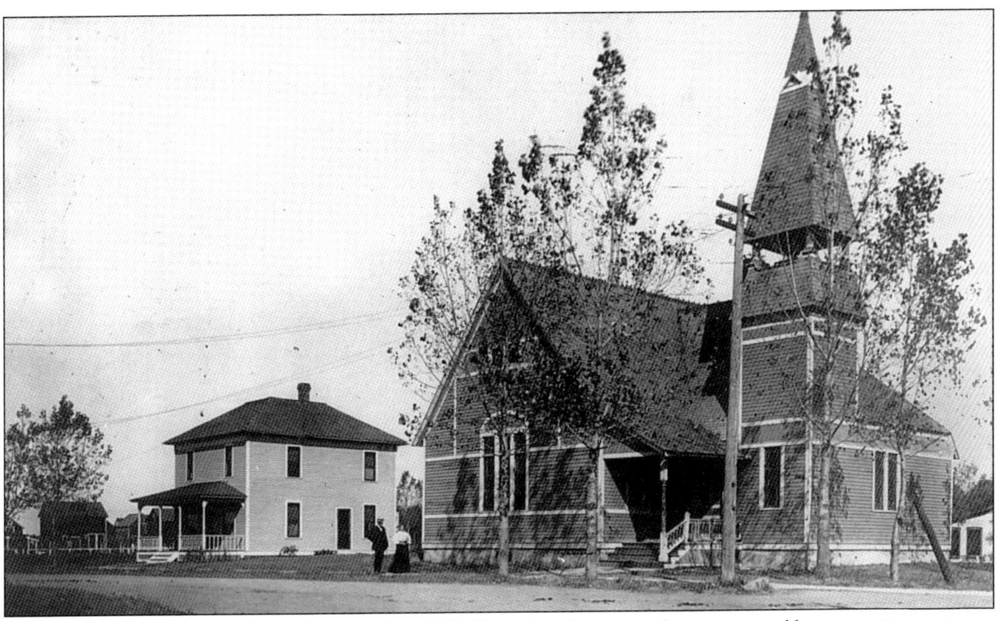

In 1879, Rev. Ruddock drove from Granite Falls to Appleton with a team and buggy to investigate the possibilities of establishing a Congregational church. The early settlers of Appleton were mainly New Englanders and preferred Congregationalism, the faith of the Pilgrims. The First Congregational Church was formed, with a house of worship built in 1891.

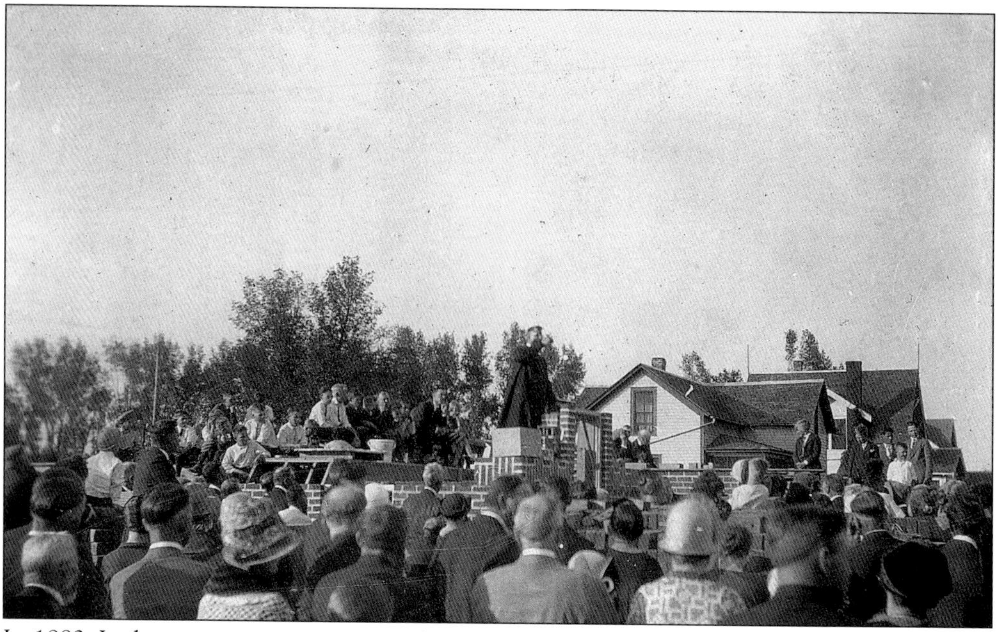

In 1883, Lutheran immigrants organized a Kerkhoven Lutheran congregation and had a small white frame church erected in 1895. It was severely damaged by a tornado in 1925. This photo was taken in September of 1926, during the laying of the cornerstone of a new brick church.

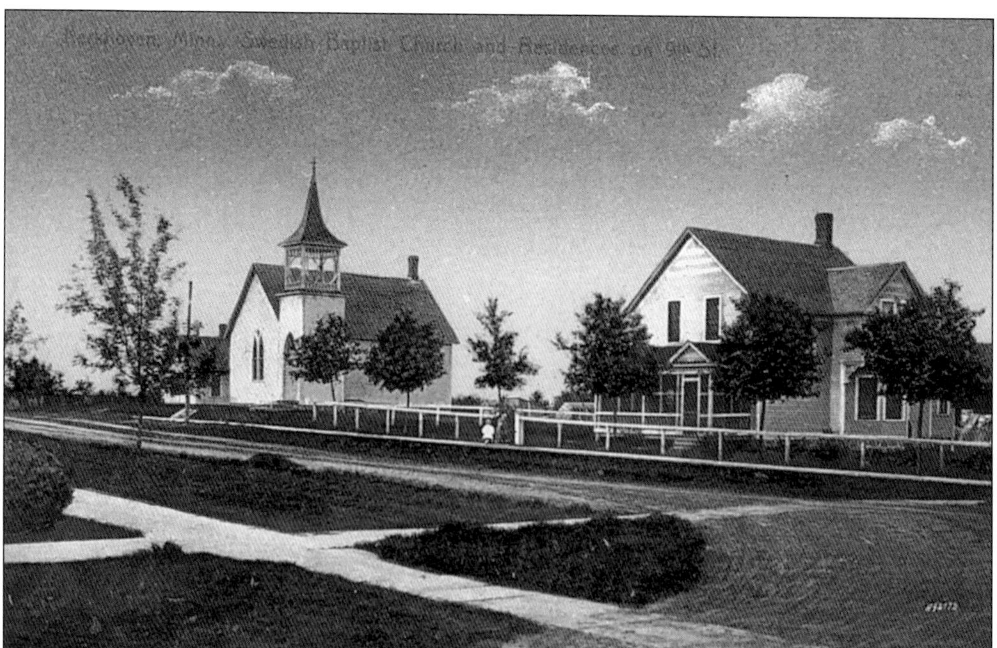

The Bethel Baptist Church of Kerkhoven was organized as the Swedish Baptist Conference in 1894. Previously, its members had to travel by horse and wagon some 18 miles to worship at the Willmar First Baptist Church. This church edifice was built and dedicated in 1905. In 1927, services were converted from Swedish to English.

St. Pauli Lutheran Church in Camp Lake Township was organized in 1877. Until 1898, when this church was built, services were held in homes, the Swift Falls schoolhouse, and for many years in the District #14 schoolhouse.

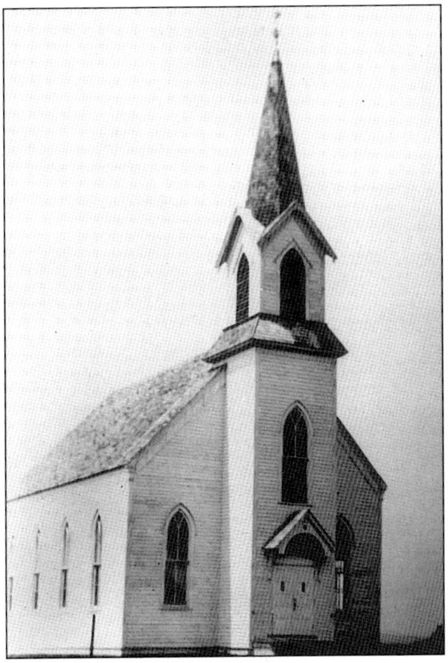

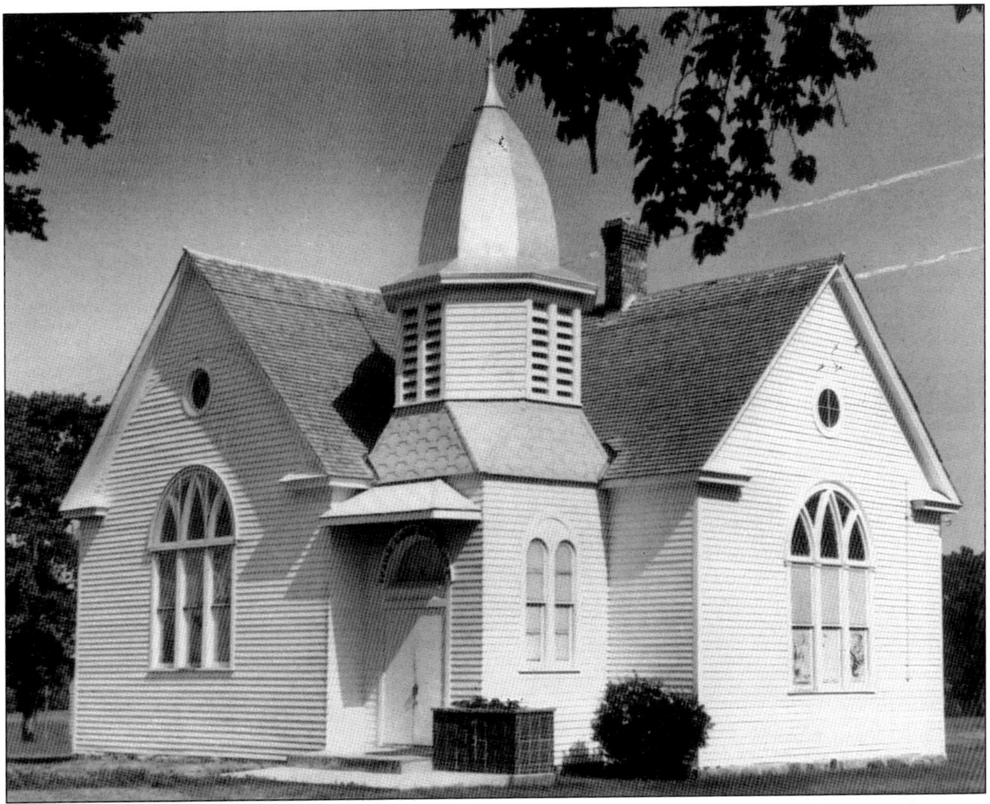

In 1884, the Swedish Evangelical Mission Church of Frank Lake in Kerkhoven Township was organized. The first church was built in 1887 and destroyed by lightning in 1900. This building was erected and dedicated several months later.

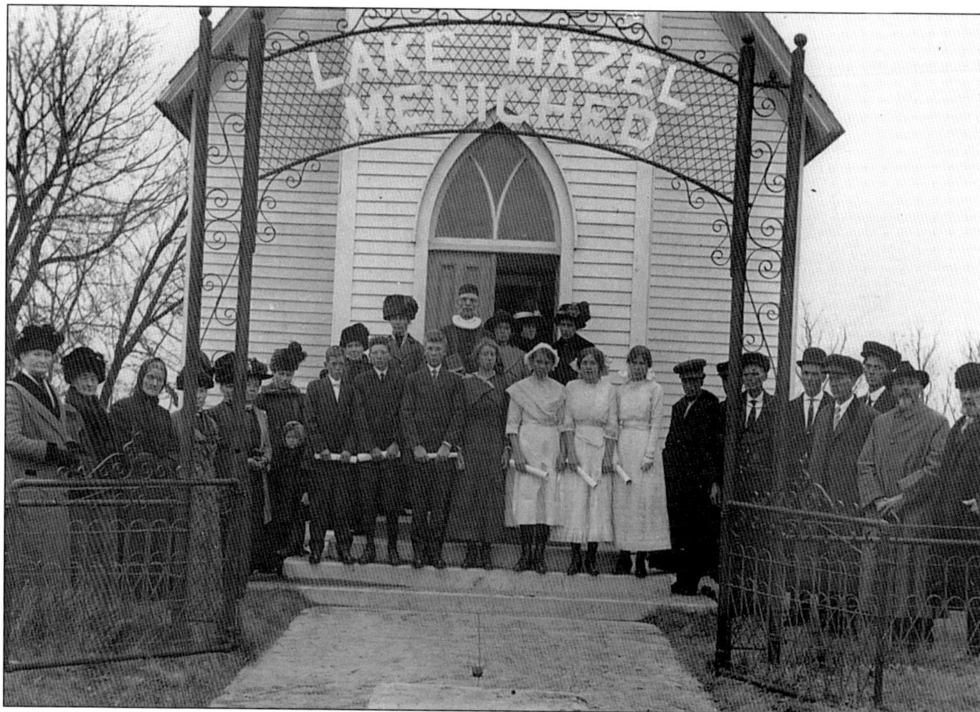

The 1913 confirmation class pose for their picture on the steps of Lake Hazel Lutheran Church in Benson Township. The church was organized in 1871, within three years of the first settlements. In 1877, a church was built.

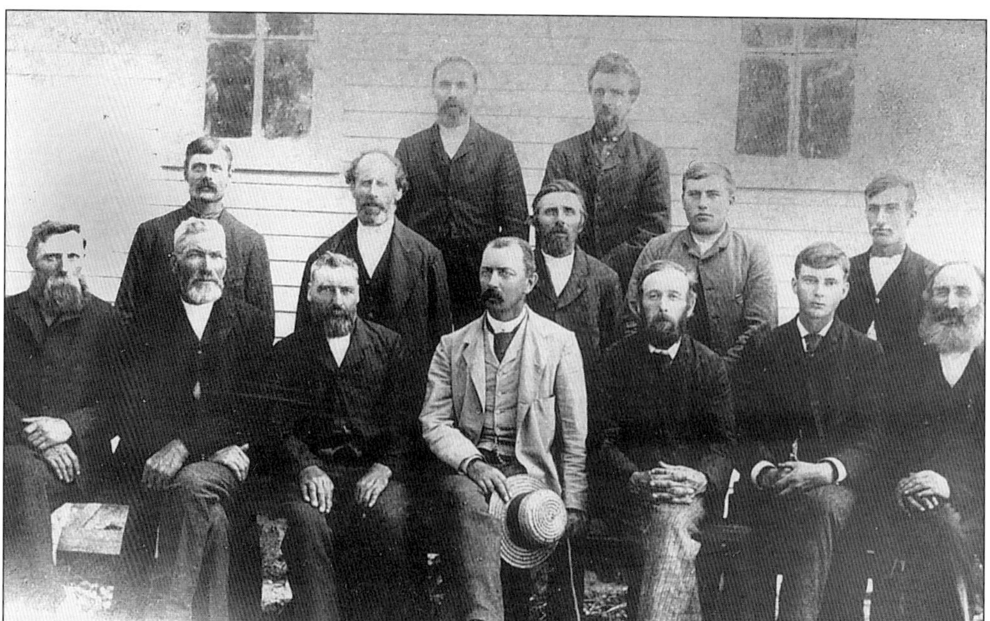

Pictured here are the members of the 1887 building committee of Lake Hazel Church, from left to right: (front row) John Olen, Johannes Torgerson, Amund Lee, Kristian Uytendahl, Eric Lee, Julius Nermoe, Lars Bagstad; (middle row) Ole Overlie, Johannes Lee, John Olson, Ole Knutson, Matthias Knutson; (back row) Rasmus Ordahl, and Paul Lee.

Seven

More Than Work

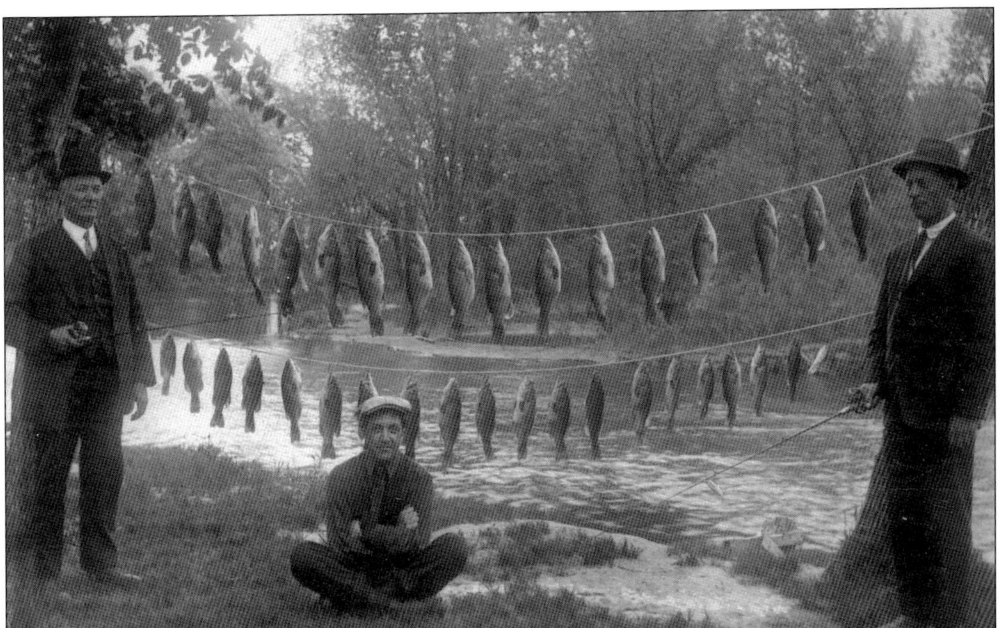

Swift County encompasses a total of 484,945 acres. When the land was surveyed in 1895, it was determined that 9,392 acres were covered with water. By 1929, numerous sloughs and several lakes had dried up. Two rivers, the Pomme de Terre and Chippewa, and about a dozen lakes are named on the maps of the county. The first settlers endeavored to locate near water because the game that followed the lake and river courses made possible income which could not have been secured from surplus crops until the coming of better transportation facilities. More importantly, fish were a valuable food. As the county prospered, fishing became more of a sport than a main source of food. This photo confirmed these men's story that they had a good day of fishing on the Chippewa River.

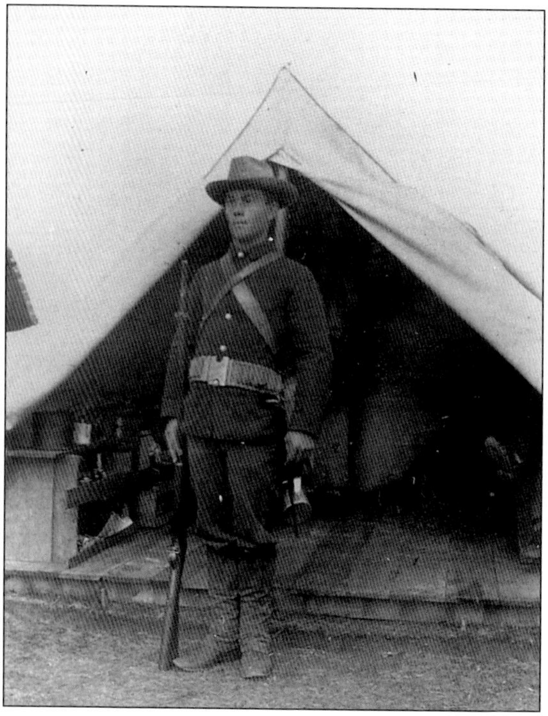

Since permanent white settlement in Swift County began after the Civil War, the first residents to leave the county to defend their country was for the Spanish-American War of 1898. Monne Hultgren from Kerkhoven served in the U.S. military in 1898. At the age of seven, Monne moved with his family to Kerkhoven. His father, Aaron, started the first drug store there in 1880.

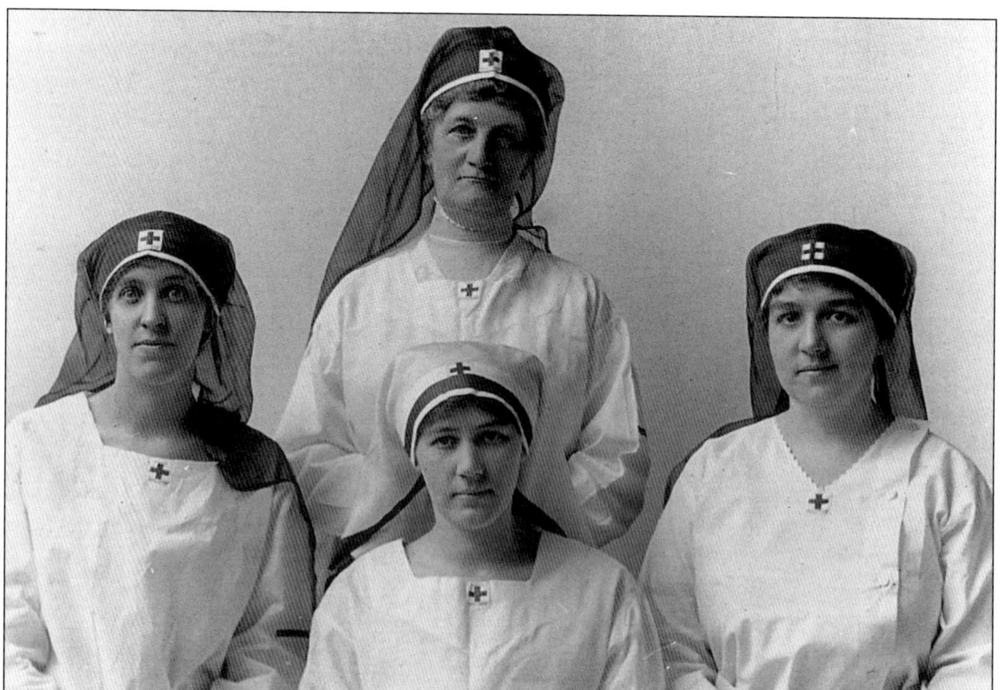

The American Red Cross was founded in 1881. This photo of Swift County Red Cross volunteers was taken *c.* 1917. The lady on the right is Vera (Smith) Harding of Benson. Women in Swift County were very active in the Red Cross, especially in war years.

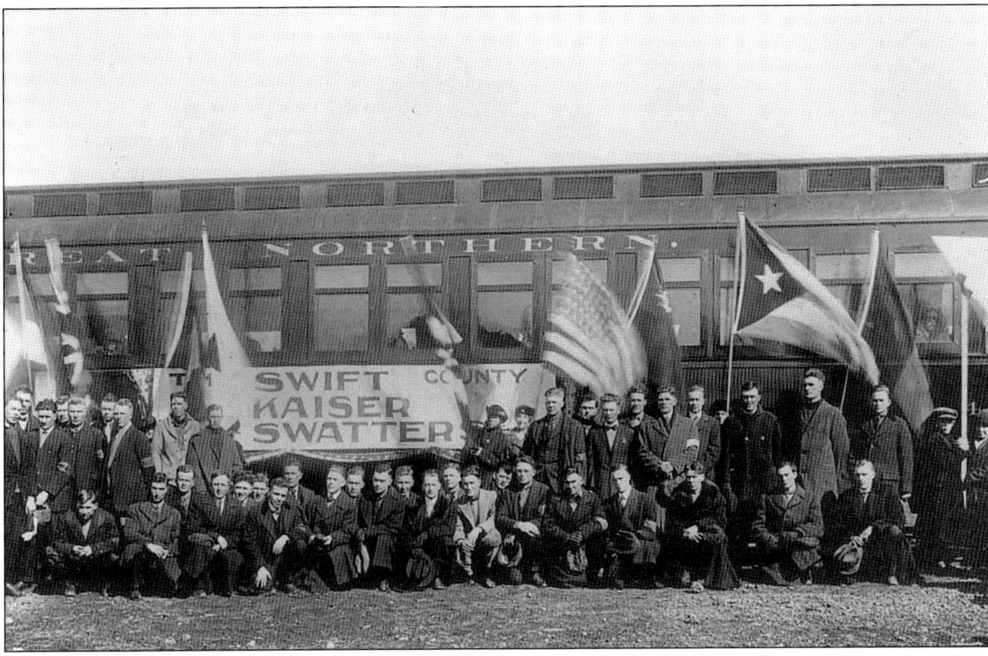

These men were leaving Benson to serve their country in World War I. Twenty-two men from Swift County lost their lives during this war alone.

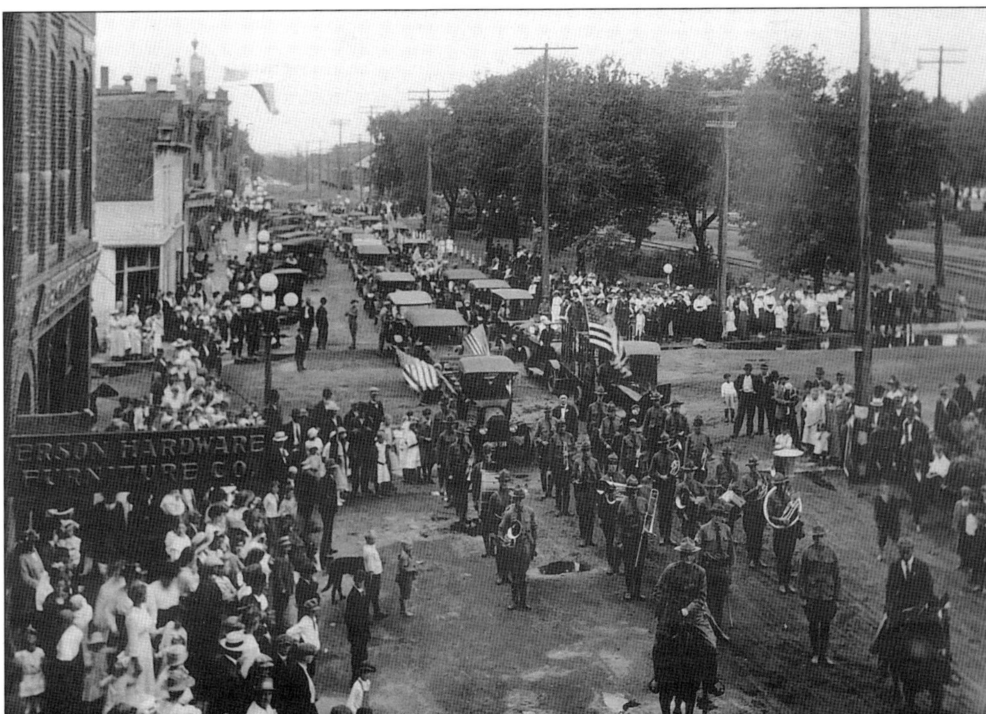

A large crowd turned out to watch the 151st Field Artillery Battalion parade down Pacific Avenue in Benson in 1918.

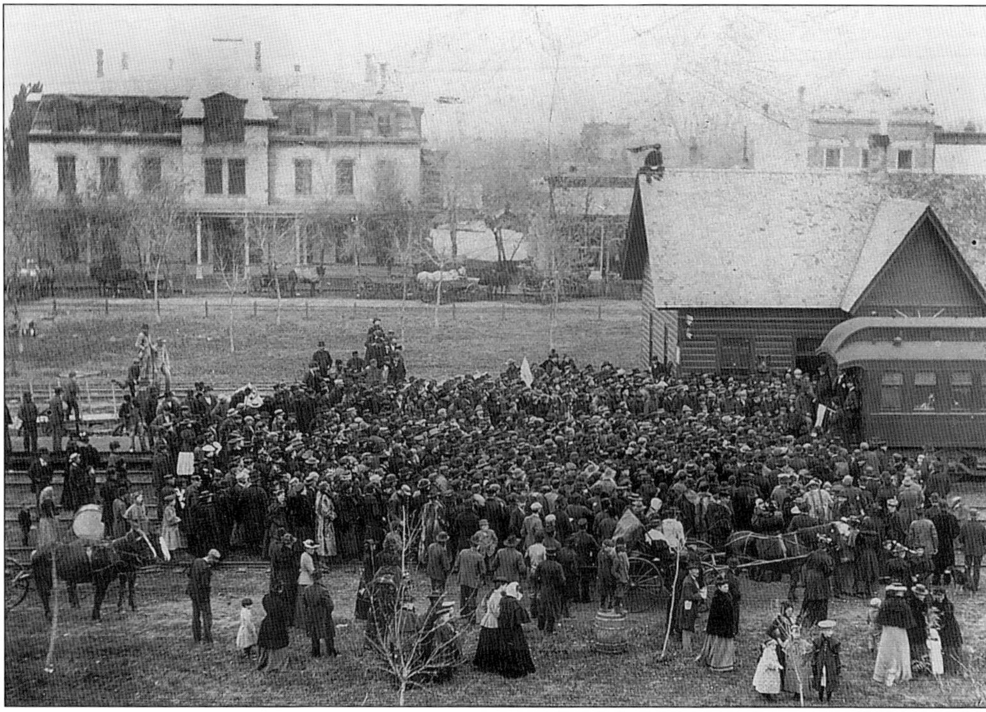

This large crowd is gathered at the depot in Benson to listen to a politician give a speech from the platform of a train. Before radio and television, this was a common method of campaigning.

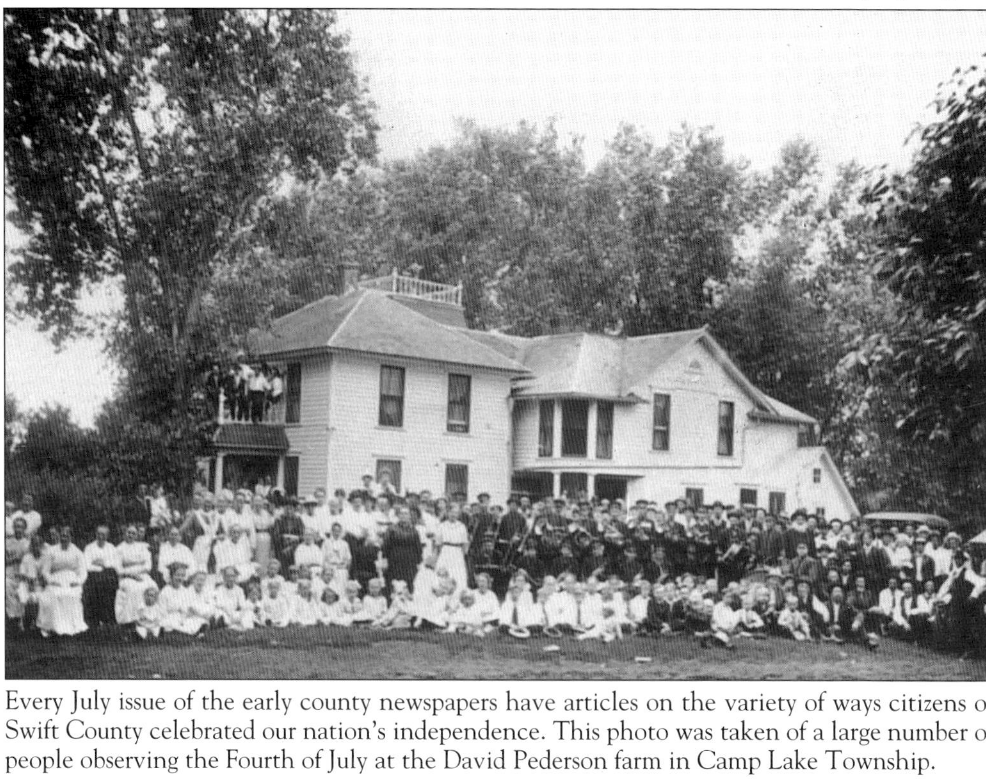

Every July issue of the early county newspapers have articles on the variety of ways citizens of Swift County celebrated our nation's independence. This photo was taken of a large number of people observing the Fourth of July at the David Pederson farm in Camp Lake Township.

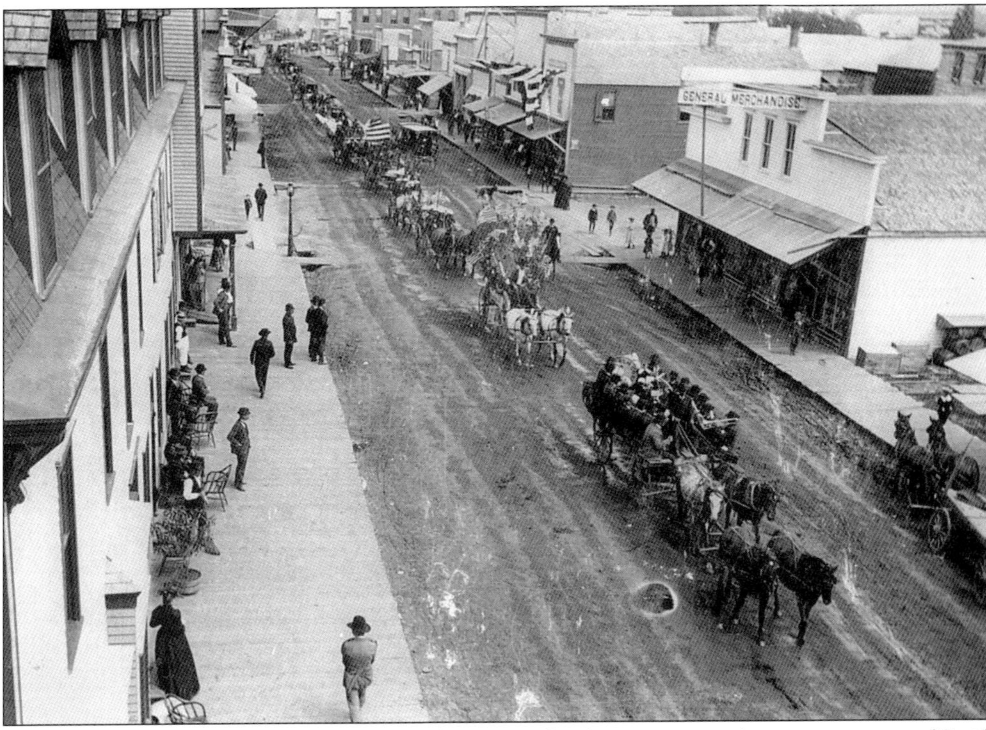

Everyone loves a parade! This must have been true for the citizens in the communities of Swift County, since many of the newspapers often mentioned parades. There are several old photos of different parades in the county; this parade was on Mill Street in Appleton.

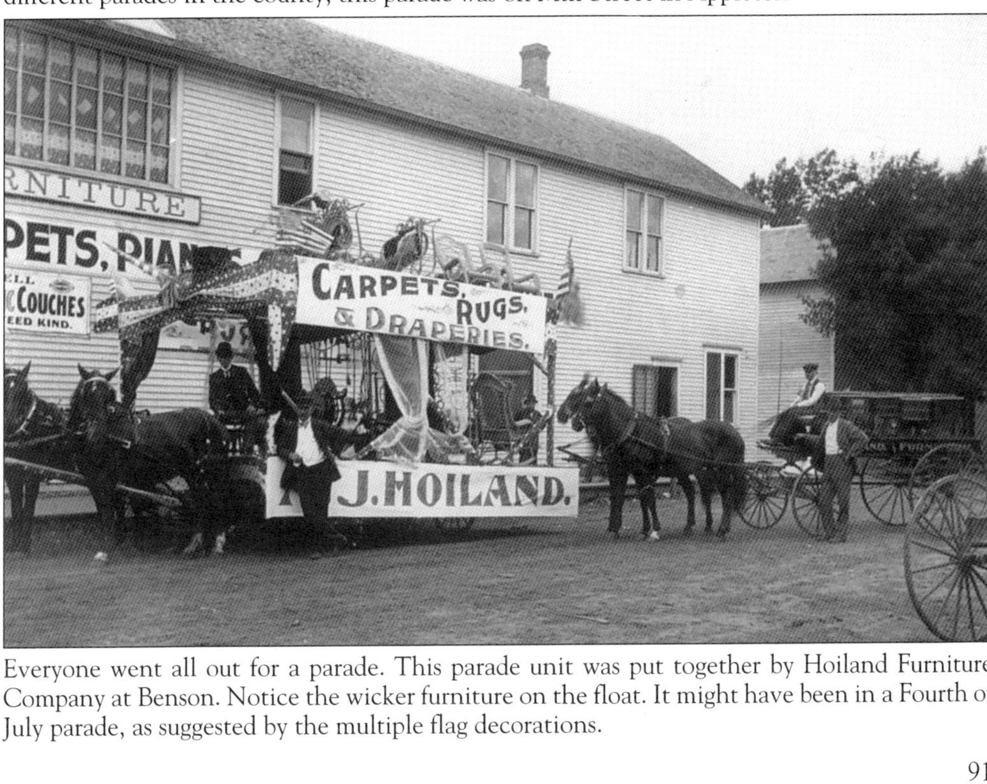

Everyone went all out for a parade. This parade unit was put together by Hoiland Furniture Company at Benson. Notice the wicker furniture on the float. It might have been in a Fourth of July parade, as suggested by the multiple flag decorations.

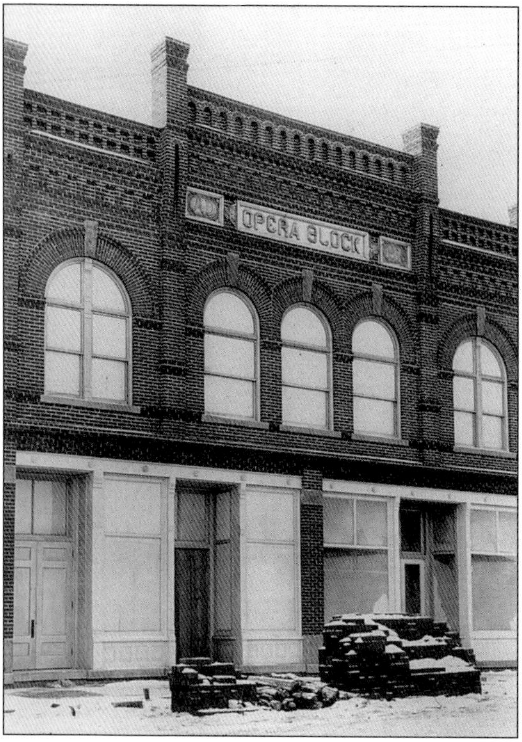

In 1895, the Opera Block was built on Pacific Avenue in Benson. It seated four hundred people comfortably. The Kickapoo Indian Medicine Company from the eastern states gave shows in this building. It was destroyed by fire in 1906, and a new opera house was built in the same location in 1907.

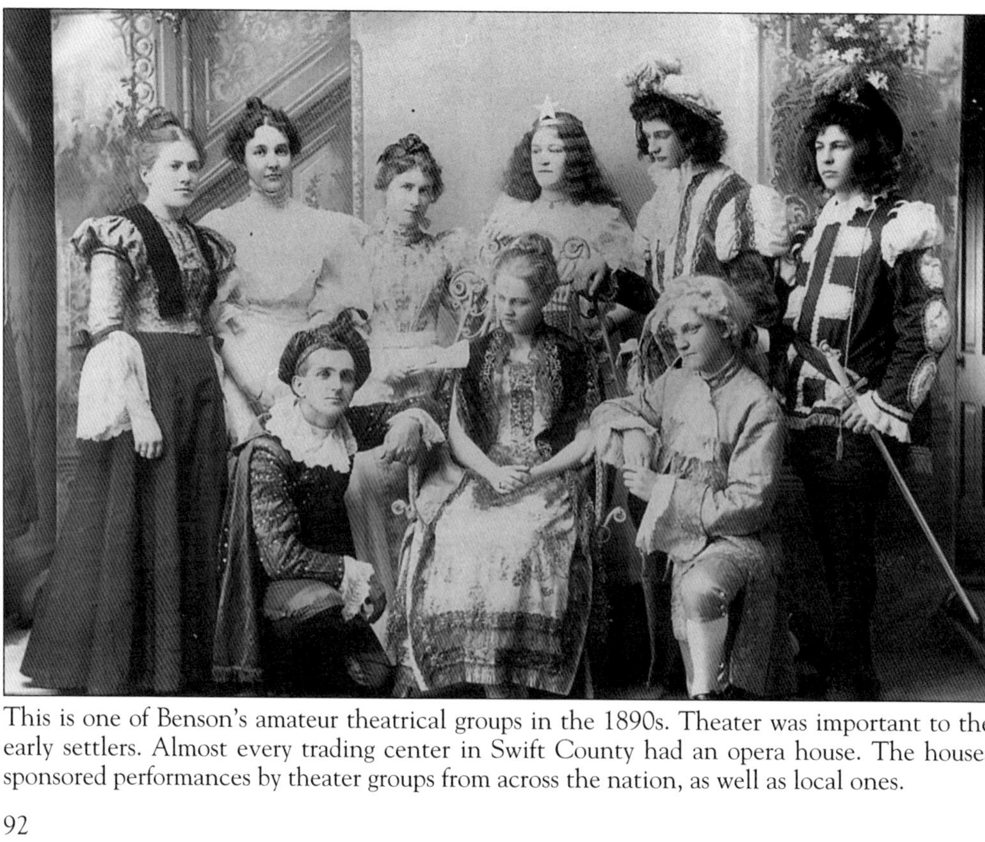

This is one of Benson's amateur theatrical groups in the 1890s. Theater was important to the early settlers. Almost every trading center in Swift County had an opera house. The houses sponsored performances by theater groups from across the nation, as well as local ones.

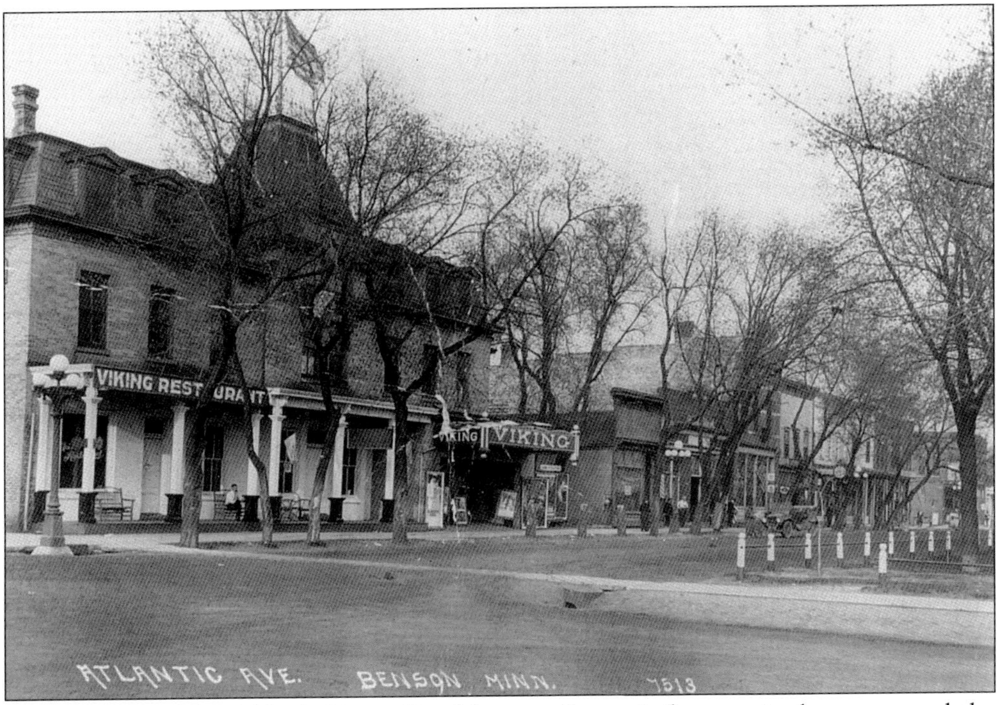

In 1916, part of the Aldrich House Hotel became Benson's first movie theater, named the Viking. A new movie theater was built after the 1930 fire destroyed the Aldrich House.

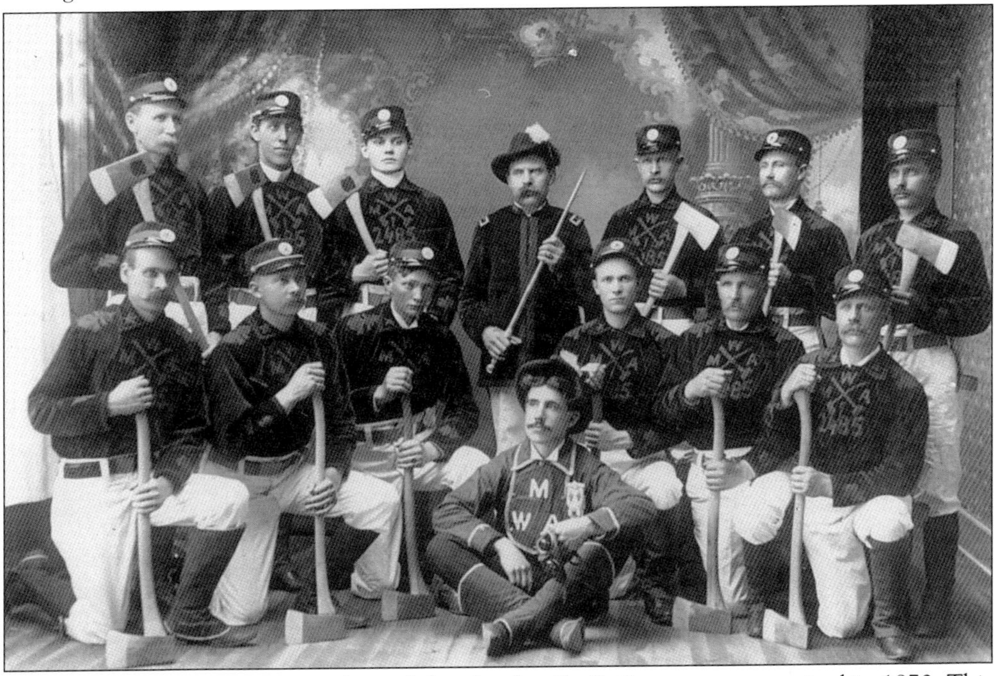

A variety of organizations were formed shortly after Swift County was organized in 1870. This photo was of the Modern Woodmen of America Lodge in Benson in the early 1900s. Lodges became so popular that in 1900, when the Hudson-Lee Block was built in Benson, the second floor had a large meeting hall with several anterooms to accommodate the lodges.

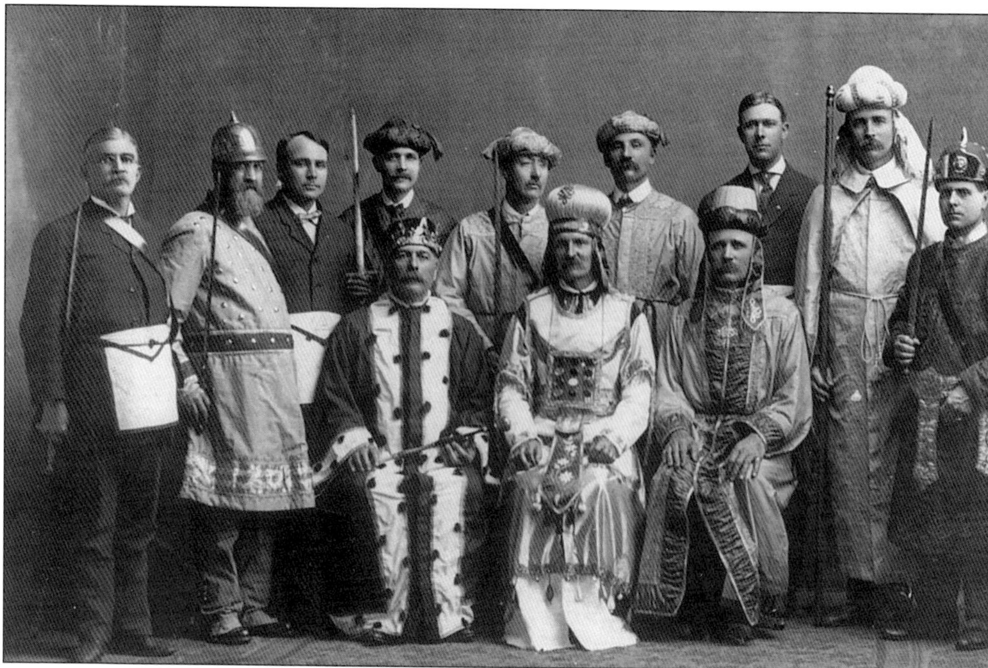

The men in this photo are members of the Masonic Lodge in Appleton, date unknown. The Appleton's Masonic Hall was mentioned in the *Benson Times* newspaper as early as 1878, before Appleton had its own newspaper.

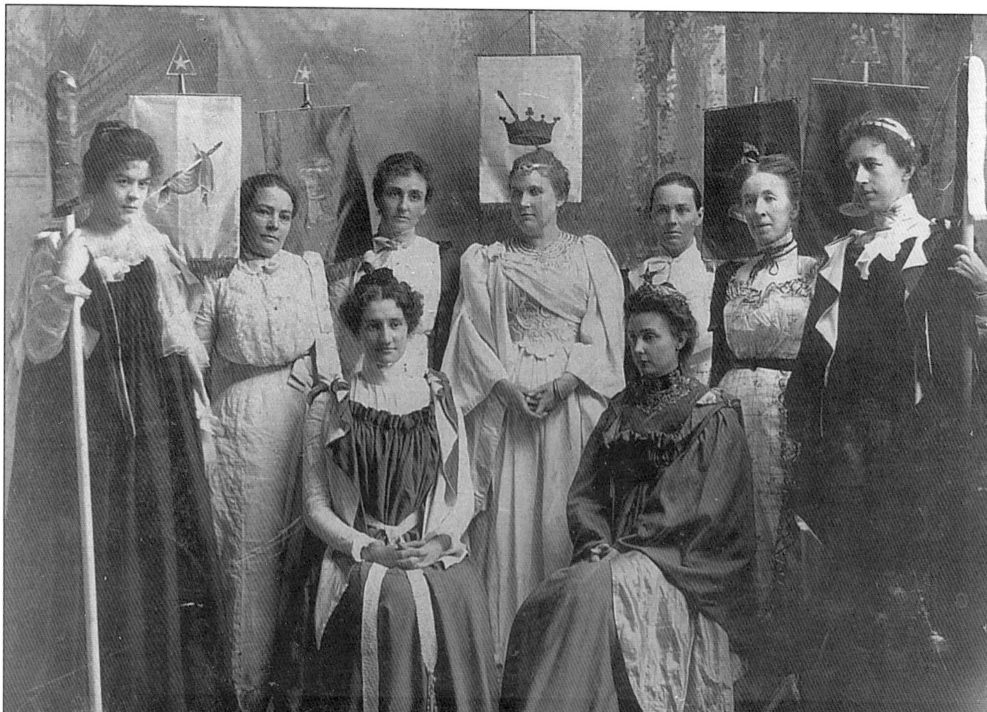

Many of the men's organizations had female auxiliaries. The women in this photo belong to the Eastern Star in Appleton, an auxiliary to the Masonic Lodge.

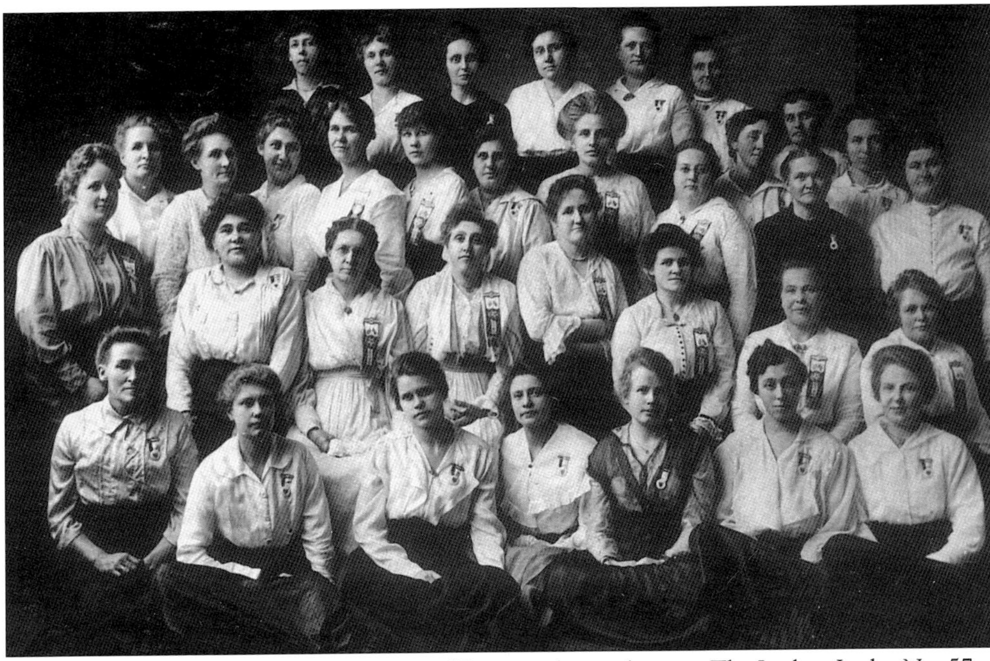

This photo is of the Daughters of Norway of Benson, date unknown. The Lerken Lodge No. 57 of the Daughters of Norway was organized on March 28, 1916. In 1927, there were 79 members.

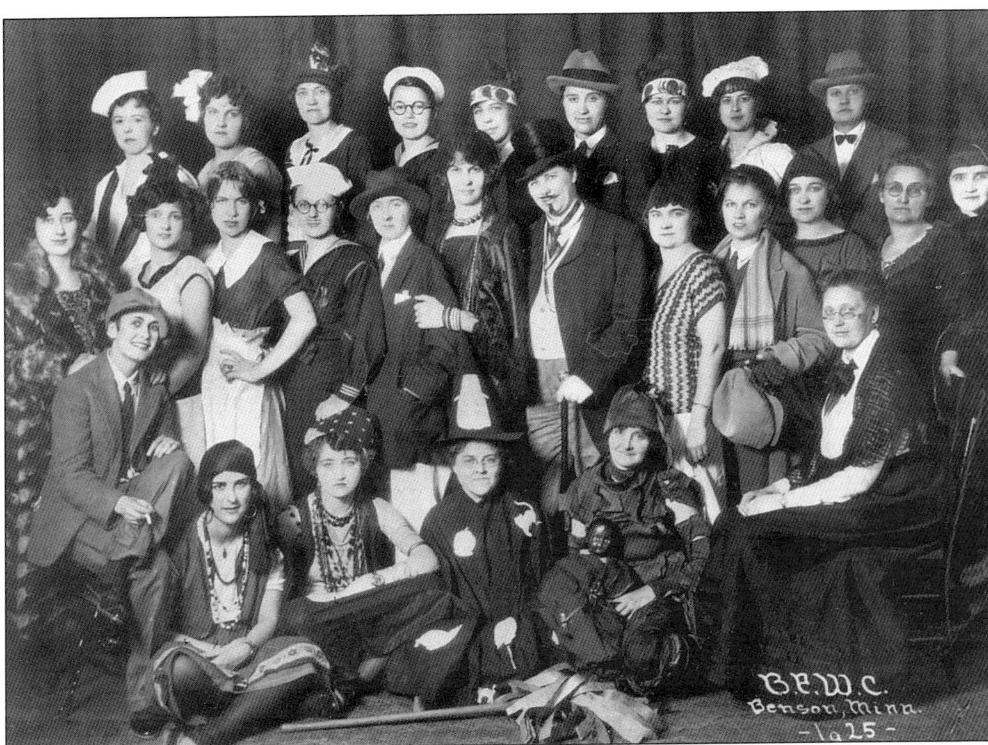

In November of 1924, the Business Women of Benson was organized. In 1925, its members, then referred to it as the Professional Business Women's Club, had this picture taken.

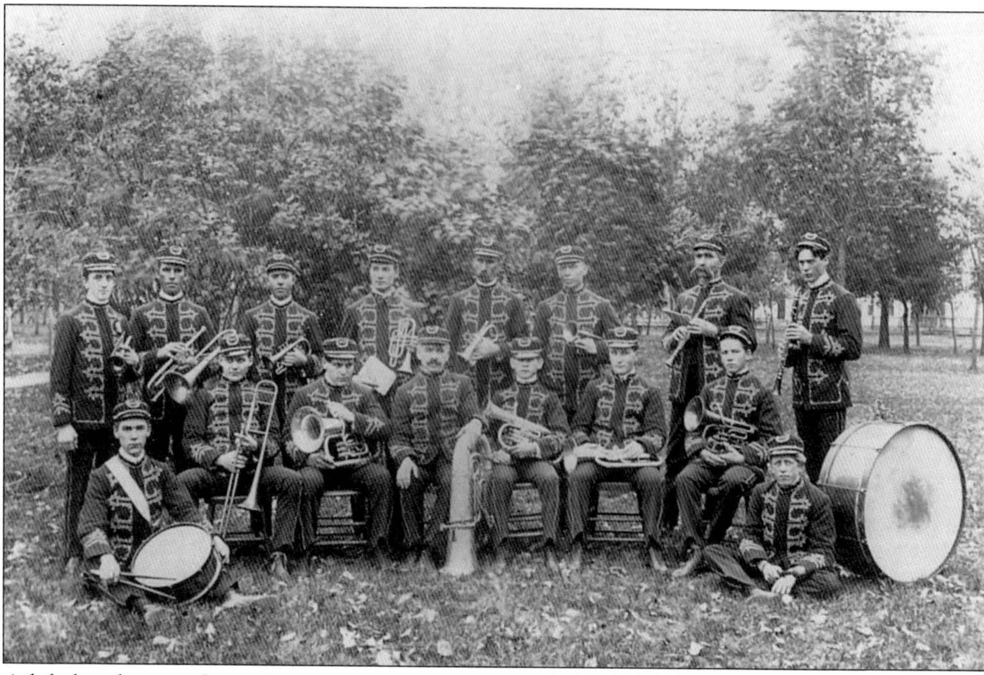

Adult bands were formed in every community and several of the townships in Swift County. Posing in Roosevelt Park in Benson are members of one of Benson's bands. The fourth person from the left in the front row is Jacob Minikus, who was director of the band for 16 years.

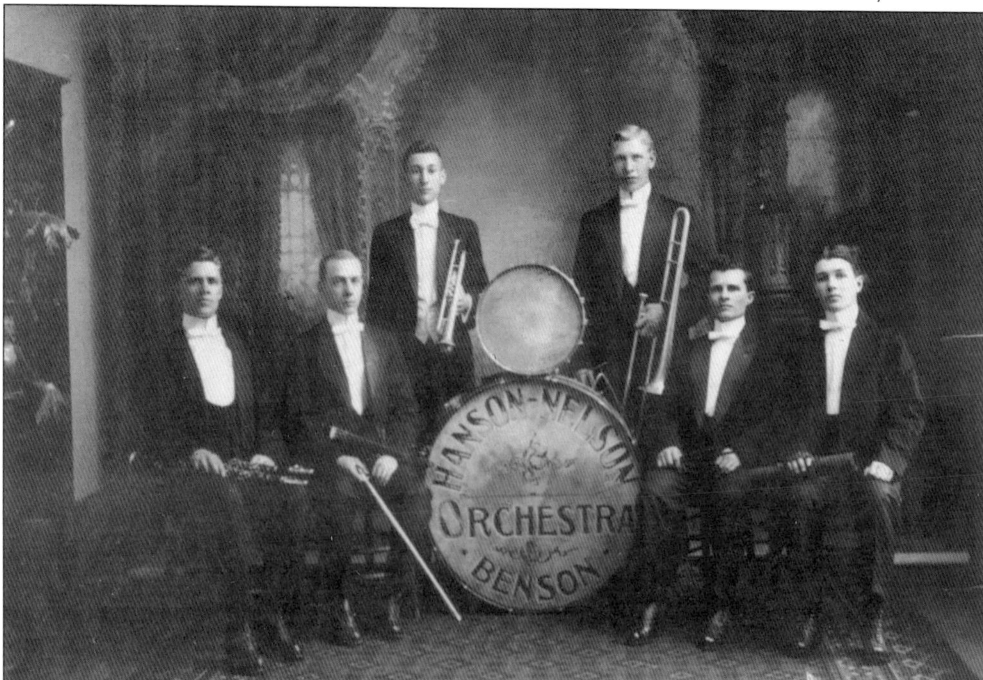

The Hanson-Nelson Orchestra of Benson was among the many musical groups in Swift County. Local orchestras and bands would play at concerts and dances. Barn dances were especially popular.

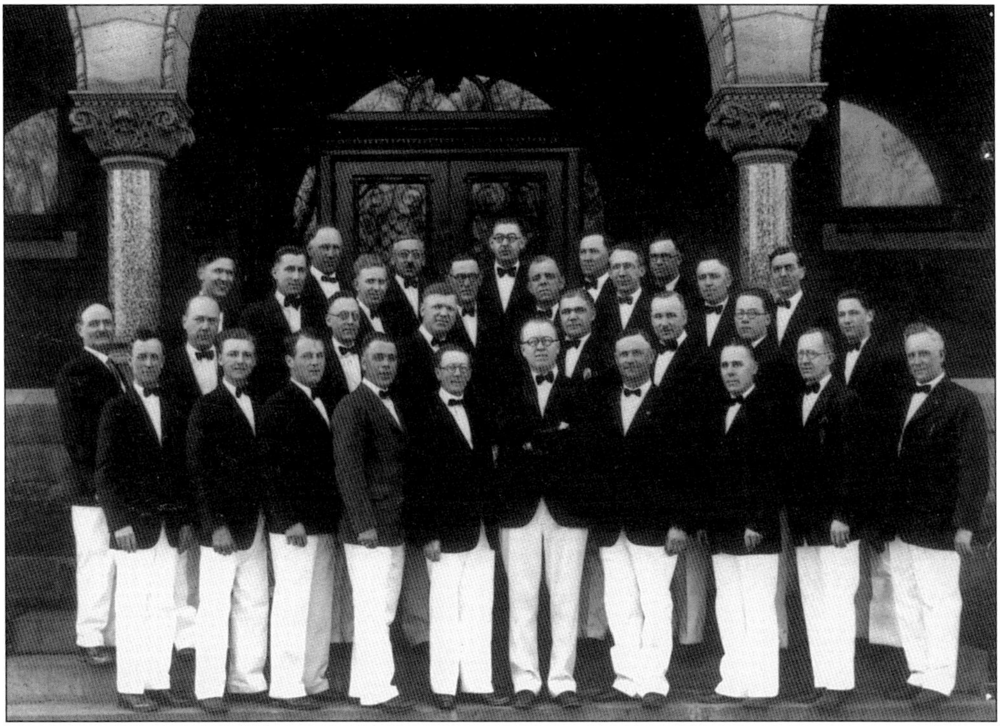

The Apollo Male Chorus of Benson poses in front of the Swift County Courthouse. The chorus was organized in 1926, with 30 male voices. G.E. Oyloe was the director.

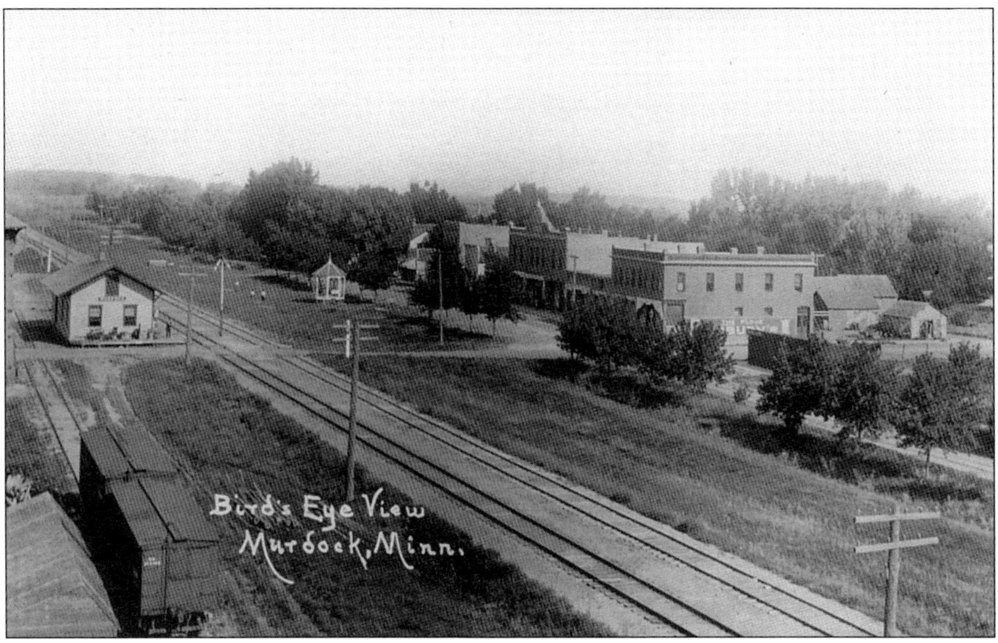

Between the depot on the left and the business buildings on the right is a small structure, Murdock's band shell. Most of the trading centers in Swift County had one. Musical groups would stand in the shell and perform to the crowds gathered to listen to their favorite tunes. Band shells gradually faded away as people turned to radios and televisions for entertainment.

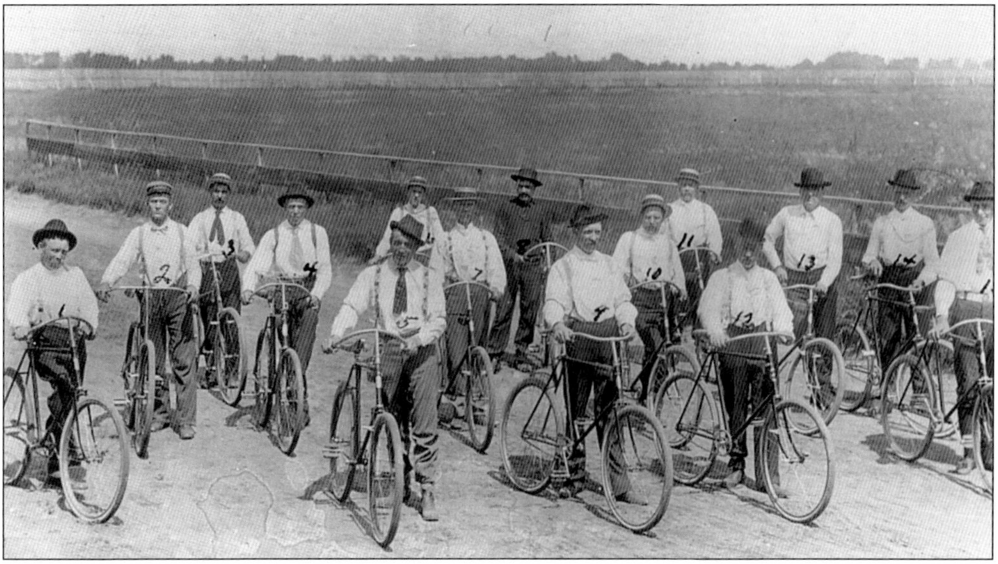

In the 1890s, bicycles became very popular among the adult population and were a deluxe form of transportation, costing as much as $100. Adult bicycle clubs were formed. This is a group of cyclists gathered for a race in 1895.

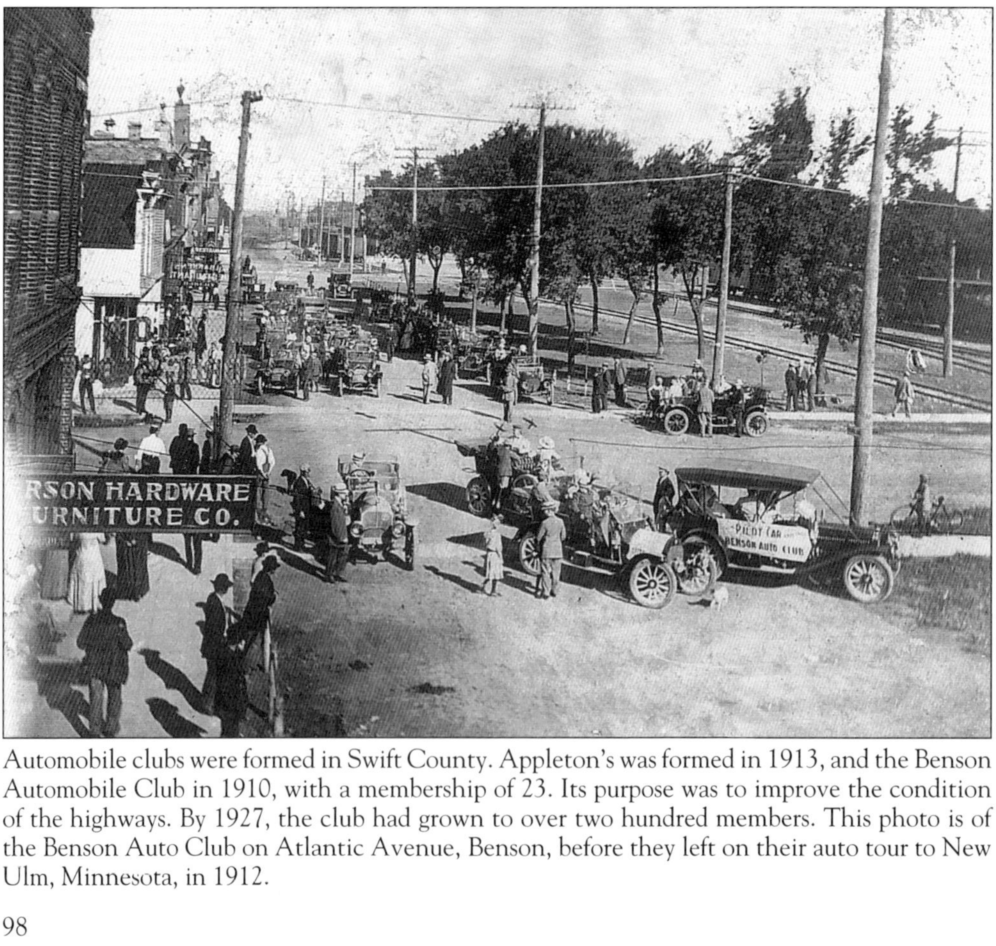

Automobile clubs were formed in Swift County. Appleton's was formed in 1913, and the Benson Automobile Club in 1910, with a membership of 23. Its purpose was to improve the condition of the highways. By 1927, the club had grown to over two hundred members. This photo is of the Benson Auto Club on Atlantic Avenue, Benson, before they left on their auto tour to New Ulm, Minnesota, in 1912.

The game of basketball originated in Massachusetts in 1891. It wasn't long before it was one of the sports played in Swift County. This is a picture of the Benson City Team of 1915.

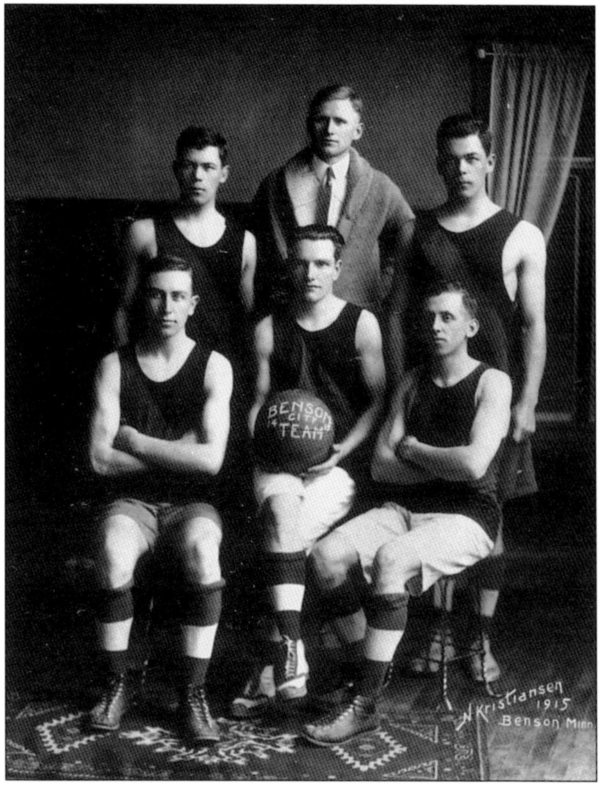

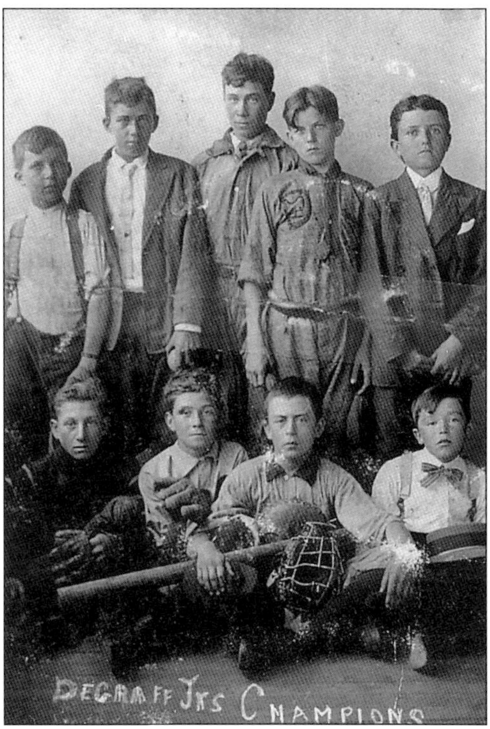

Perhaps the most popular sport, and one of the first organized in Swift County, was baseball. In 1909, these were the young boys who played on the DeGraff Jr.'s baseball team. They are, from left to right: (top row) Joe Boyle, Jimmie McNellis, Irvin Acher, Jimmie Boyle, Pete Hughes; (bottom row) Ernest Speiss, Neil Wall, Jack Sheridan, and Francis Kelly.

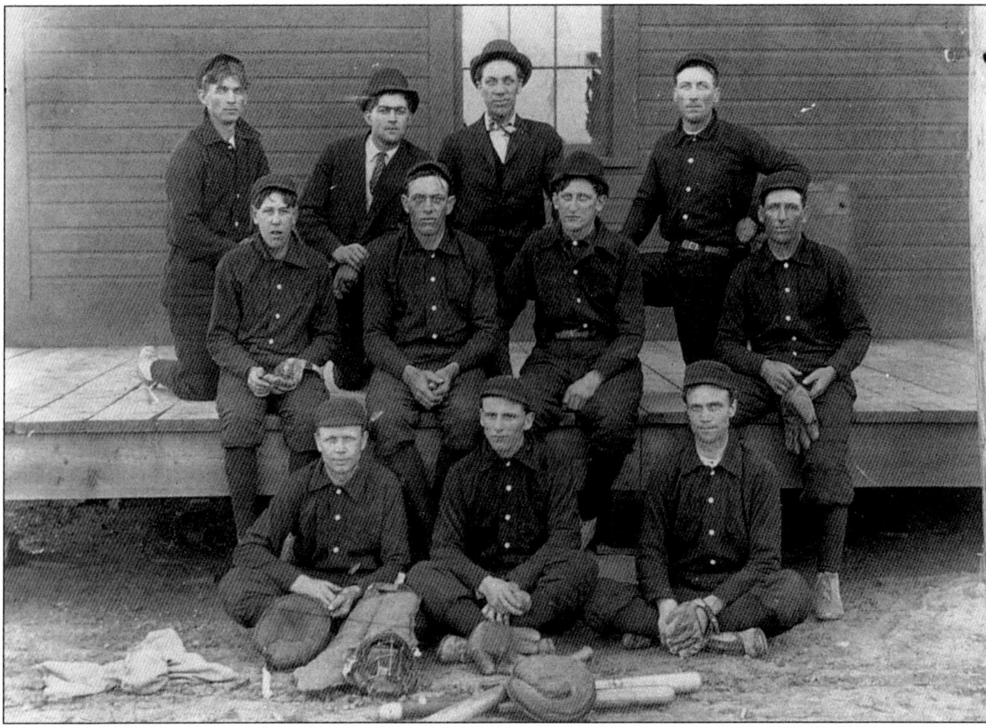

Baseball teams were formed throughout Swift County. Newspapers carried articles about upcoming games and details of past games. Sometimes the newspapers became involved in heated debates over how a game was played or the calls. The group of men in this picture played for a Swift Falls baseball team.

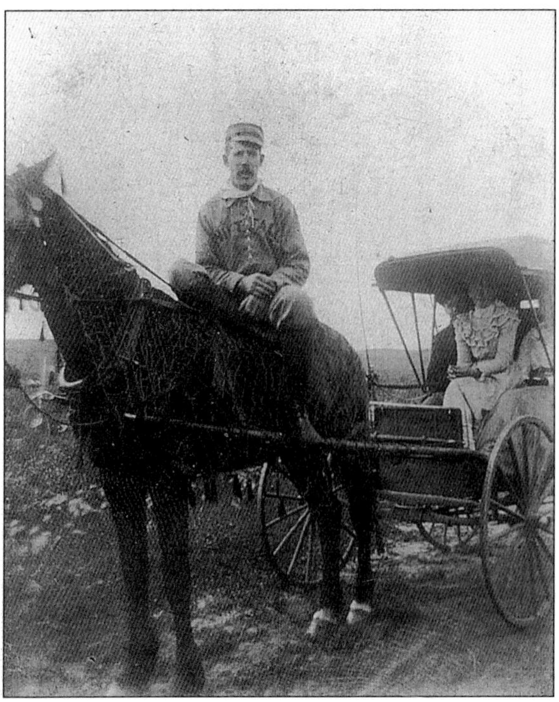

"Take me out to the ball game" is the familiar cry, and that is just what this horse and buggy is doing for the young people in the photo. The man on the horse is dressed in his baseball uniform and ready to play for a Swift Falls team.

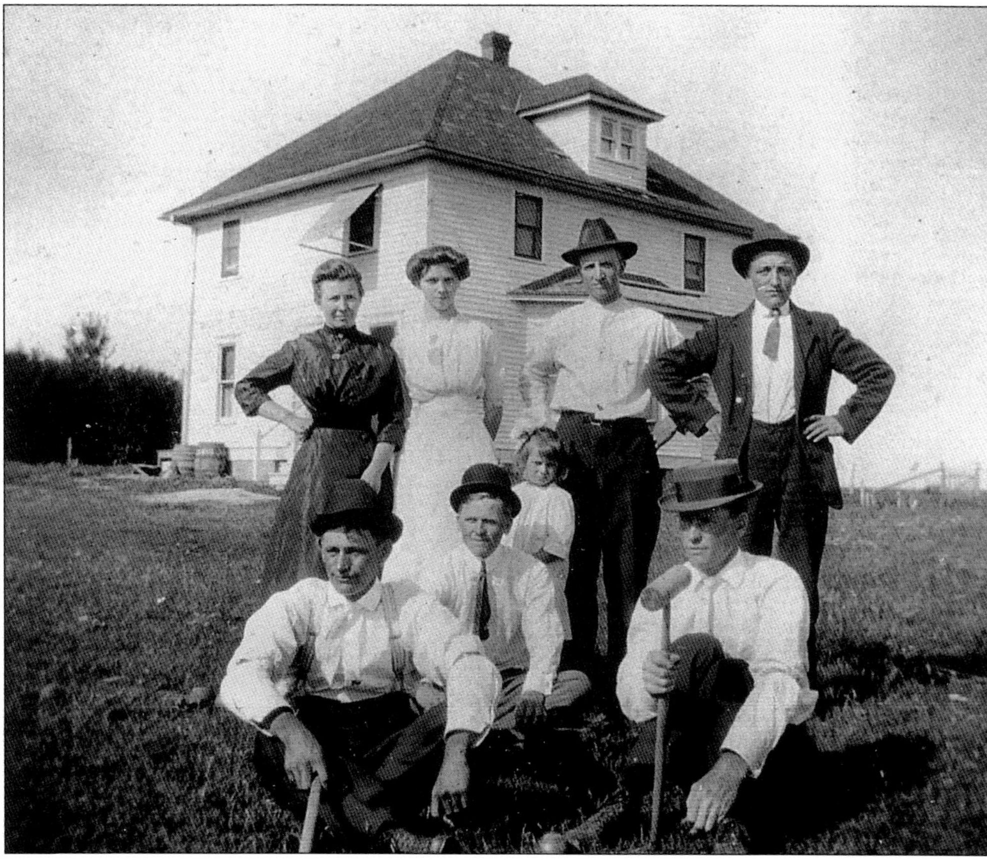

A game of croquet is stopped at the Rodberg farm in Torning Township to pose for a picture.

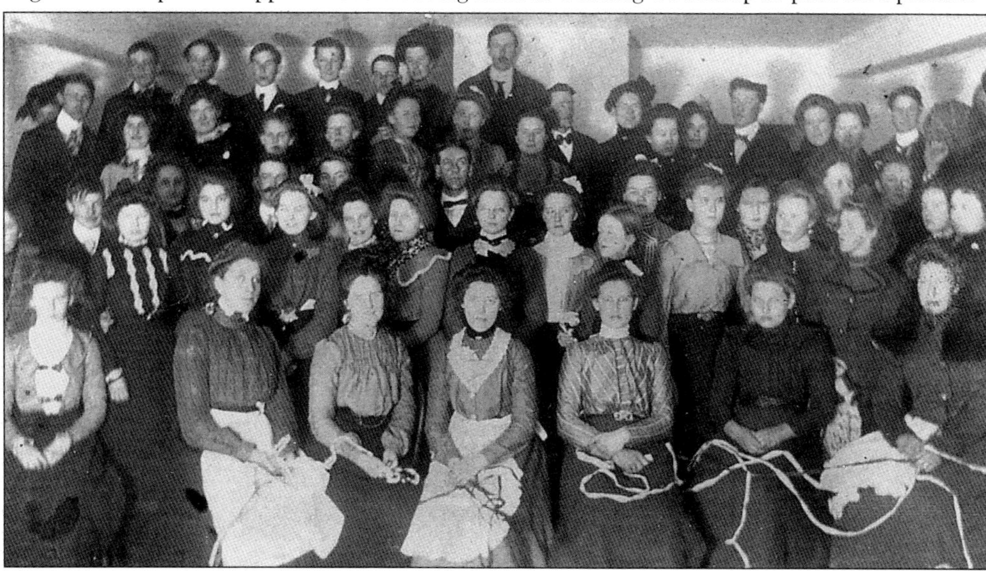

There were a variety of socials held in the early years. Socials were a great way to get together with neighbors and friends. This rag ball social was held at District 16 in Torning Township about 1901.

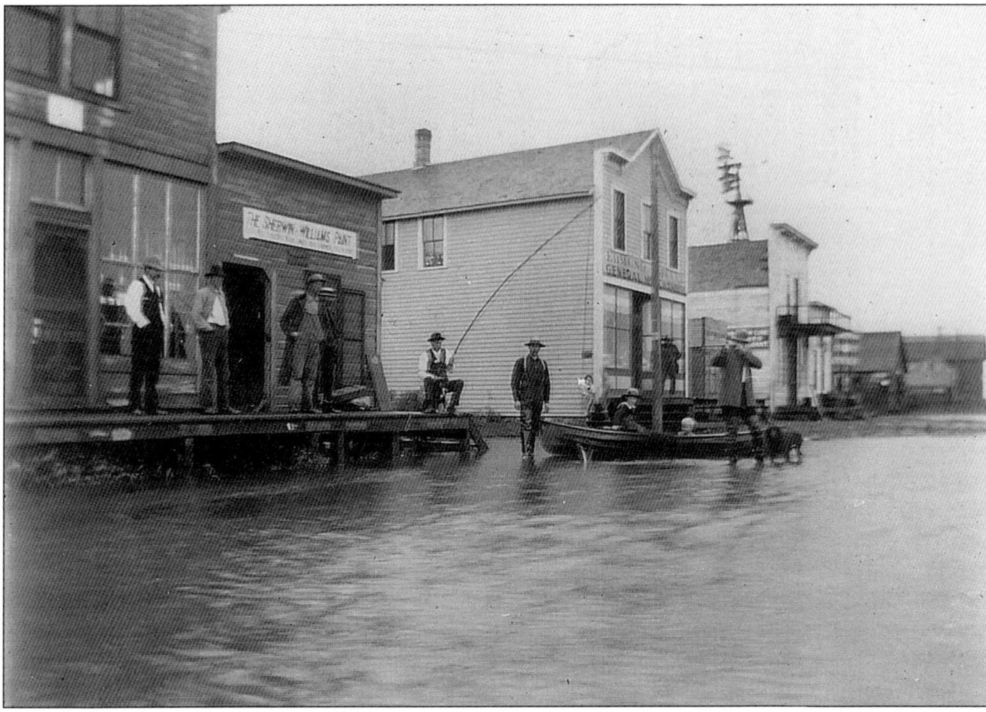

This is not Venice, Italy, but Main Street, Danvers, during a very wet season. The man with the fishing pole is having some fun, but it is very doubtful that he will have any luck as there were no lakes, streams, or rivers anywhere close to Danvers.

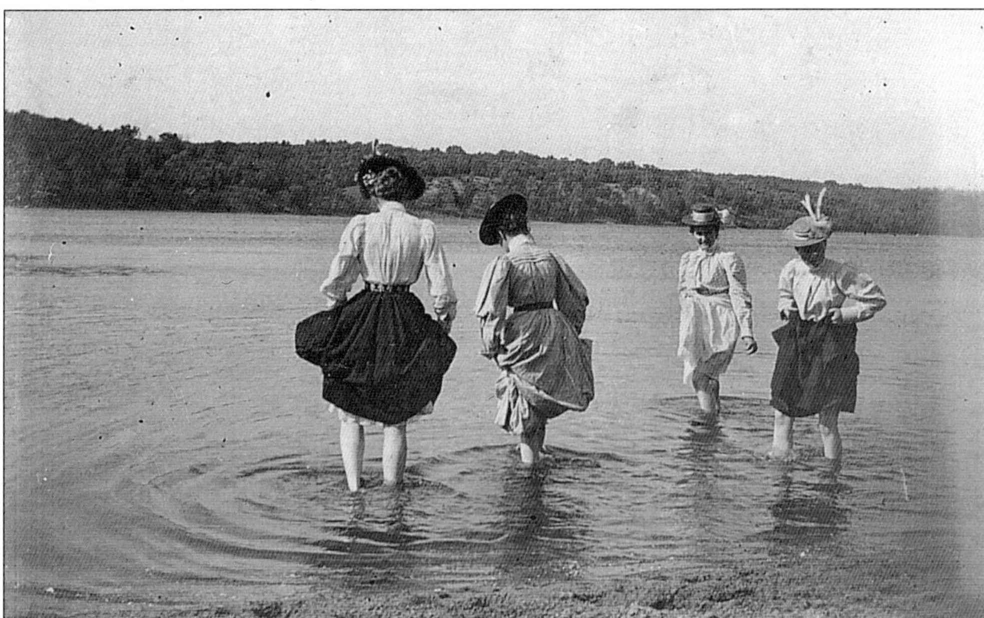

These ladies decided to put aside the strict rules of modesty of the era (*c.* 1900) to wade in the water of Lake Hazel in Benson Township. They removed their shoes and stockings but kept on their hats. Ladies never left their homes without a hat.

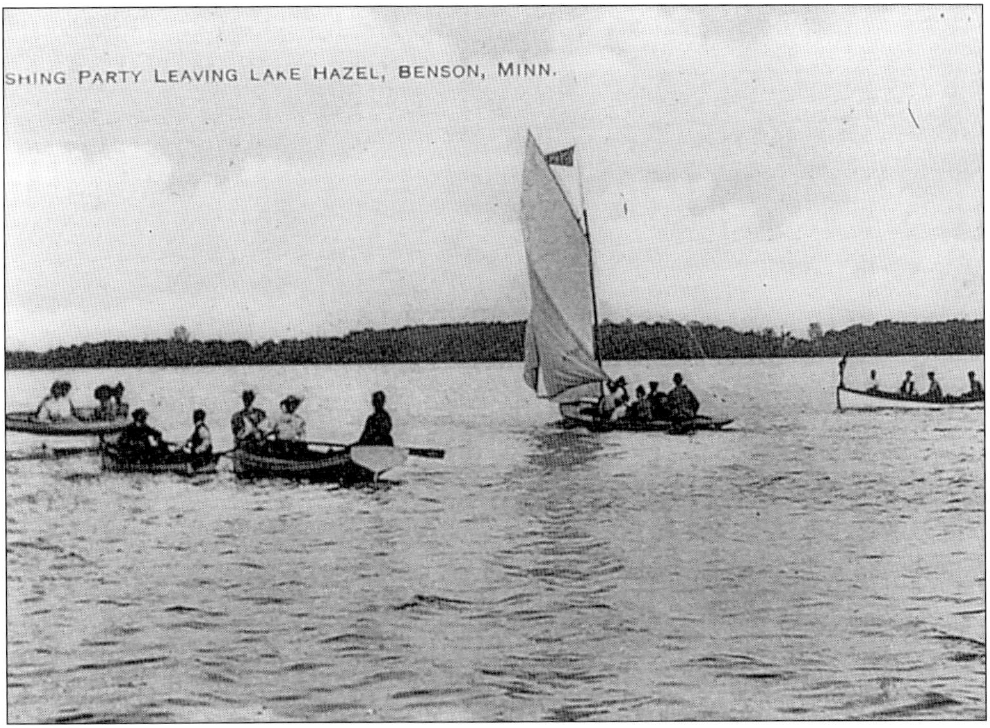

Local residents and people from the metropolitan area, 150 miles away, would sail or row their boats on Lake Hazel in Benson Township. During the drought of the 1930s, the lake went dry and was mowed for hay. Water did return to Lake Hazel, but not enough to attract tourists.

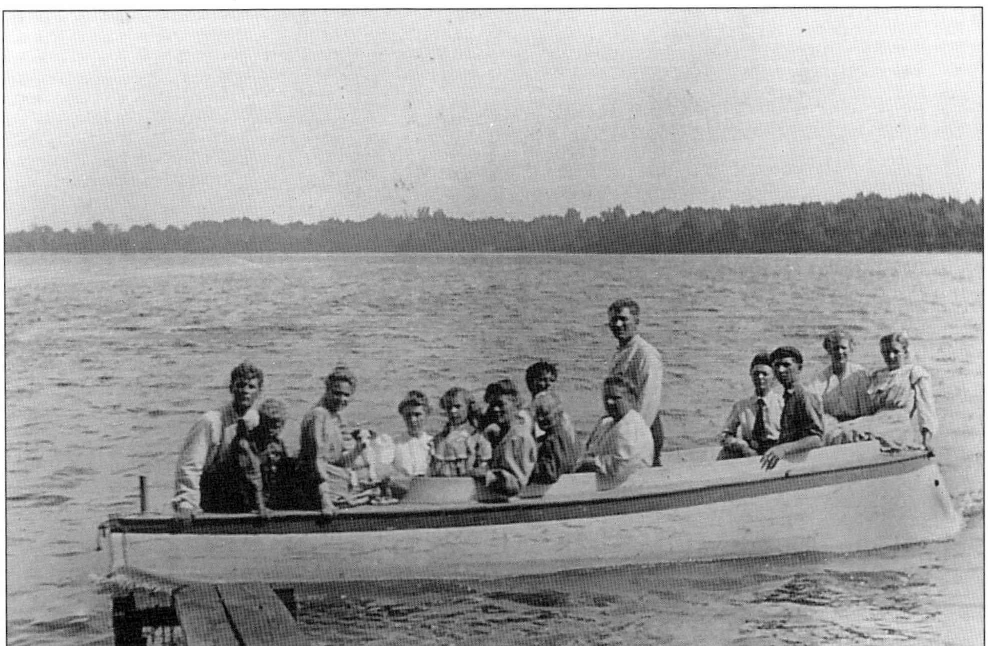

Dr. Scofield of Benson owned the island that was located in Lake Hazel. The boat in the picture belonged to him.

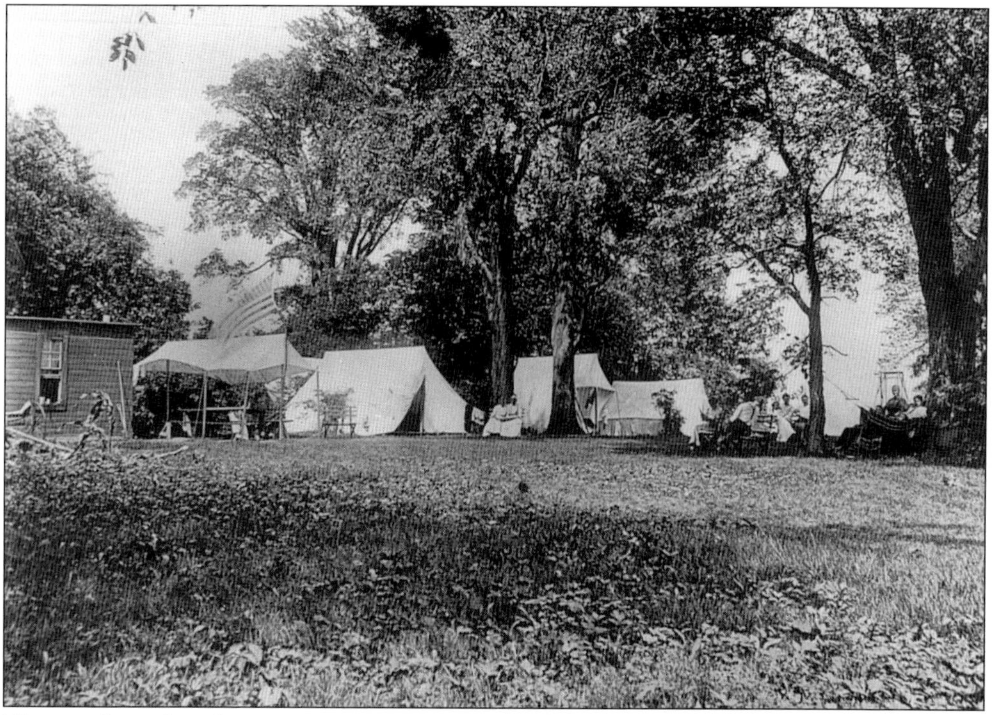

The people in this photo are enjoying camping on the island in Lake Hazel located in Benson Township. The Boy Scout Troops were allowed to use the island for meetings and camping. In later years, the owners of the island turned it over to the Scouts.

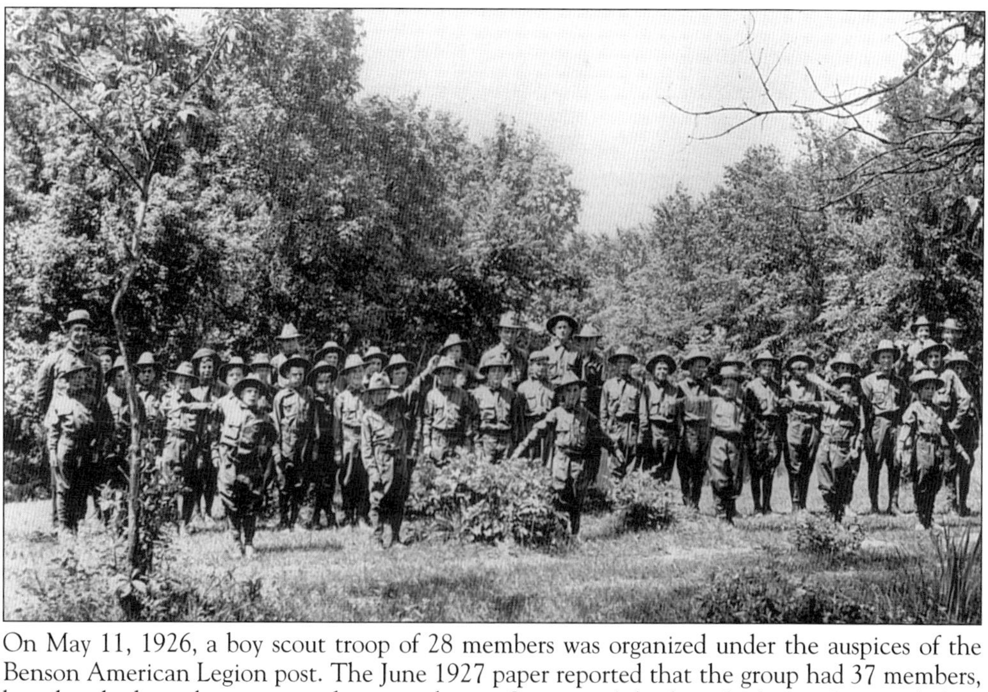

On May 11, 1926, a boy scout troop of 28 members was organized under the auspices of the Benson American Legion post. The June 1927 paper reported that the group had 37 members, but they had not been assigned to patrols yet. Sixteen of the boys had already passed their tenderfoot tests.

The first settlers that arrived in Swift County depended on their hunting skills for their meat supply. Hunting began to be more of a sport than a necessity after the railroad reached the communities. More businesses had been established, and farms were raising livestock for butchering. These three men were so proud of their hunting success that they had a photo taken.

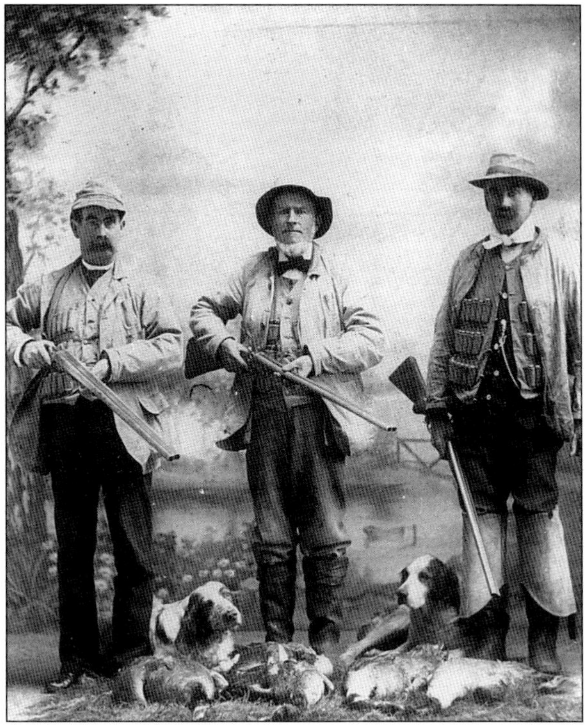

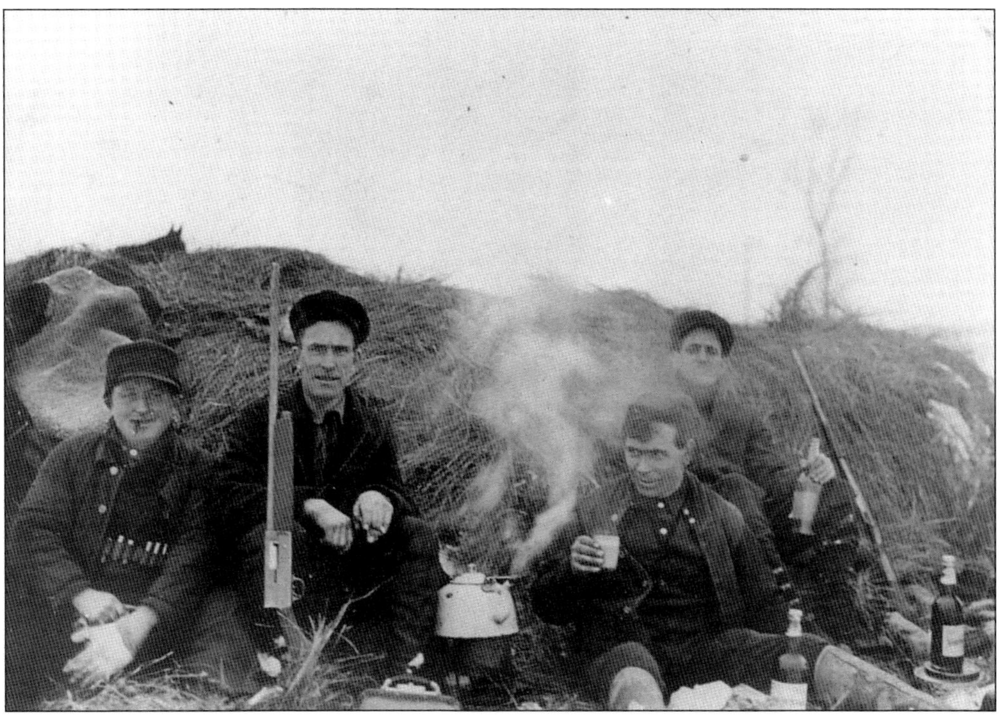

There were so many rabbits in Swift County that some communities made rabbit hunting an event. Large numbers of hunters would gather and participate in the day or days set for the hunt. These gentlemen were taking a break during a 1904 rabbit hunt.

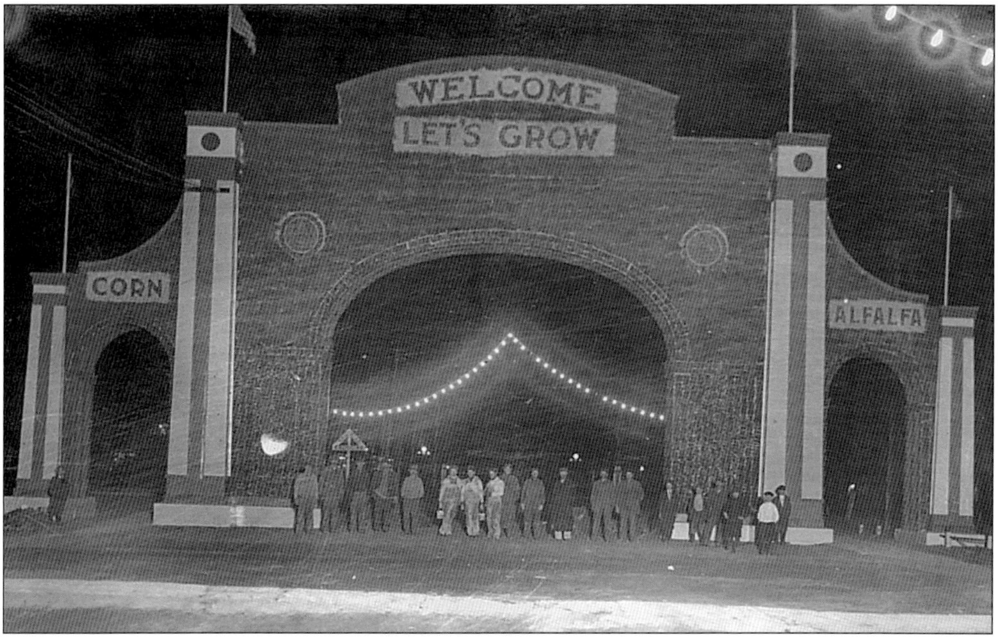

In 1914, the West Central Minnesota Development Association held its Corn and Alfalfa Exposition in Benson. This arch made of alfalfa bales and corn welcomed thousands of people representing 16 counties and the Twin Cities. Special trains were run for the three-day event.

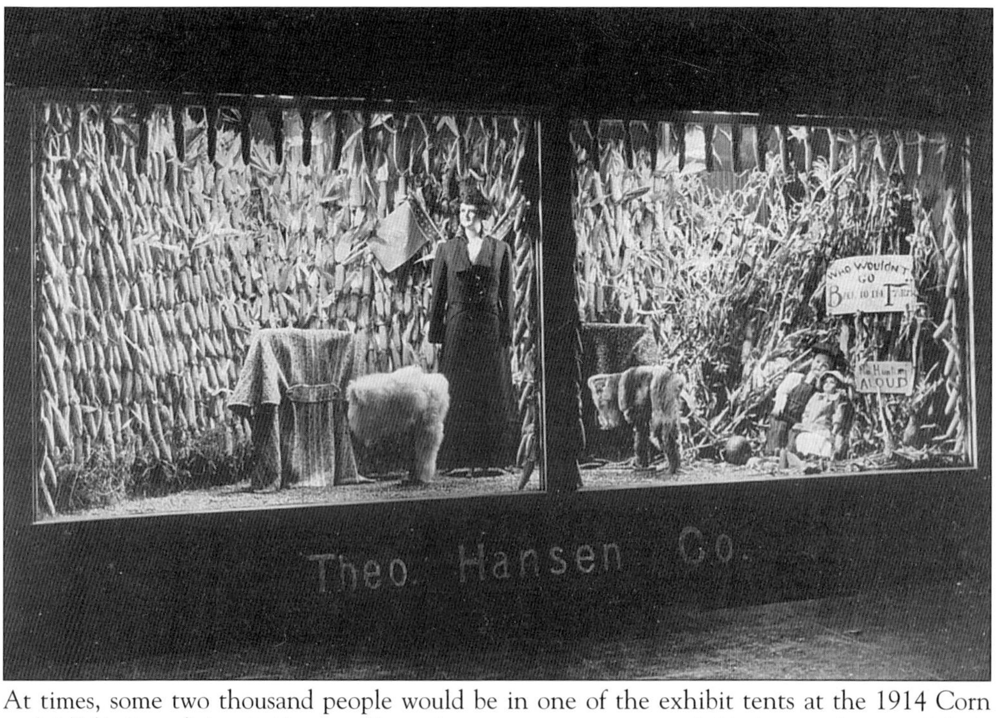

At times, some two thousand people would be in one of the exhibit tents at the 1914 Corn and Alfalfa Expedition in Benson. Several contests were sponsored. Businesses decorated their windows as seen in this photo of the Theodore Hansen store.

Eight

TRANSPORTATION

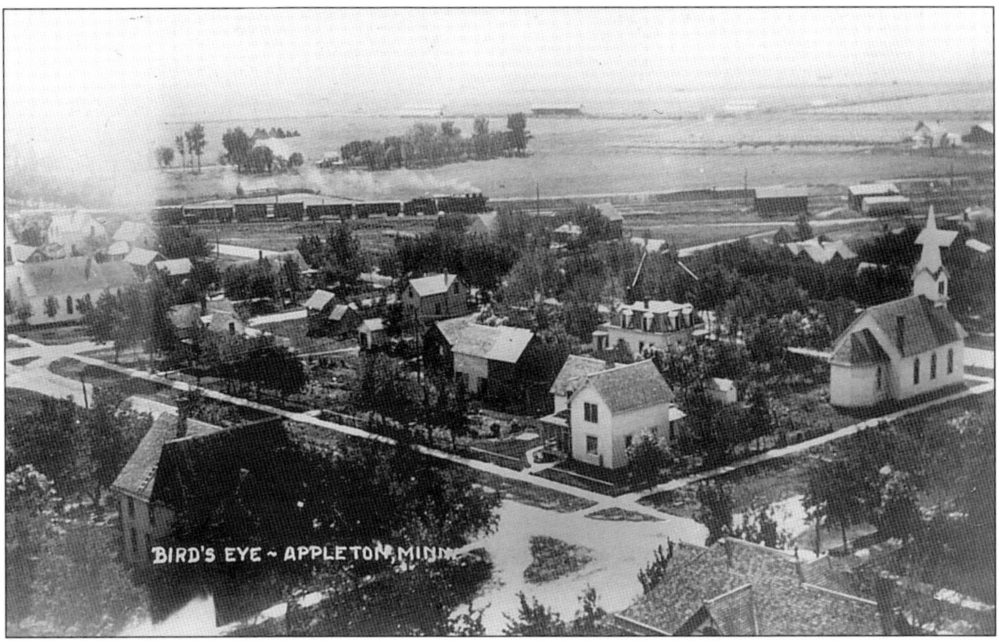

In the background of this birds-eye view of Appleton is the form of transportation that played such an important role in the growth of Swift County. However, the railroad did more than provide transportation. The St. Paul and Pacific Railroad advertised that it would transport, free of charge from St. Paul, all the saplings that the settlers would plant. The black prairie loam held so much water that streets became impassable. The railroad offered to load empty "deadhead" freight cars with sand and gravel and drop it free of charge at depots along the line. After the 1877 grasshopper invasion, the railroad postponed payments on its land until after the next harvest.

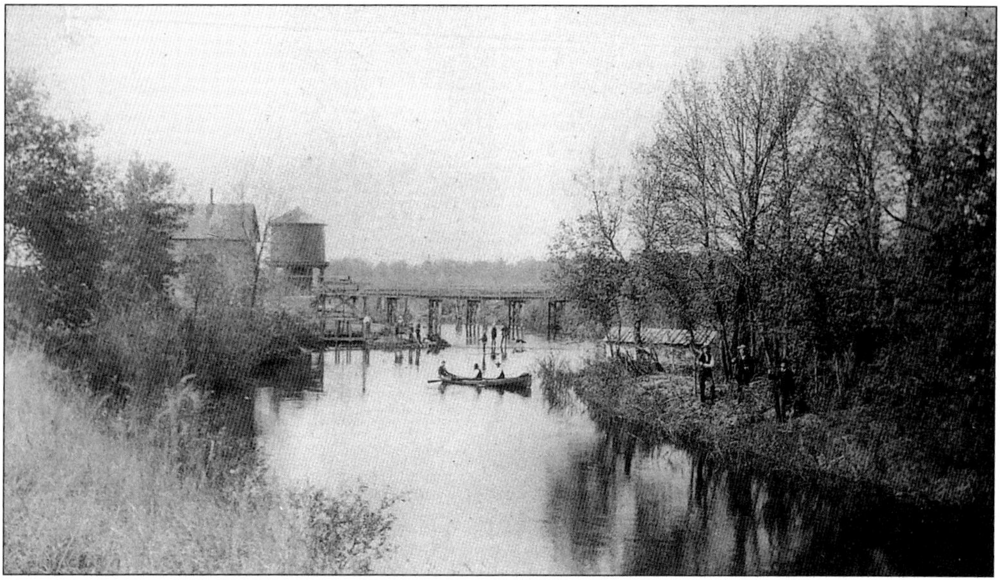

The Chippewa and Pomme de Terre Rivers in Swift County were too narrow or shallow for large water vessels. They were obstacles for travel by land until bridges were built. This is the first bridge on the Chippewa River near Benson. There was a ferryboat in this location before the bridge was built.

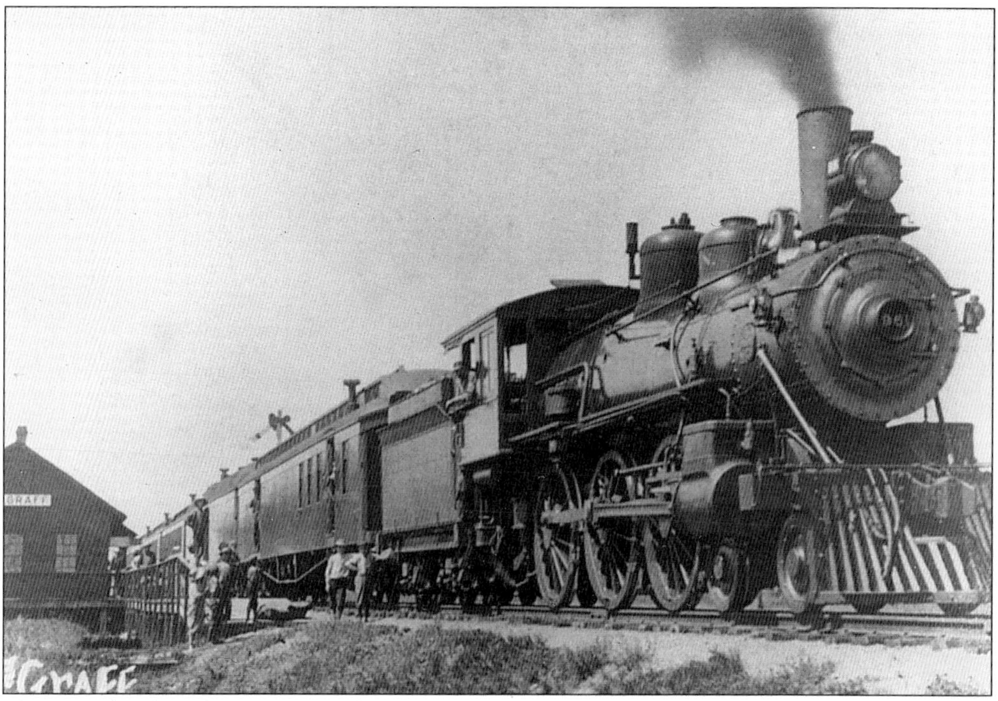

The growth of Swift County can largely be credited to the railroad. Settlers were attracted to the area knowing that there was a railroad for transporting supplies. This train was parked in front of the DeGraff depot. Railroad cars were pulled by steam locomotives in the first years of settlement in Swift County.

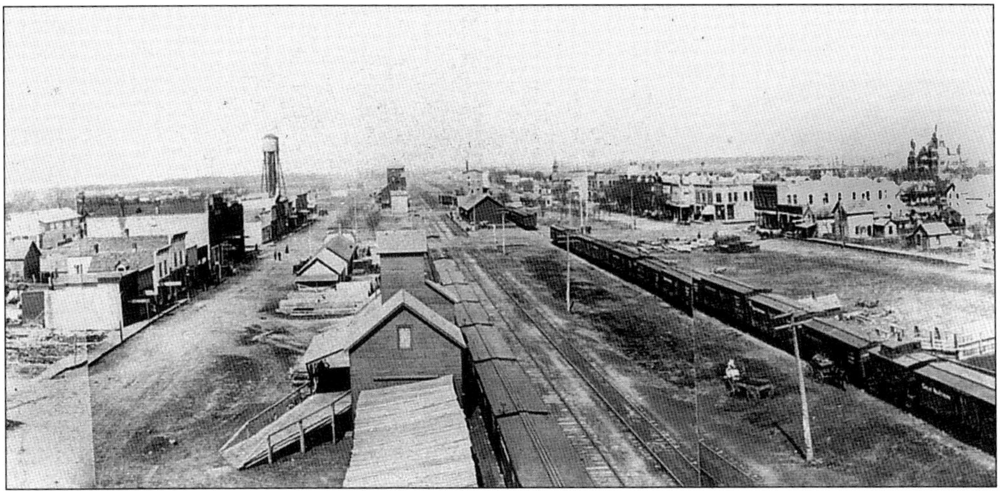

This 1900 photo of Benson shows how the business districts would develop next to the railroad tracks. Tracks dividing a city were inconvenient. "Afraid she would be late for church, Mrs. Anna Trank decided to climb between two freight cars that were tying up the tracks. Just as she got on the bumpers, the train started to move. For fear of falling under the wheels, she stayed where she was. She rode 40 miles to Willmar on the bumpers."

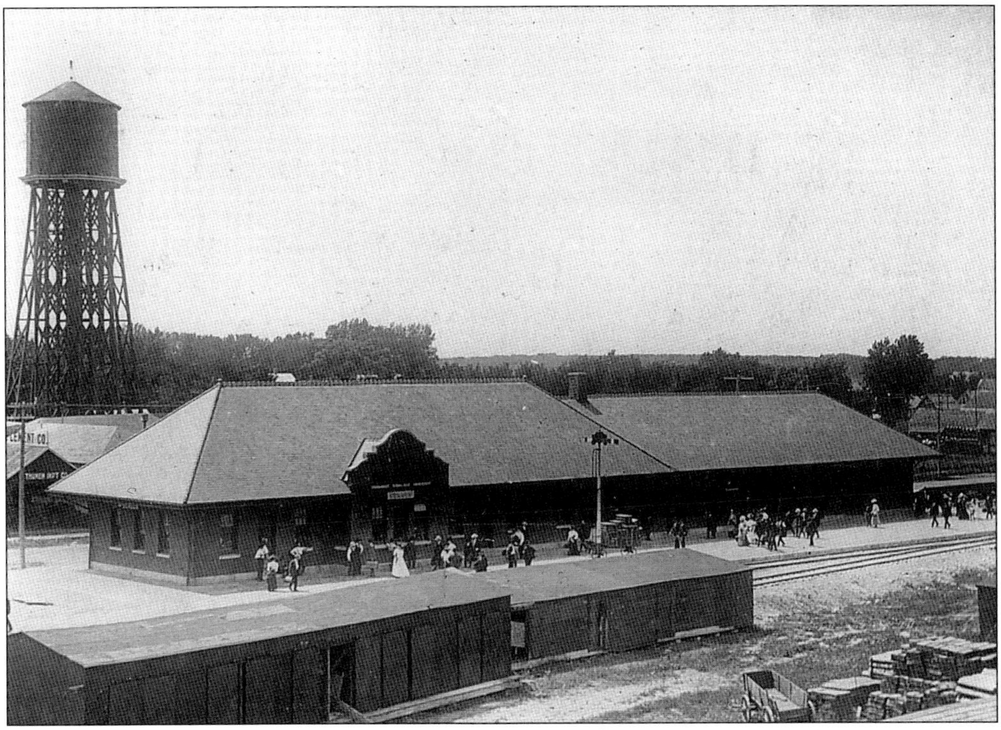

This Great Northern Depot, built in 1906 at a cost of $35,000, was located in Benson. Men and women each had their own waiting room with a drinking fountain between the two rooms. Offices were connected with a private telephone system, and the floors were tiled with marble.

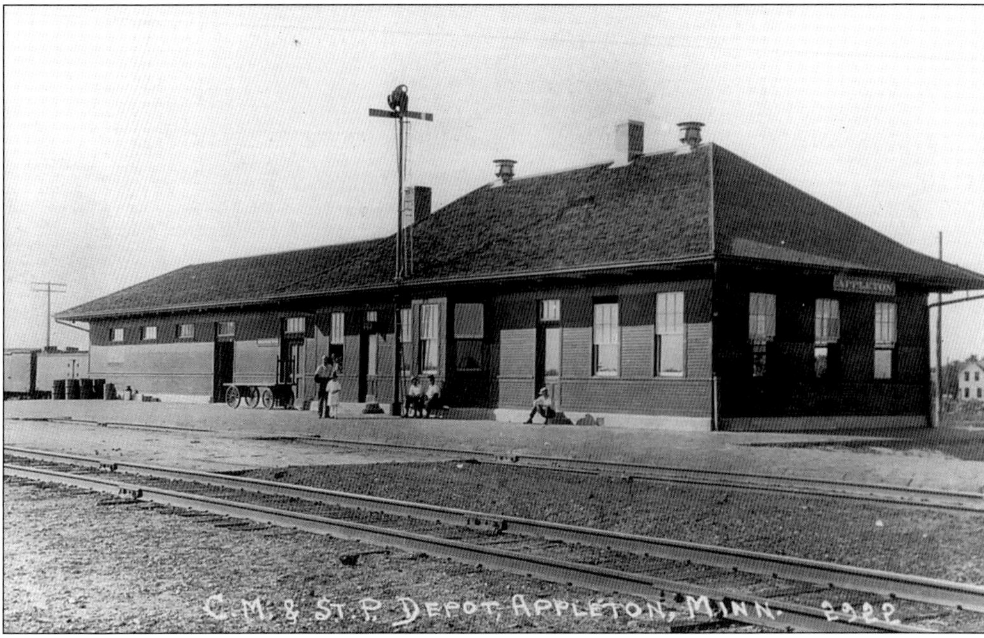

Appleton was served by two railroad lines, and each had its own depot. This is the Milwaukee Depot. In 1879, the Hastings and Dakota (later the Milwaukee) from Chippewa County went through Appleton as far as Ortonville, Minnesota. The Great Northern Railway reached Appleton on its way to Watertown, South Dakota, in 1887. Before this, a stage carried passengers and mail twice a week to and from Benson.

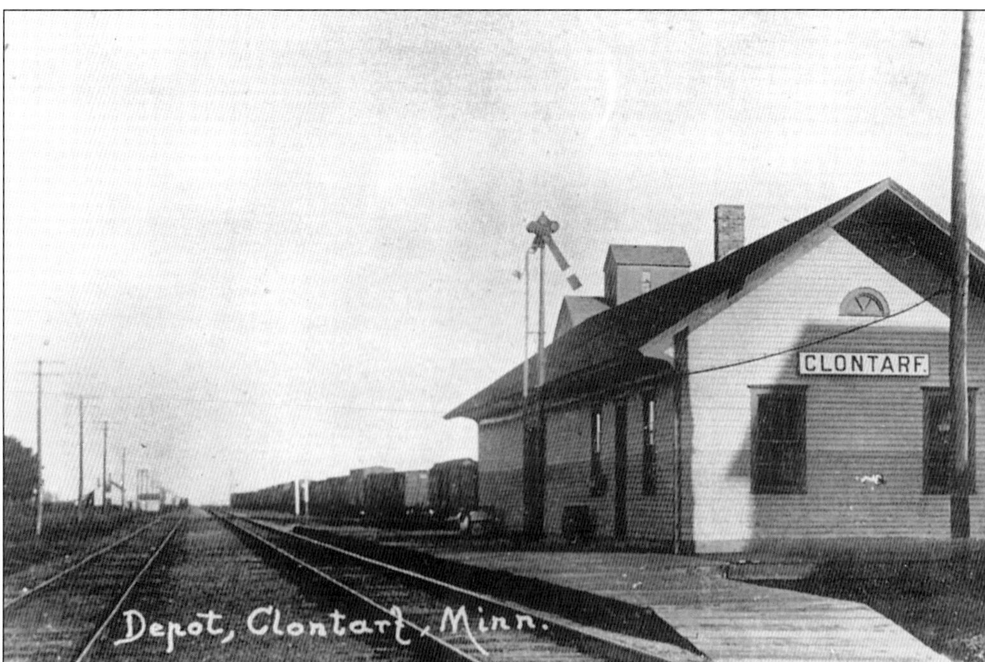

The railroad site at Clontarf was established in 1876, with a new depot built in 1878. Due to lack of business, the depot closed in 1901.

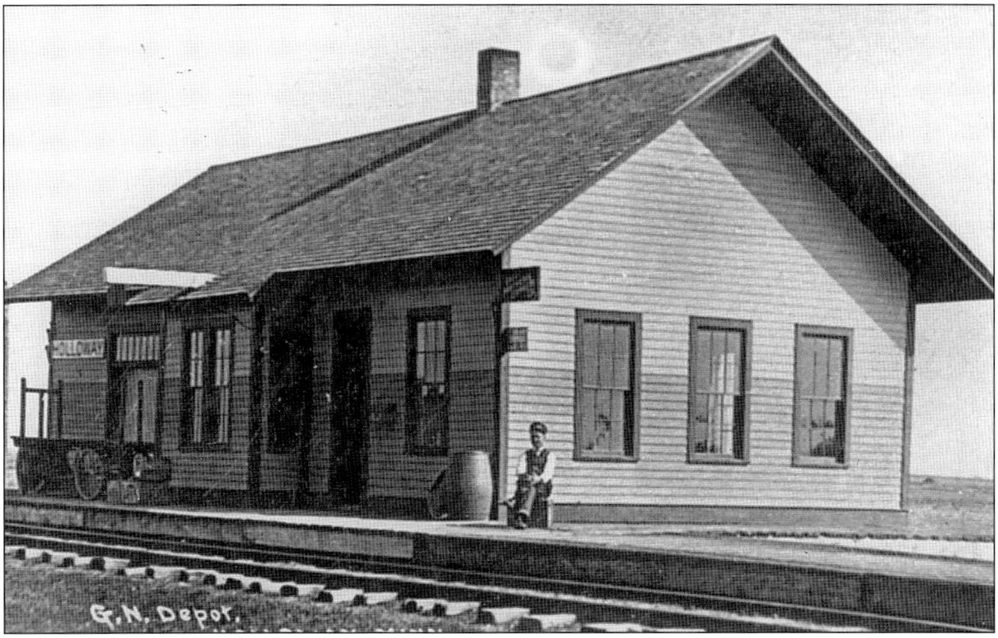

In 1887, construction of the Great Northern Railway from Benson to Appleton was completed. Two additional railroad towns, Danvers and Holloway, were platted with depots built in 1898. Newspapers reported a depot being built in Holloway in 1901, which is believed to be the one in this photo.

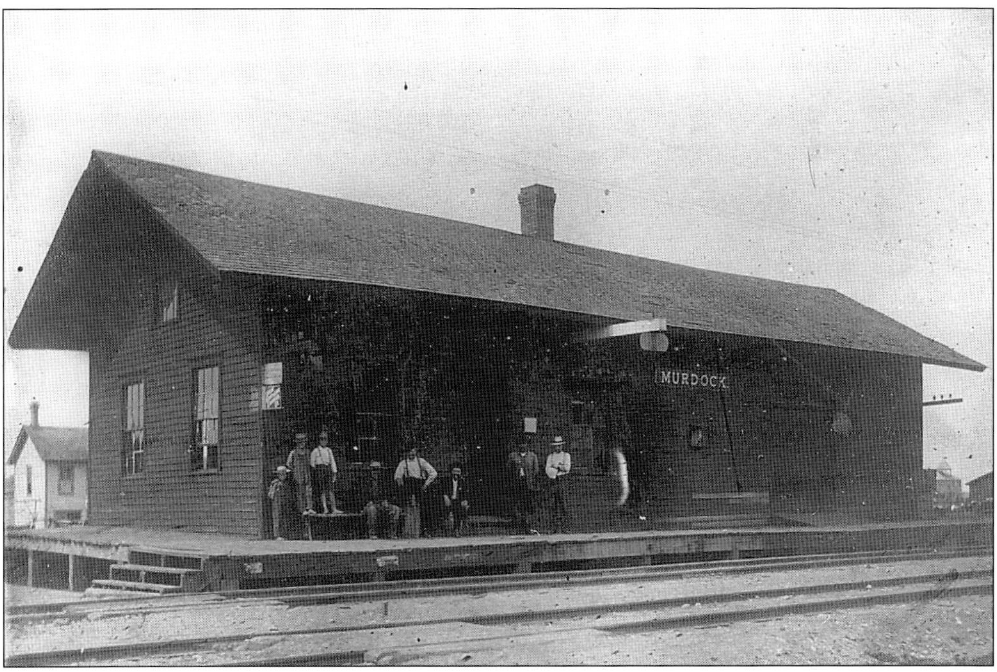

In 1876, S.S. Murdock was convinced that there was room for another trading center between DeGraff and Kerkhoven. The railroad didn't agree, but did lay a sidetrack there with Mr. Murdock responsible for expenses. After one year, the site was so successful that the railroad took it over. This photo was taken in 1906. The depot burned in 1918, and a new one was built.

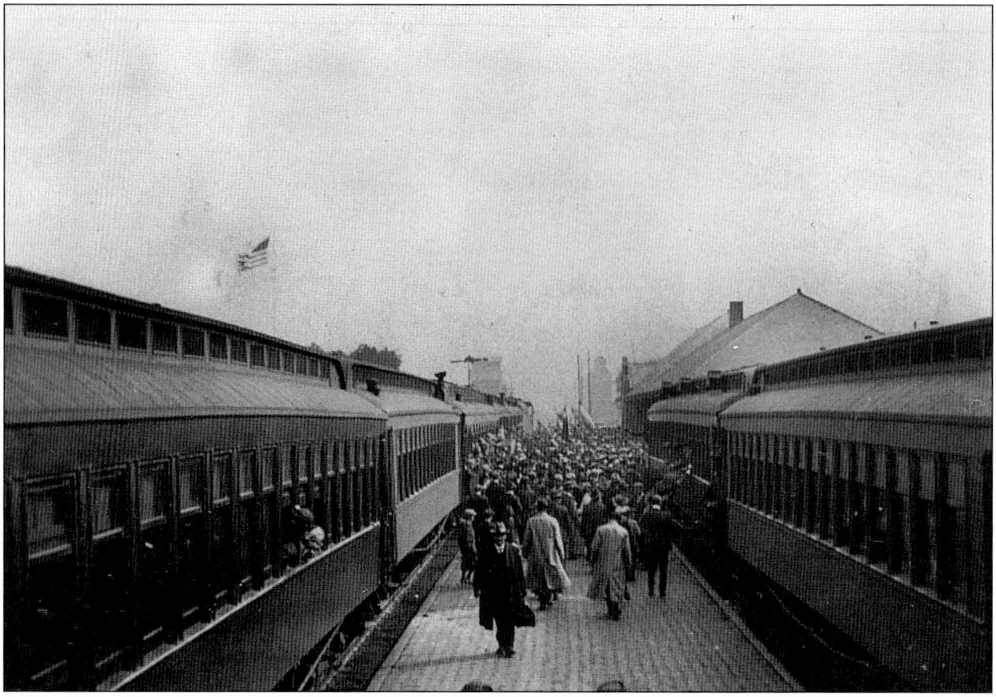

Before the automobile, trains were the main source of transportation to and from Swift County. This picture of train passengers was taken in Benson at the Great Northern Depot. The depot in the background was built in 1906.

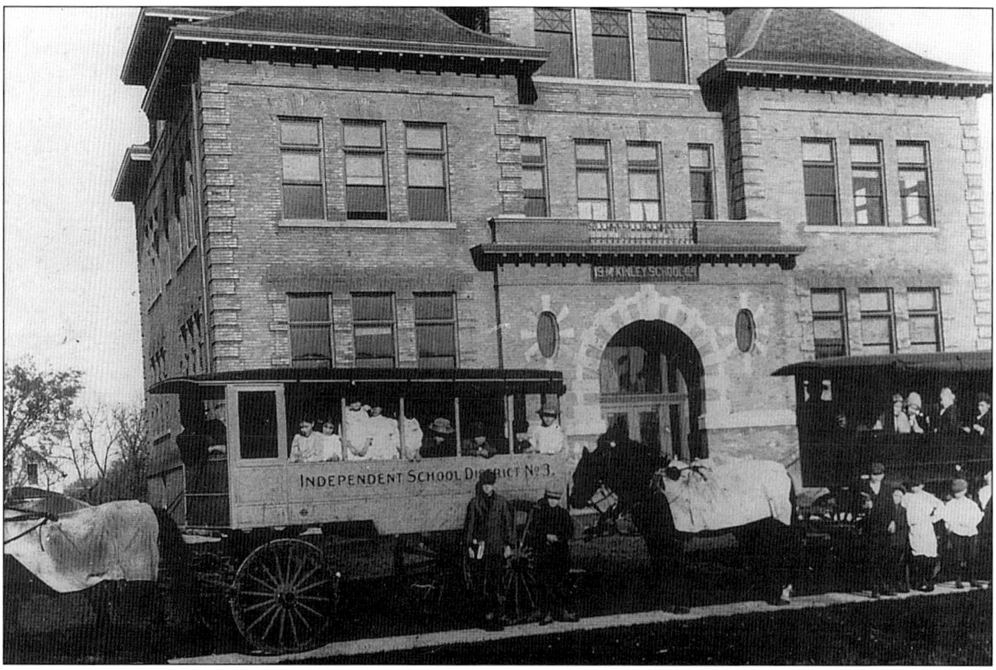

The Kerkhoven School District provided transportation for their students as early as 1904. As more students came into the high school, it was necessary to provide more vehicles. The first drivers furnished the horses and were paid $1.50 per trip.

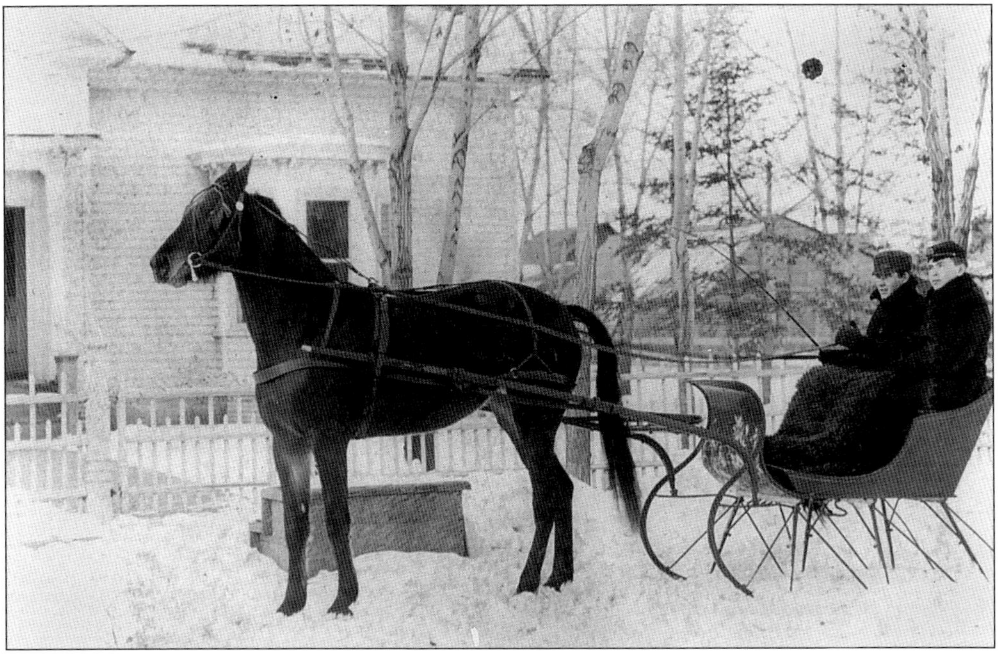

During the winter months in Swift County, horses would often be hitched to a sleigh or bobsled. Sleighs and bobsleds had runners instead of wheels making them easier to pull on snow or ice. A small one-horse sleigh like the one in this picture was called a cutter.

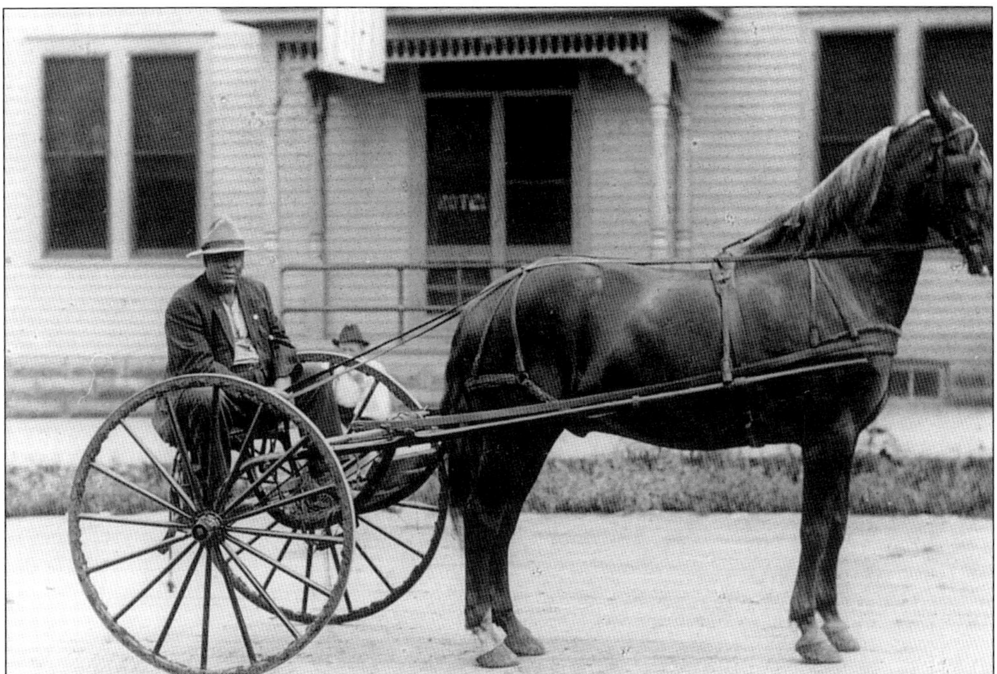

Horses were very important to the settlers. Owners took great pride in having a good steed or team. This gentleman was so proud of his horse that he stopped in front of the Kerkhoven Hotel to have a picture taken.

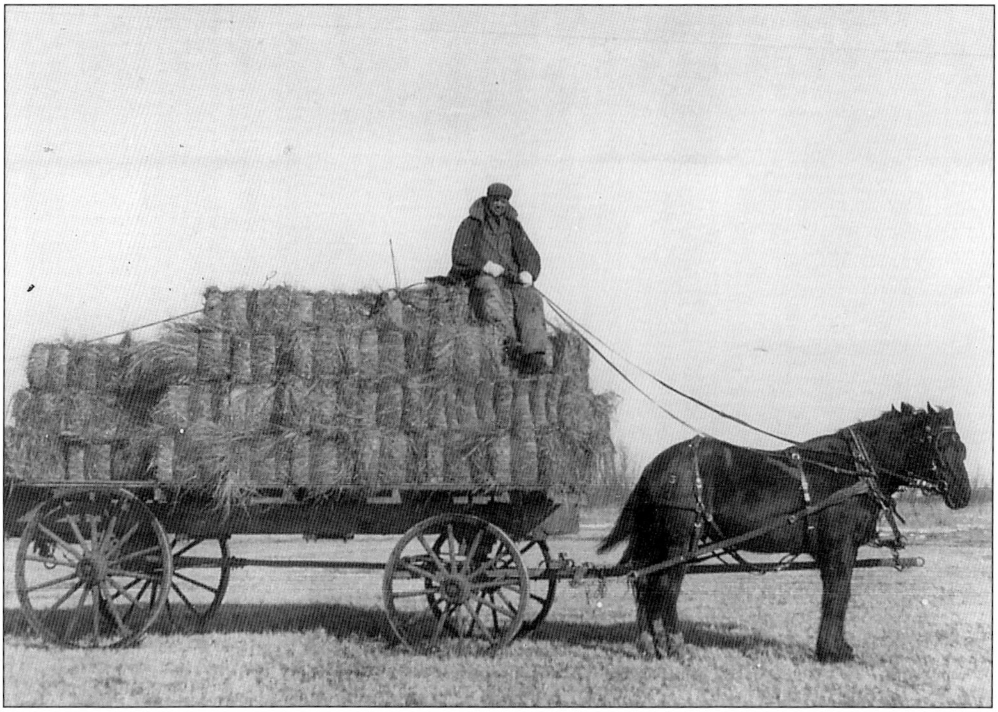

Many of the first settlers used oxen when they first arrived in Swift County. Horses replaced oxen, because the open level prairies and the use of modern machinery made it necessary to have a speedier work animal.

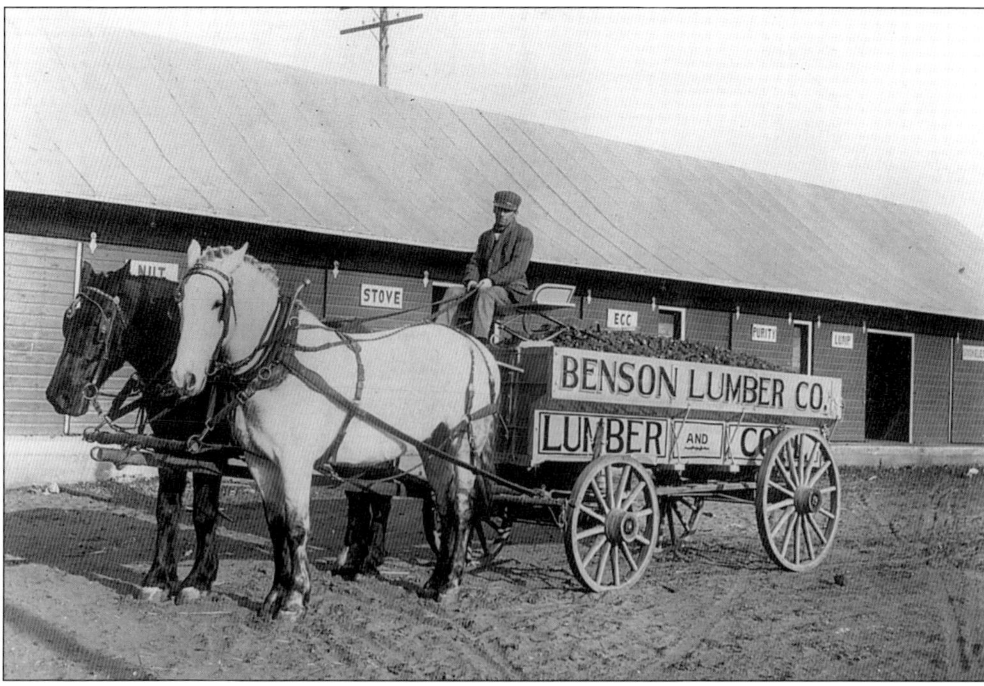

Horses were used to haul the fuel for cooking and heating homes. Since Swift County was a treeless prairie, there was a shortage of wood for fuel. Many of the homes burned coal.

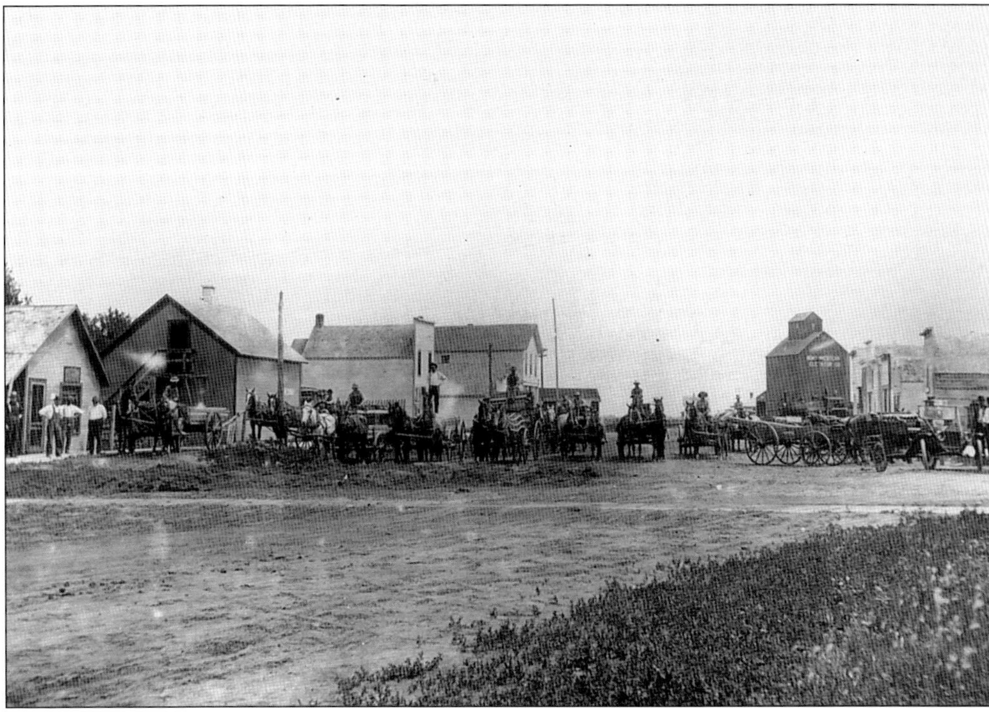

The demand for lumber was great. In 1875, in Benson alone, 1.5 million feet of lumber was sold. This photo was taken at Clontarf of Peter Forbord and a crew of men hauling lumber for his home. Mr. Forbord had arrived in the area from Norway in the 1880s.

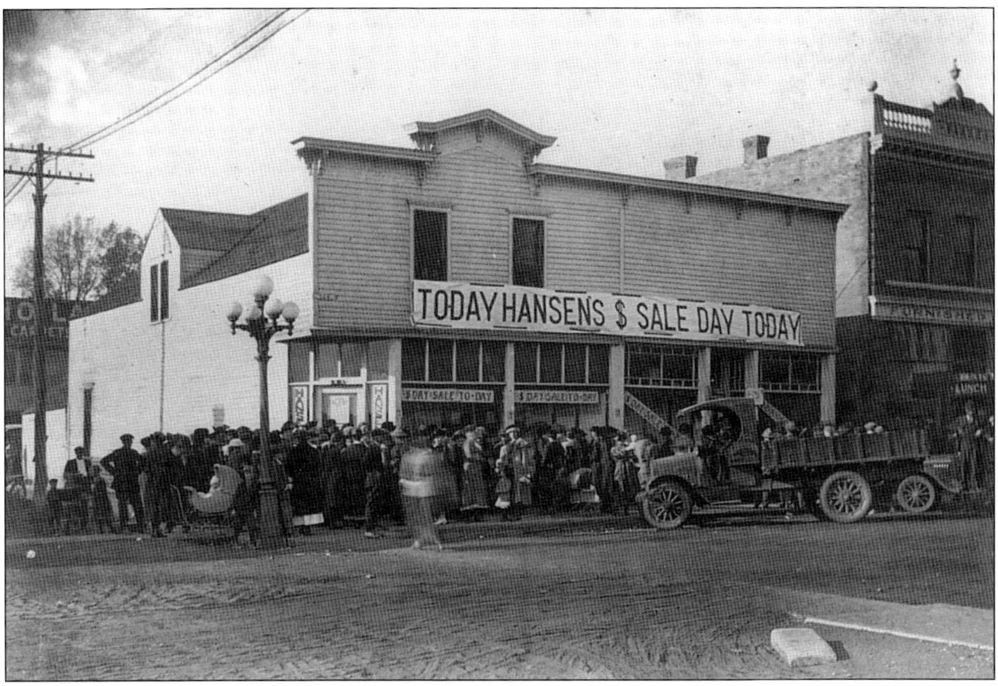

By the 1920s, trucks were beginning to replace the horse and wagon. In later years, the efficiency of hauling by truck would result in a decline in the need for the railroad.

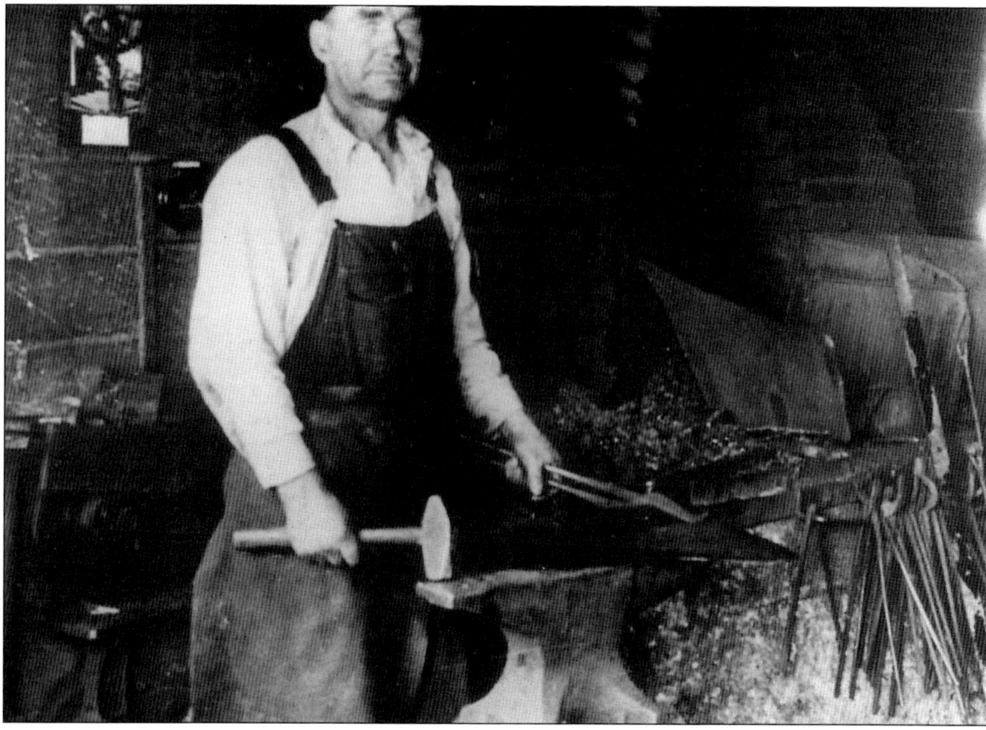

An important part of transportation were the people who kept things going. Horses needed shoes, and the blacksmiths took care of this need. Joe Halvorsen was a blacksmith in Danvers, moving there in 1900. He also was a dealer of buggies and plows.

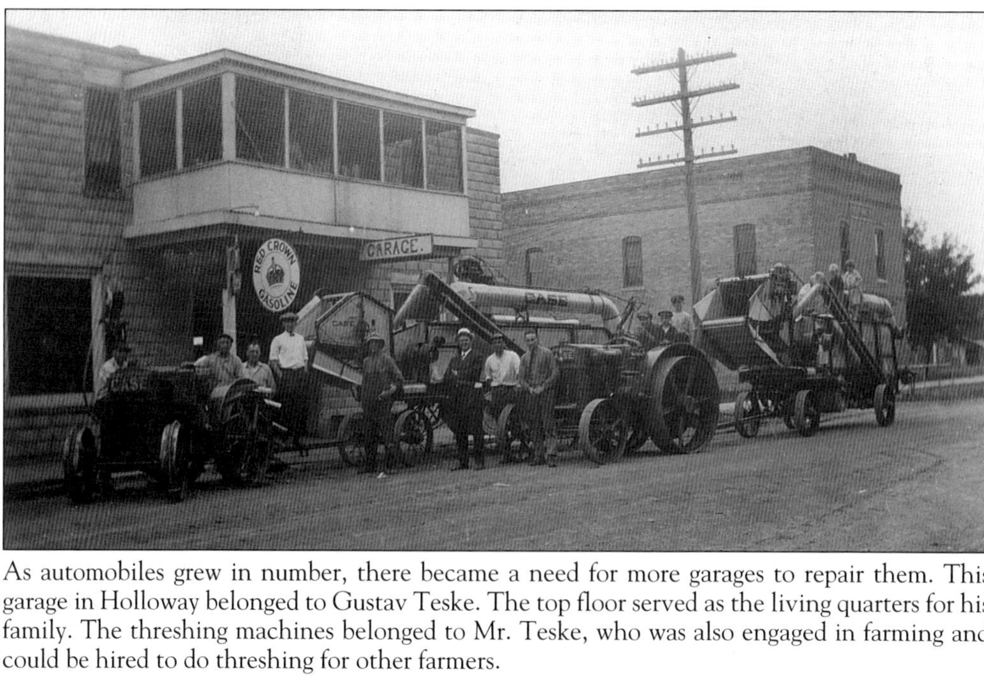

As automobiles grew in number, there became a need for more garages to repair them. This garage in Holloway belonged to Gustav Teske. The top floor served as the living quarters for his family. The threshing machines belonged to Mr. Teske, who was also engaged in farming and could be hired to do threshing for other farmers.

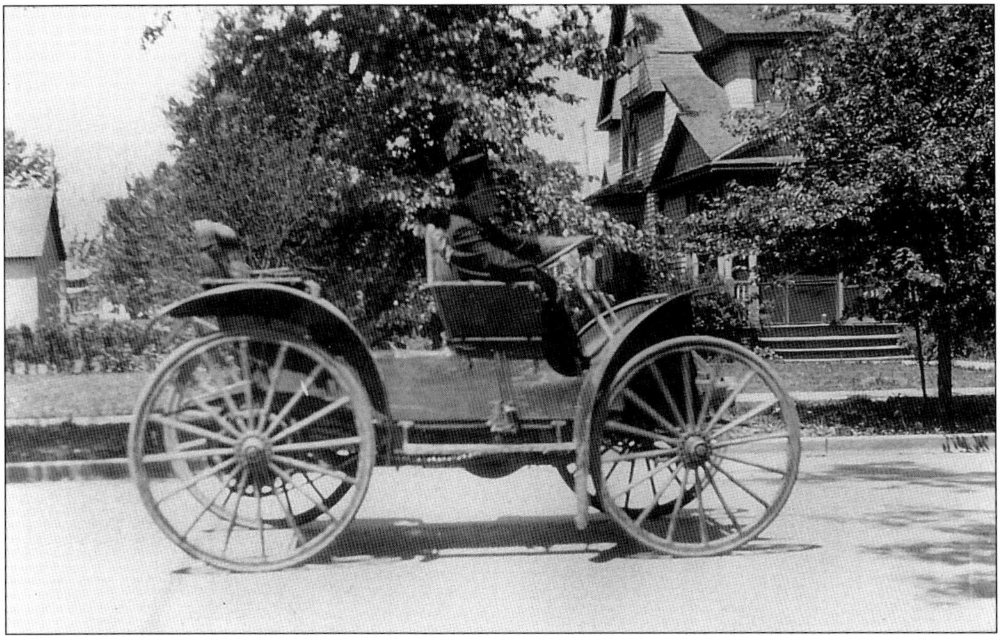

The first automobiles in Swift County were an attraction for everyone. They looked quite a bit different than the cars manufactured in the 1930s. This car is being driven by Dr. C.L. Scofield of Benson.

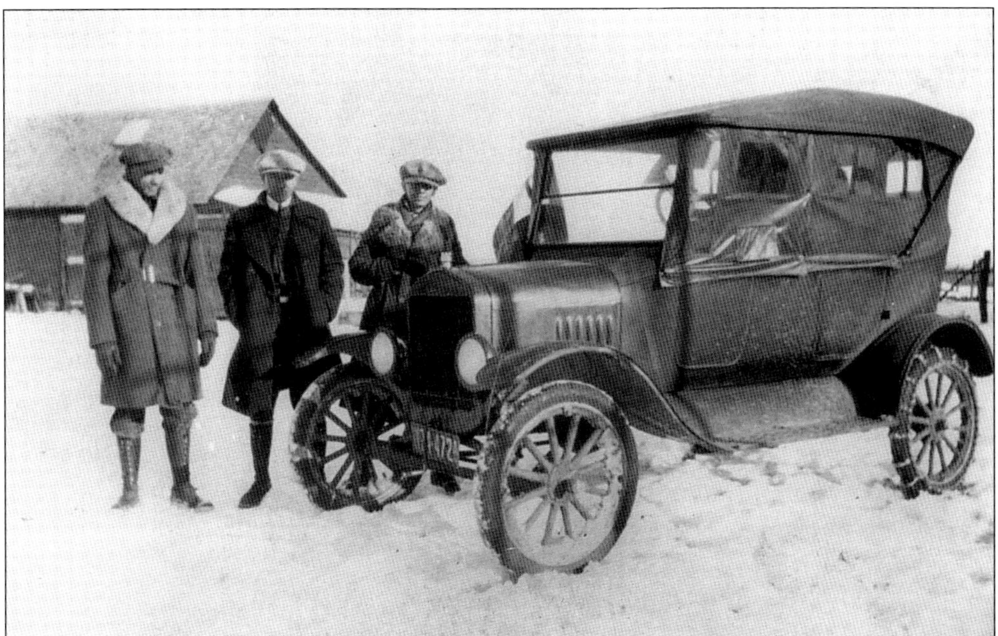

Standing by this 1924 Model T Ford are, from left to right: Ole Tollefson, Ray Tollefson, and Oscar Kronberg. Winter in Swift County meant putting a top on your auto. It still was a cold ride, because there were no heaters in the cars.

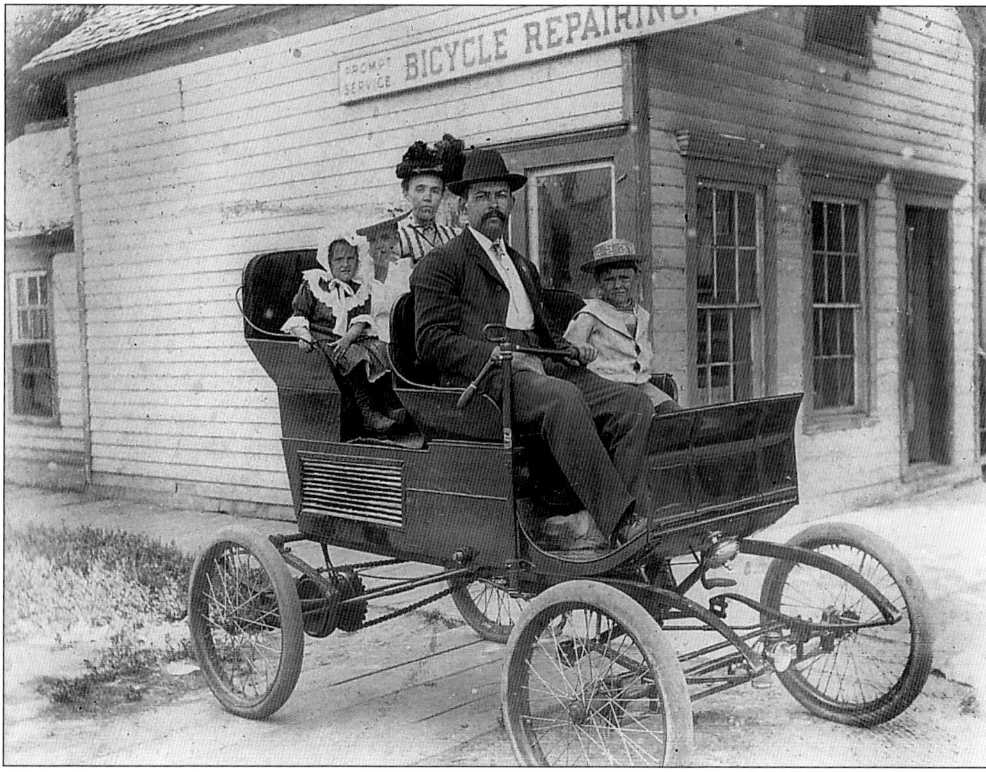

Pictured is J.B.A. Benoit with his family in the car he made in his bicycle shop in Benson in 1902. All the parts were turned out in wood with a turning lathe and sent to Minneapolis to be cast in iron. Benoit polished and finished the rough castings and assembled them into this auto.

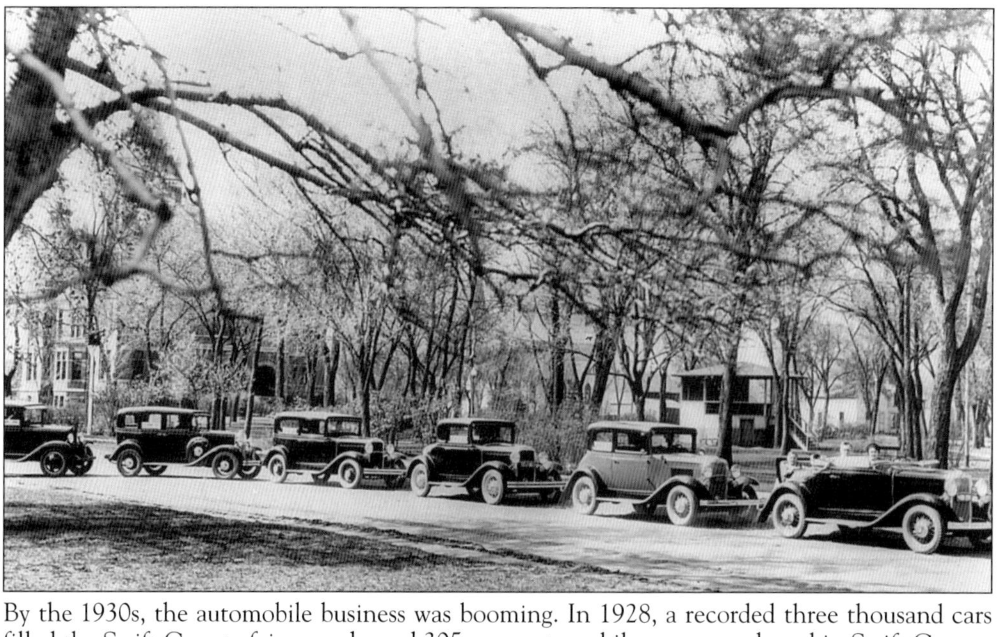
By the 1930s, the automobile business was booming. In 1928, a recorded three thousand cars filled the Swift County fairgrounds, and 305 new automobiles were purchased in Swift County alone. These cars were lined up across the street from the Swift County courthouse, c. 1932.

Nine

They Lived Here

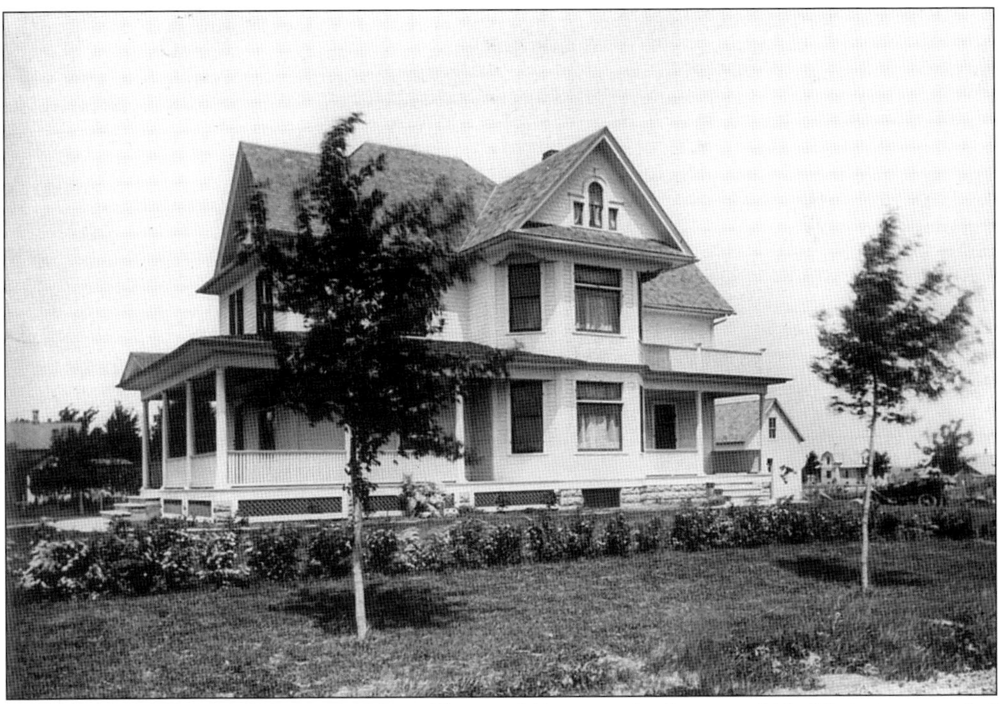

Christine Evenson was born in 1859 in Olmstead County. At the age of 13, Christine traveled by covered wagon pulled by oxen among a caravan of wagons, oxen, cattle, and whatever the settlers in the company brought with them. They traveled over unmarked trails and uncertain footings. It took three weeks to get to her new home in Hayes Township. On January 31, 1883, she married Ole Backlund. Their first home was located over the store where Mr. Backlund was in business. Later they were able to build this beautiful home in Kerkhoven.

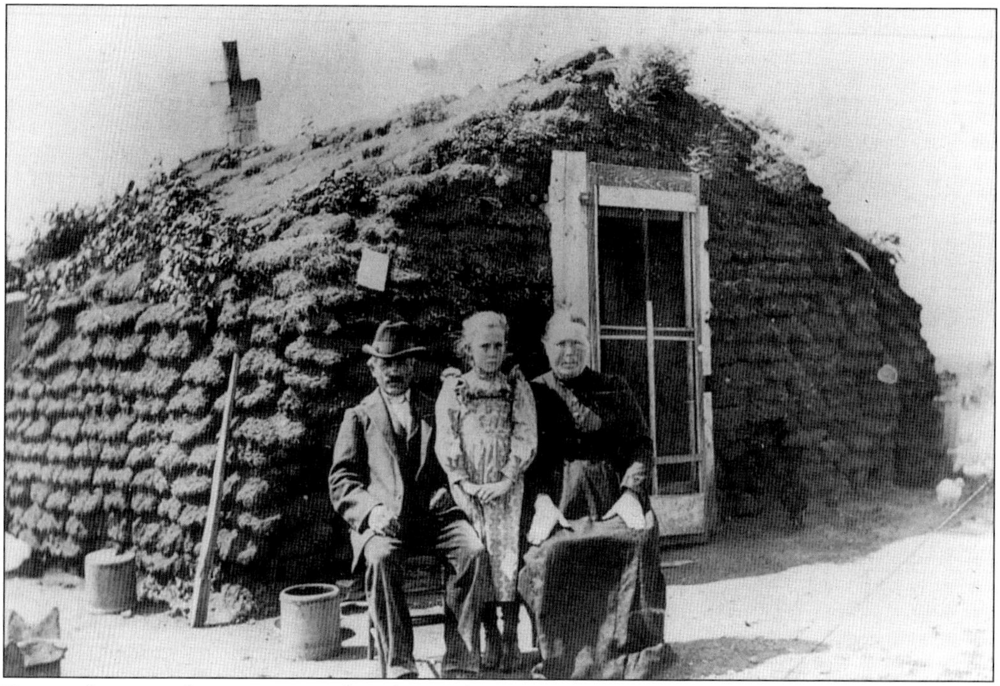

Few settlers were fortunate enough to live in log cabins in Swift County, because it was a treeless prairie. Pioneers resorted to making homes from the only natural resource they had—sod. This house was built by Ole Groven, who settled in Swenoda Township in 1892. Seated are Mr. and Mrs. Groven with their daughter, Inga.

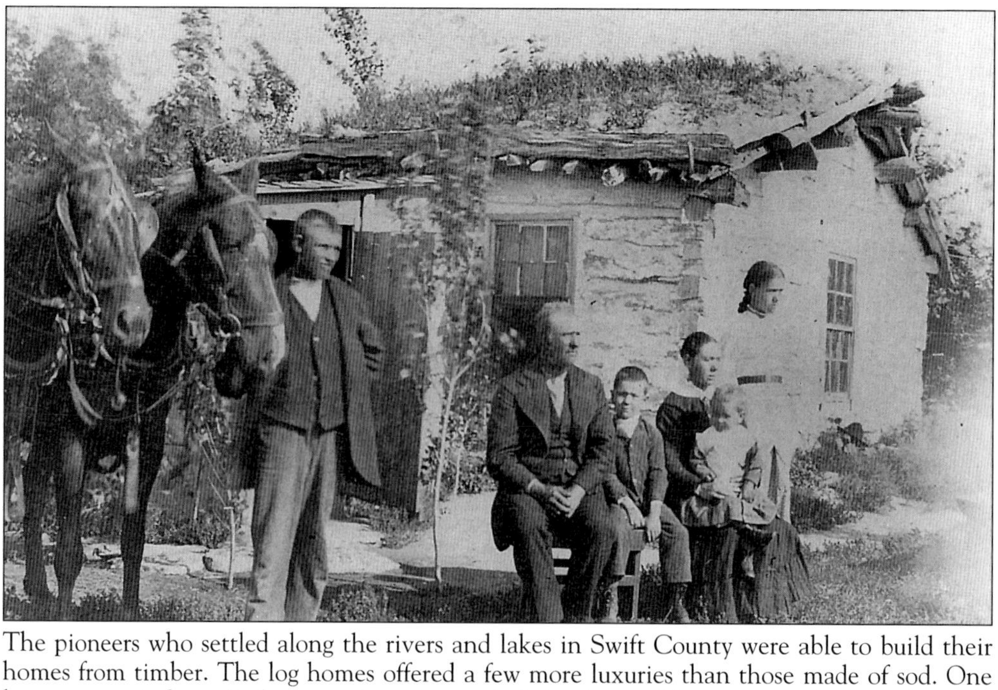

The pioneers who settled along the rivers and lakes in Swift County were able to build their homes from timber. The log homes offered a few more luxuries than those made of sod. One luxury was windows. Sod was used on the roof of this home. This log cabin belonged to Ole Monson, who filed his claim in 1876 in Camp Lake Township.

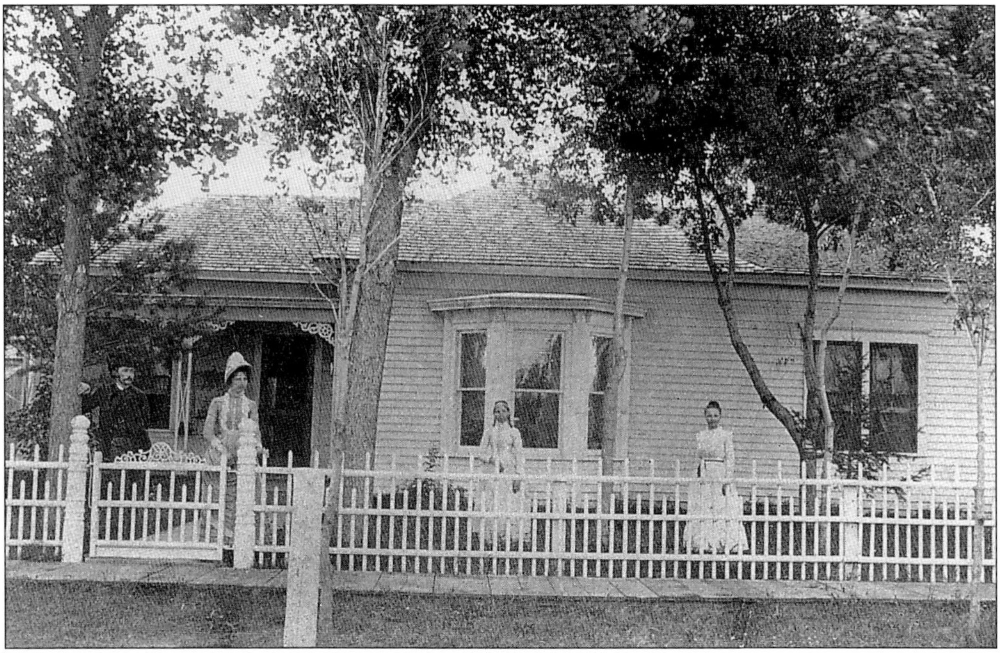

This is the home of C.H. Colby, who moved to Benson in 1877. This photograph was taken before the fall of 1894, when Mr. Colby rebuilt the house, changing every particular. The homes built in the villages were much different from the dugouts, sod, or log homes on the open prairie.

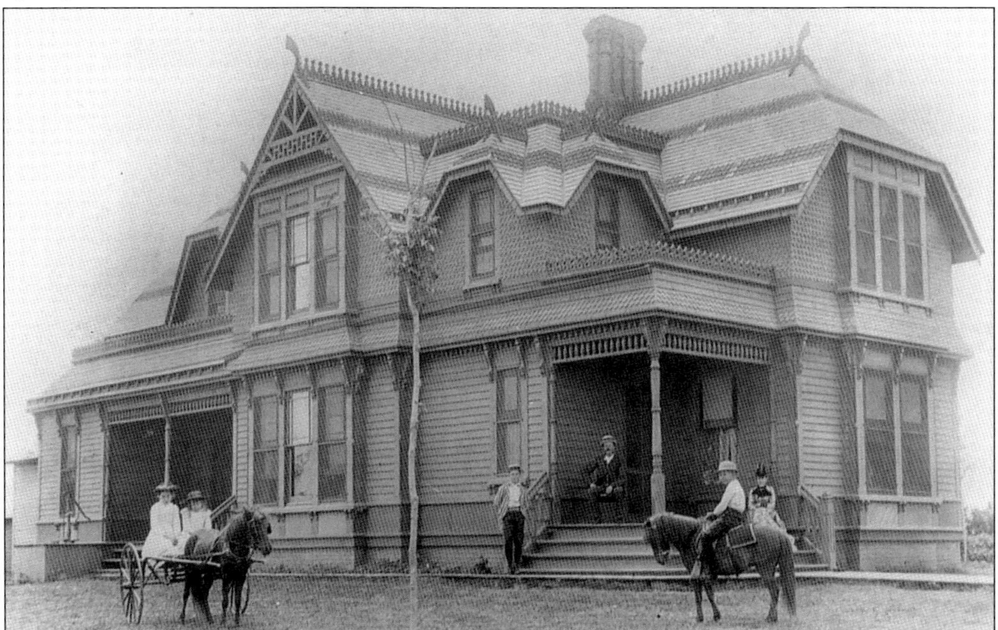

This photo of H.W. Stone's home was taken in Benson in 1891. Seated on the porch are Mr. Stone and his wife, Clara. Mr. Stone acquired this home in 1888 from Mrs. Z.B. Clarke, whose husband had the 15-room mansion of Queen Anne style built in 1885. Mr. Clarke died of consumption in 1886.

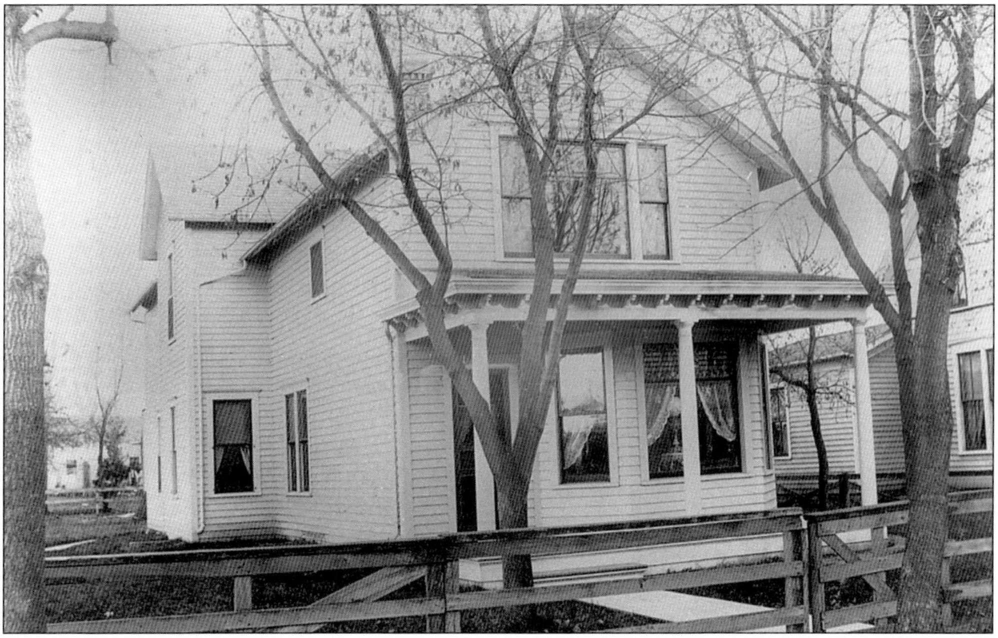

In 1885, W.R. Smith, his wife, and daughter moved to Benson. He purchased this home in 1897. Their daughter, Vera, married Thomas Harding in 1919. The Hardings made their home with Vera's parents. The Smiths and the Hardings lived the remainder of their lives together in this home.

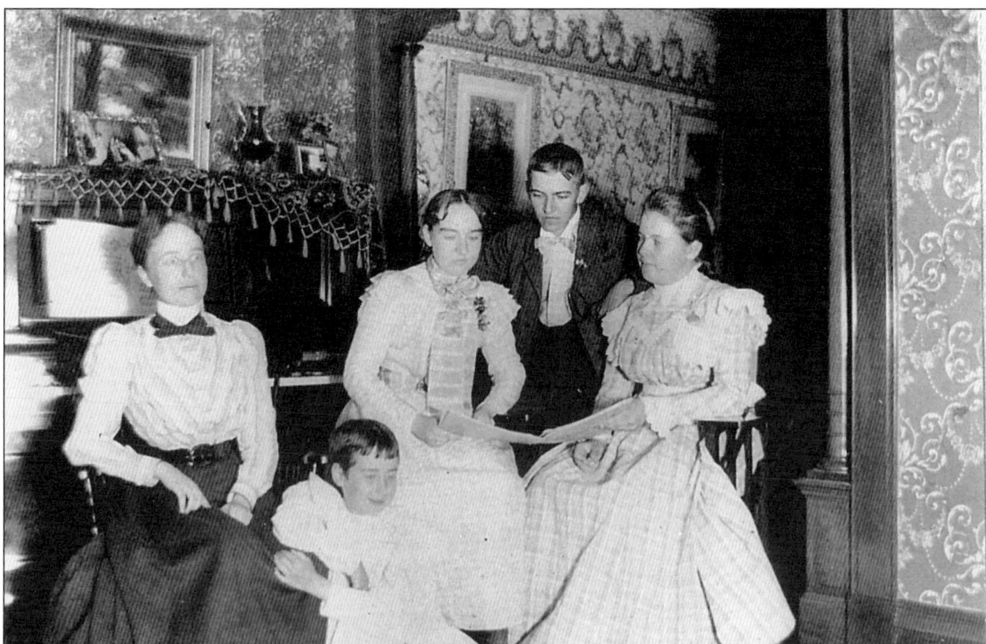

This is the interior of the W.R. Smith home in Benson. Vera Smith is believed to be the girl to the left of the young man. Music was a very important part of people's lives. Newspapers advertised teachers who gave music lessons.

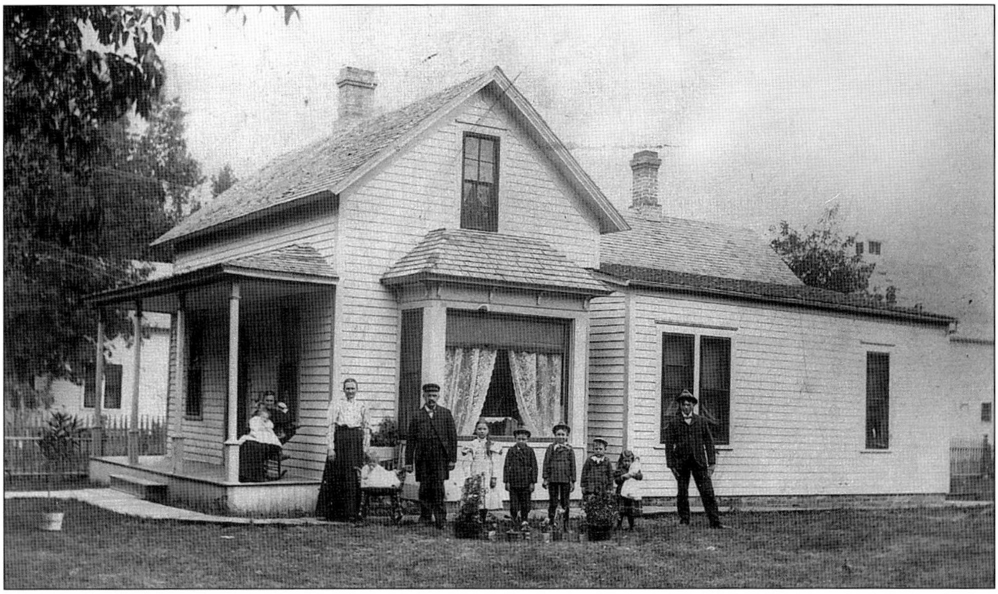

Jacob Minikus was born in Germany and served as an apprentice to a barber. In 1884, he came to Benson and opened his own barbershop. Mr. Minikus organized and directed the Benson Municipal Band and was a member of the Benson Volunteer Fire Department for 39 years. He and his wife, Mary, had seven children.

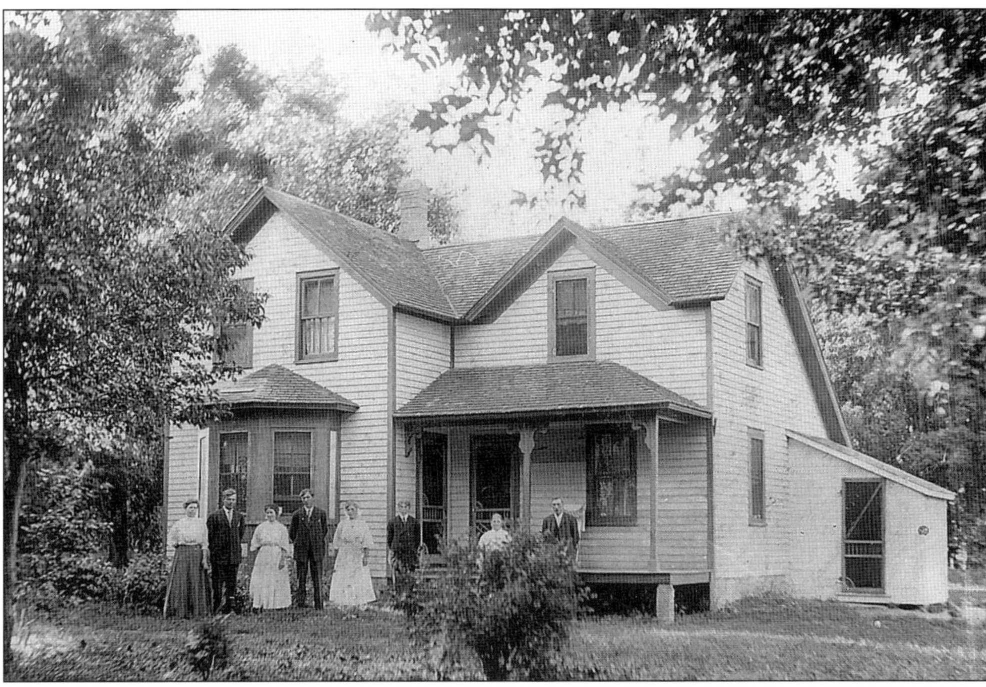

This is the family of Leonard Bergstrom in front of their home in Hayes Township. Leonard and his wife, Mary, were married in 1884 at Frank Lake in Hayes. They built this beautiful home where they lived until 1915, when Mr. Bergstrom took a position at the Farmers State Bank of Murdock and moved there. He was one of the county commissioners when the Swift County Courthouse was built in 1897.

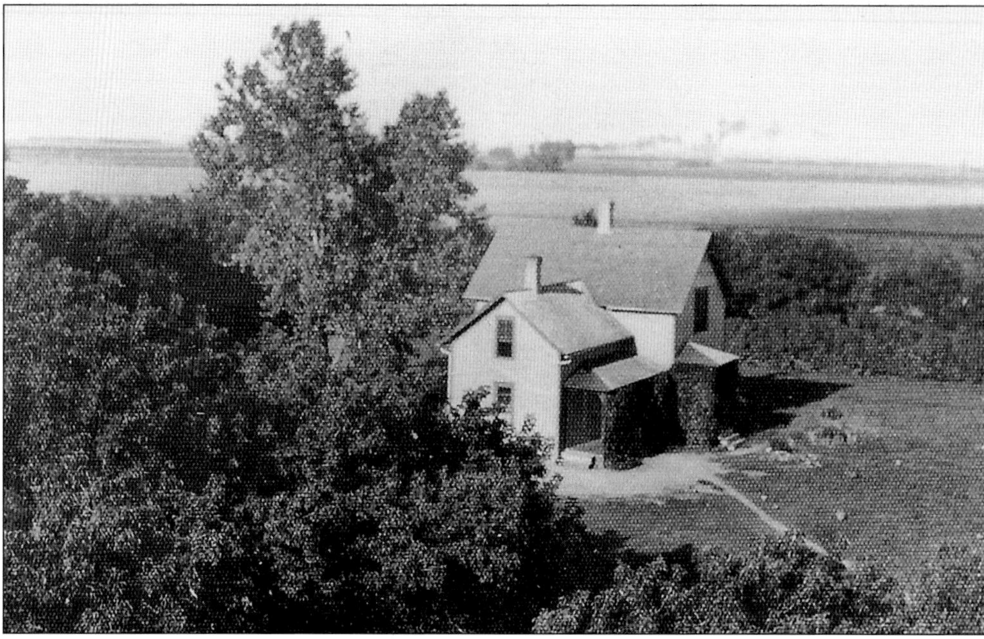

August Roll came to Swift County in 1877, and settled in Section 8 of Clontarf Township. In 1883, August married Victoria Bach from Marysland Township. Victoria's mother lived with them from 1886 until her death in 1905. This photo was taken about 1904.

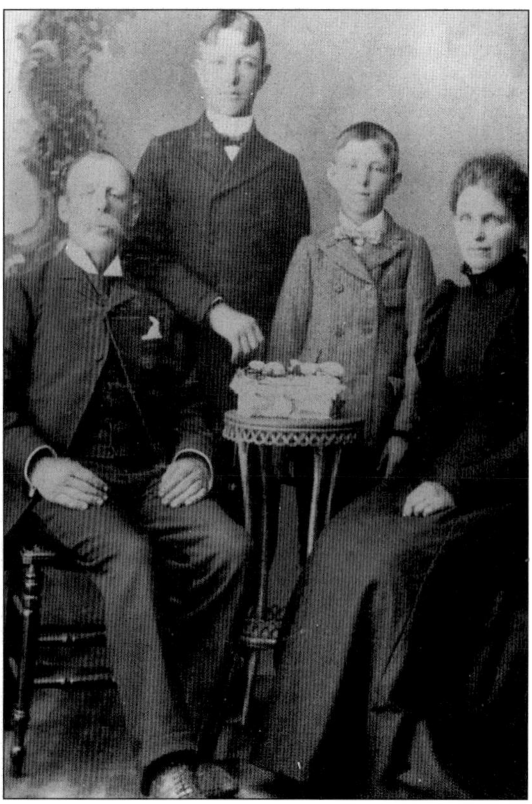

August and Victoria Roll had three children, two sons and a daughter, who died in infancy. One of the hardships that faced the pioneers was the loss of so many young children.

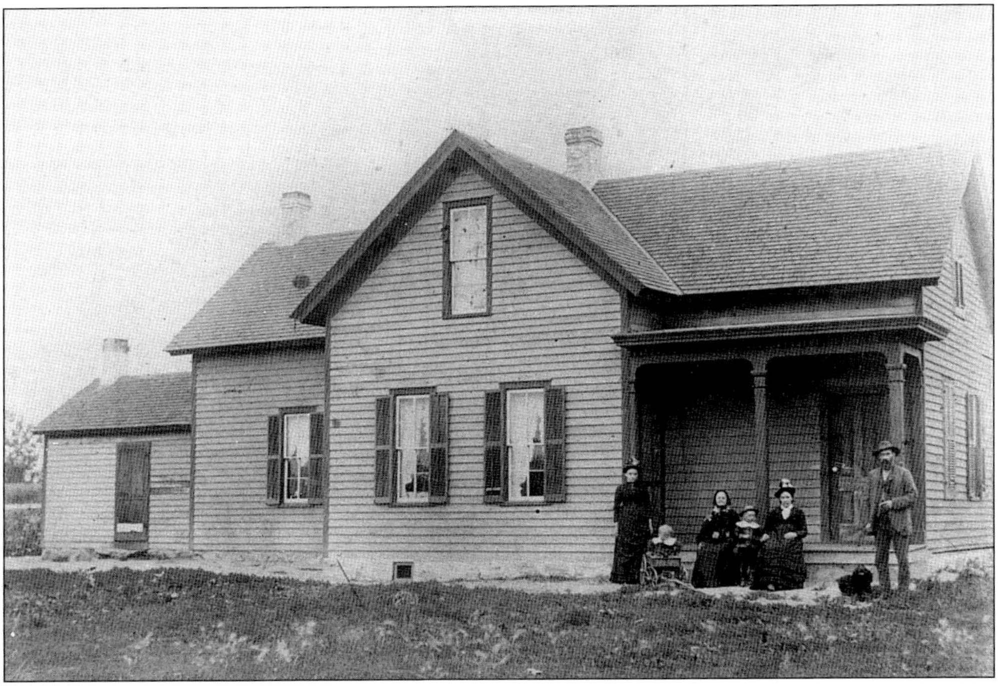

J.M. Danelz staked his claim in Section 10 of Camp Lake Township in 1870. He had two carloads of lumber shipped from St. Paul to Benson. First he erected a shanty to house himself and his mother. Then he commenced work on a mill. Mr. Danelz was married in 1873, after which this house was built. This picture was taken of him and his family in 1904.

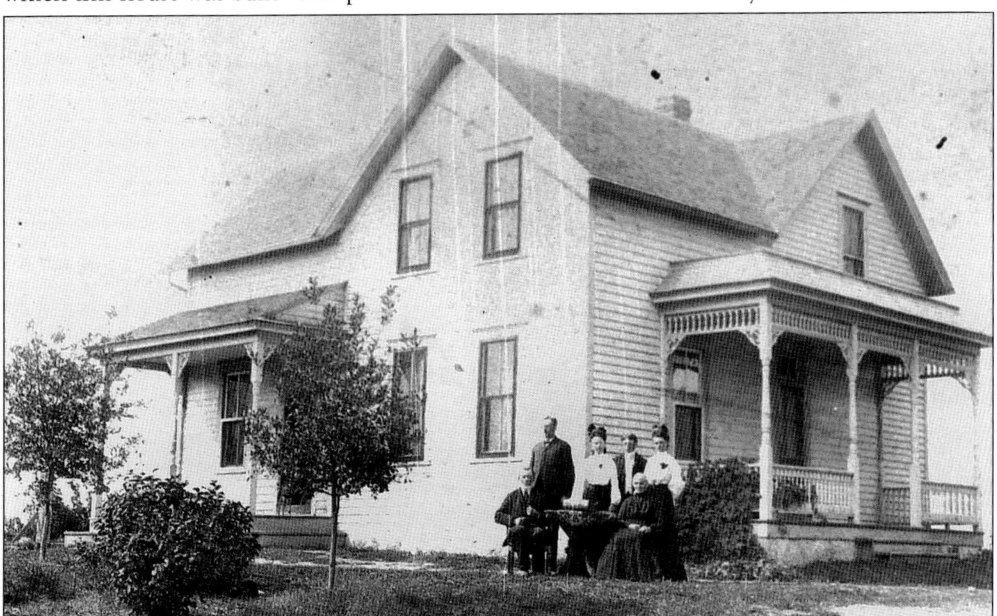

In front of this Torning Township home is the Anton Pederson family. Anton and his spouse, Brita, were married in 1877, and made their home here the rest of their lives. Anton died in 1907. Brita continued living in this home with her daughter, Mrs. Edwin Larson, and family until her death in 1934.

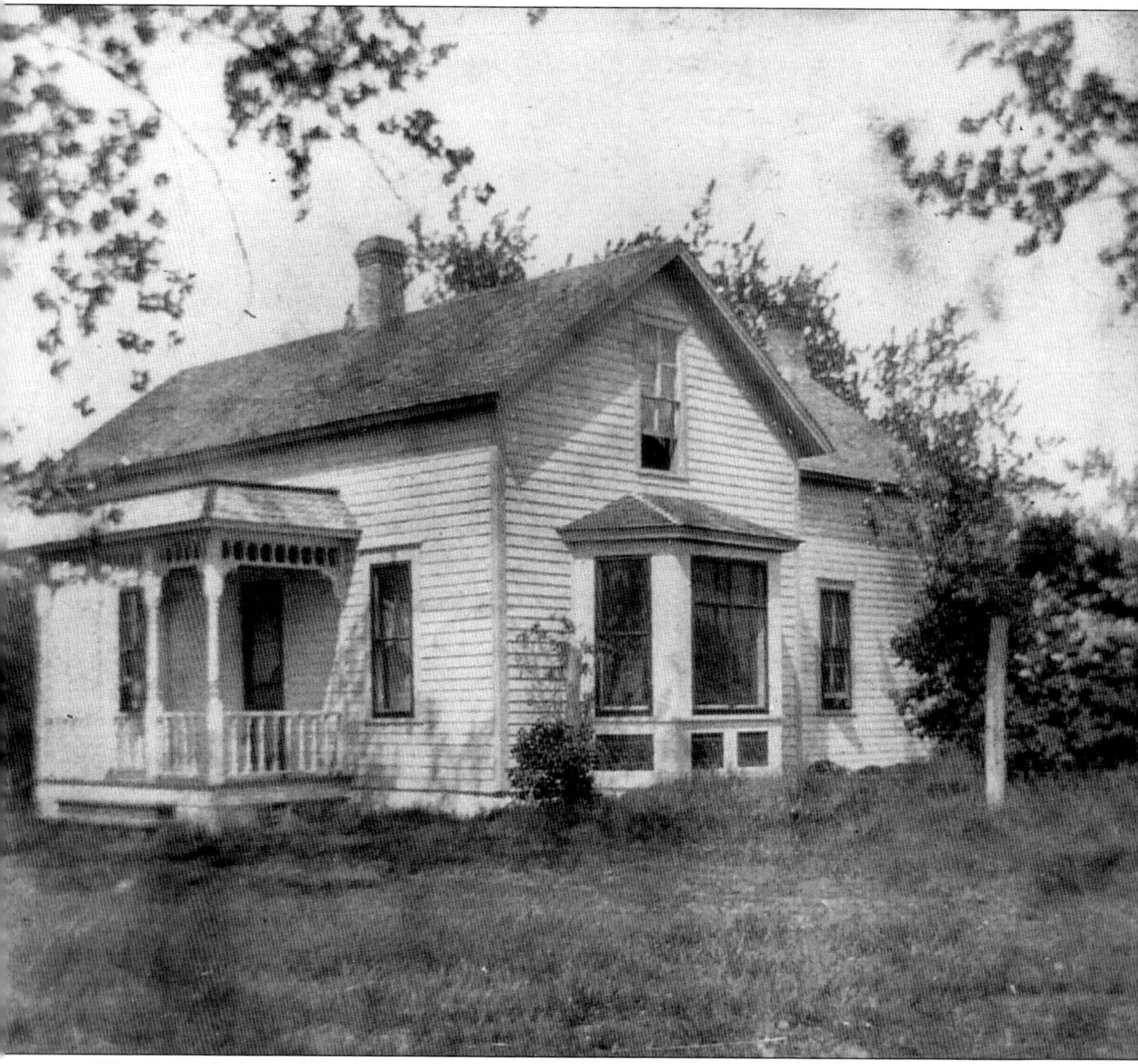

This home belonged to Peder and Karen Nermoe. Peder Nermoe was one of the first settlers of Benson Township, arriving in 1869. The following story has been told about Karen Nermoe. "When Indians were camped by their home, a squaw took the Nermoe baby to her camp. Karen went right after and took her baby back. The Indians did nothing, but evidently admired Karen for her courage."

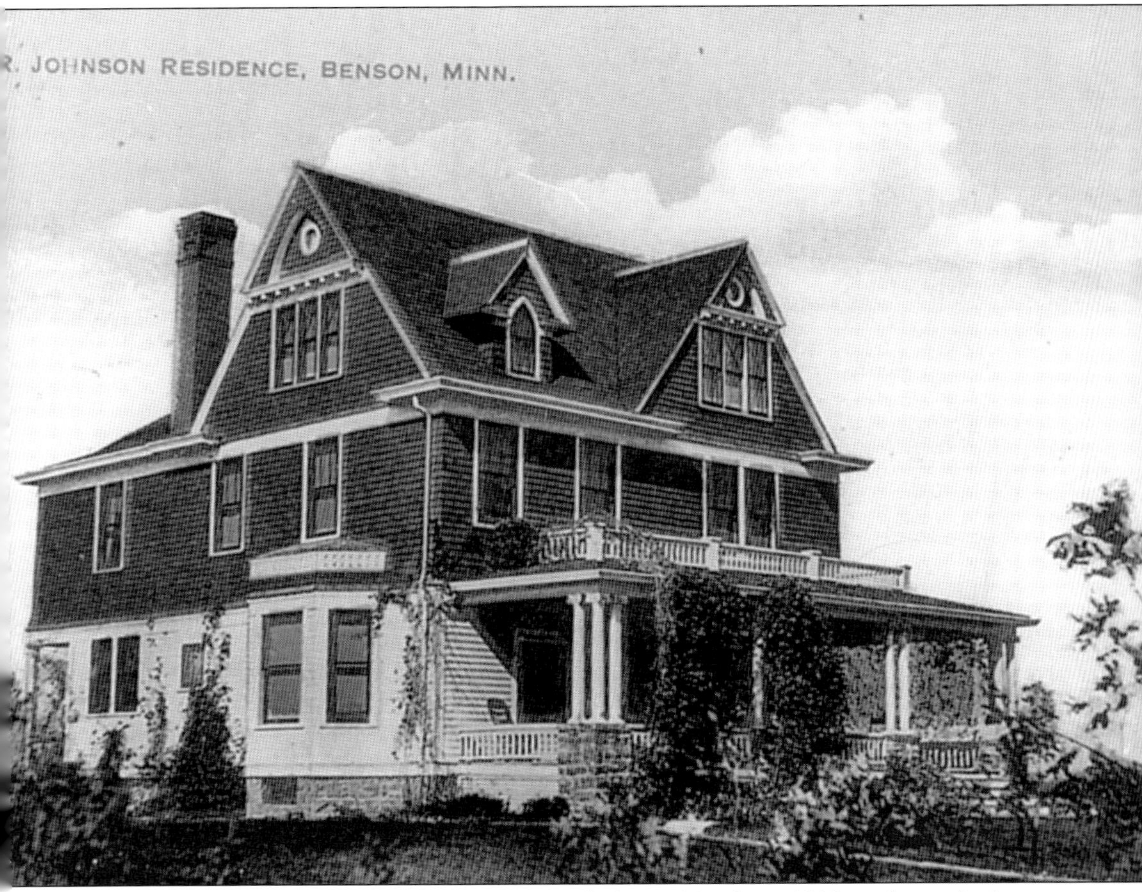

This beautiful home was built in Benson on 13th Street North in 1900, and was the home of R.R. and Emogene Johnson. Mr. Johnson came to Benson in 1875. He spent many years as county surveyor, and for 20 years handled the sale of railway lands in Swift, Pope, and Chippewa Counties.

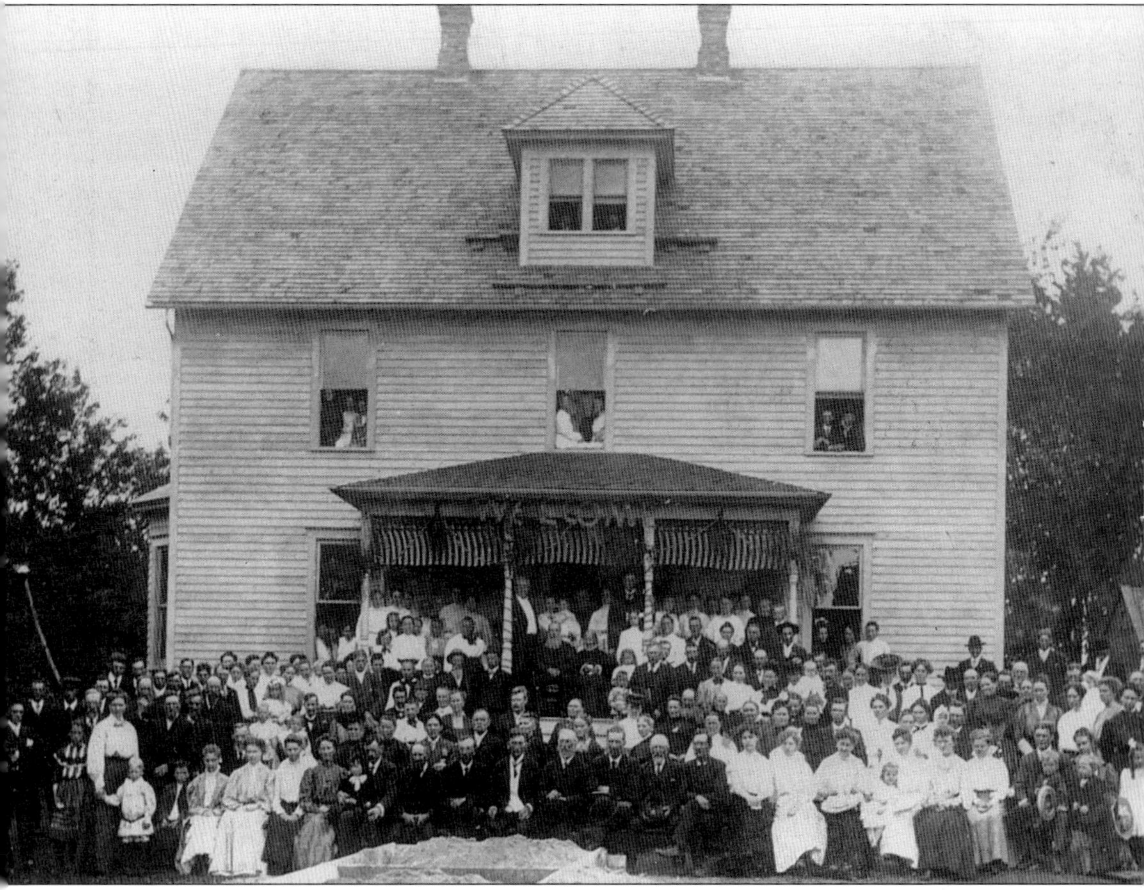

In 1906, a large group of relatives and friends gathered at the Ole and Kari Hatledal home in Torning Township to celebrate the golden wedding anniversary of Ole and Anne Hatledal. Ole and Anne and six children sailed to America in 1871 on the sailing vessel, *Argo*. It took ten weeks to get to Quebec. A short time after, they arrived in Swift County and secured a homestead in Section 22 of Torning Township. Their first home was a dugout, 12-by-12 feet. They used course slough hay for the roof. Their "house" was well built and stood for ten years. Later Ole built a smaller house. To make a living, Ole worked on the railway and would be gone for weeks. Anne wanted to mail Ole a letter, so she walked 2.5 miles to Benson pushing a baby carriage and carrying two pails of butter. The storekeeper would exchange the butter for groceries but would not give her money to mail the letter. Their son, Ole, took over the farm in the early 1900s and built the large home in this photo.